Simple Things

Daily Thoughts, Stories, and Inspiration to Live Life More Fully

Lori Nawyn

Covenant Communications, Inc.

Covenant

For women the world over who want to believe they are of worth—you are! Who want to know they can make a difference—you can! Who want to hope they have a bright future—you do!

And for my daughters and granddaughters: you are my love and my light. Thank you for teaching me!

—

Cover image: *Flowers with Watering Can* © Susabell, istockphotography.com.

Cover design by Christina Marcano © 2014 by Covenant Communications, Inc.

Published by Covenant Communications, Inc.
American Fork, Utah

Printed in the United States of America
First Printing: January 2014

19 18 17 16 15 14   10 9 8 7 6 5 4 3 2 1

ISBN: 978-1-62108-666-6

FOREWORD

DO YOU CONSIDER YOURSELF PERFECT?

If not, you're in good company! At points in our lives, we may reach what might be considered precision: a level of spiritual and emotional equilibrium that enables us to move confidently toward our goals. Yet often we have to grapple for a foothold or handhold just to keep ourselves upright. We stumble and fall as we battle fear, guilt, doubt, lack of self-worth, and disillusionment. We fight frustration over both real and perceived deficiencies. What we might view as perfection remains elusive.

That's okay!

Our journey through life wasn't intended to be easy. It was designed to teach us how strong and capable we are. Even if gaining a testimony of the gospel comes late in our lives, even if we're still working on comprehending our divine destiny, we are counted as beloved daughters of God. Joy and happiness, peace and serenity, confidence and self-respect are ours for the choosing.

Though the journey is difficult, discovering who we truly are ennobles and enables us to enjoy life. We have a birthright of immeasurable potential. Limitless possibilities and blessings await!

INTRODUCTION

MY NAME IS LORI NAWYN. I'm married to a fireman, and I'm a mother of four and grandmother of four. Early in my life, I was taught that I was of little or no value. I struggled with debilitating self-doubt. I felt alone, inferior, and hopeless. As the years progressed, I became increasingly critical of myself and believed God's love and blessings were intended for everyone but me. Simply put, I was convinced I was not—and would never be—good enough!

A wise and loving Father in Heaven gave me life experiences that helped me see myself in a new light. As my heart softened, I came to understand that hardships and adversity are not punishments. Rather, they provide unique opportunities for us to realize we are truly miraculous beings.

This collection of thoughts, stories, quotes, and scriptural references focuses on key elements that can help you navigate your journey through life with confidence and success. My goal is to persuade you to refine your state of heart so you can grow to love, forgive, and believe in yourself and come to realize what an extraordinary person you are. Within these pages, you can discover how it is possible to know that you are a daughter of God and know how to face and overcome trials and challenges to thrive instead of merely survive. I share ideas for how to take action and glean the resolve to emerge from the shadows of discouragement, despair, and doubt so you can celebrate your life and blessings. In addition, the *Making the Most of* sections each month provide ideas for nurturing yourself and those you love, and the special recipe sections give you a unique taste of each season.

You are important—you matter. You deserve to live in peace, joy, happiness, and hope. Come journey with me as we claim the privilege of living life to its fullest!

—Lori Nawyn

JANUARY

The First Steps

Knowing You Are a Daughter of God

STILL. QUIET. JANUARY. GRAY SKIES, silver frost, white snow. Trees slumber. Flowers rest. Ice-encrusted grass crunches underfoot. Yet beneath winter landscapes, anticipation simmers. Bud, leaf, and blossom wait for sun-filled days. We wait too for sun and warmth, reflecting on the preceding year and resolving to make the months ahead better. Within our hearts, contemplation nourishes the mustard seeds of faith that have been stored up in joyful expectation of future growth and blessings.

This month as you affirm or reaffirm to yourself that you are a beloved daughter of God, commit to reapportioning your time so you have an ample amount for study, pondering, and prayer. Equip yourself with tools to help you: scriptures, a journal in which to record your thoughts and impressions, a willing heart, and a desire to believe. Believe, or at least consider, that wherever you are on your life's journey, your efforts to learn about your heavenly ancestry will be of great benefit. Before you can effectively touch the lives of your family, friends, and others you meet, you must know for yourself of God and His love.

Making the Most of January

* If you don't have a journal, plan a special shopping trip and find one that appeals to you. Or create your own. Use a spiral notebook; cover the front and back with decorative scrapbook paper. Get a journaling pen and markers. Keep your journal in a special place where it's easily accessible.

* Ring in the new year by making a personal or family time capsule. Put photos, cards, letters, and mementos in a small box or tin, and stash it away until a predetermined opening time.

* Write down your heart's desires for the new year. Include aspirations for spiritual, emotional, physical, and financial well-being. Make firm plans to get your credit card debt under control. Doing so will put you in charge of your fiscal destiny and security.

* Reorganize the refrigerator. Get rid of holiday foods that are past their expiration dates and those that are packed with calories.

* Read the book *Walk with Me* by Greg Olsen. It reminds us the kingdom of God is a spiritual destination as well as a place. The eighty-four paintings in the book, along with quotes and scriptural insight, will touch your heart and lift your spirits.

* Organize holiday photos, and make CDs to give to loved ones.

* Shop after-Christmas sales. With a budget in mind, stock up at sales on sheets, towels, and blankets. January is also a good time to purchase wedding gifts for the coming year.

* Start a tradition of a family snow day or winter Olympics. Include events like snowball fights, snowman and snow-fort building, sledding, skiing, tobogganing, or skating. Ahead of time, use a family home evening to make Olympic medals, ribbons, or awards. Make an Olympic torch out of an old Tiki torch or lantern. Have a thermos of hot chocolate on hand and fresh-baked cookies. Or have a family service day and shovel walks and driveways for neighbors.

* Get out a calendar and plan when to make your important appointments for the coming year—gynecologist, mammogram, dentist, optometrist, and others. Determine what appointments family members need. Don't forget car and home maintenance. Gather all the necessary phone numbers and set aside a time to schedule everything.

* Reorganize your desk. Clear out the old and add new items. A whimsical pencil holder; a decorative card file; fun or fashionable stationery and stickers; colorful pens, pencils, highlighters, and markers.

* Ward off January blahs by spicing up the month with salsas and dips. Try different kinds of tortilla chips. Have a fiesta night with friends and family and hold a salsa contest. Decorate with lots of bright colors.

* Write about your favorite winter memories. Enter a short story or poetry contest.

JANUARY 1

Choosing: Earthly versus Eternal Goals

We look not at the things which are seen, but at the things which are not seen: for the things which are seen are temporal; but the things which are not seen are eternal. —2 Corinthians 4:18

In his painting *Living Water*, artist Simon Dewey depicts Christ's encounter with the Samaritan woman at the well. Clothed in humble attire, she bears only the vessel she carries in her search for water. The gentle intensity of Christ's love for the woman is evident as is her wonder at His words. The Jews had no dealings with Samaritans; she marveled He would speak to her. Her request to have her thirst quenched was granted (see John 4:4–42). The scene is a poignant reminder that nothing can compare to the living water Christ offers: His gift of the Atonement, the gospel, and the love of God.

The experiences and possessions obtainable during our earthly existence can enhance our lives in many ways, but they often rob us of precious time that would best be used to acquire knowledge that will help us meet eternal goals. Whether you are seeking for the first time to feel confirmation of your divine identity or if your knowledge of your eternal nature has somehow been weakened or lost, determine to take whatever time necessary to know the truth. No matter your circumstances, you can receive, or have strengthened, a sure testimony that you are God's own beloved and cherished spiritual offspring.

If, like the Samaritan woman, you consider yourself somehow less than others or an outsider, earnestly seek to discover God's plan, purpose, and love for you. Not discerning for a certainty your divine identity and role is, in itself, a choice. Choosing to become acquainted with our true potential and birthright is the first step on our journey.

JANUARY 2

Learn: Seek to Know about God

Thou hast said, I know thee by name, and thou hast also found grace in my sight. Now therefore, I pray thee, if I have found grace in thy sight, shew me now thy way, that I may know thee, that I may find grace in thy sight. —Exodus 33:12–13

Have words spoken in a church meeting impressed you as having been delivered specifically to you? Has the Spirit touched your heart when you've realized your prayers have been answered? Such experiences can help you reconnect with Heavenly Father as you sense His presence. Your association with Him is not new. Your bond with Him was forged long ago. However, just like you might get to know a new friend, becoming reacquainted with Him while in this mortal realm—both a choice privilege and a vital need—takes time and effort.

The scriptures affirm that if we seek God, He will be found. Daily time spent searching is essential. Prayer is our side of a communication equation that enables us to stay in contact with Him and receive guidance and direction. Paying close heed to evidences of His hand in our lives leads us to discover His loving nature.

Nothing will bless your life more than having a personal relationship with God. Nothing will bring more abundance and immeasurable joy, more direction and sense of worth, more depth and meaning to your relationship with yourself and others. This month is characterized by new beginnings. Begin your life anew by seeking to learn about your Father in Heaven.

JANUARY 3

Come unto Me: Accepting the Invitation

Why art thou cast down, O my soul? And why art thou disquieted within me? hope in God: for I shall yet praise him, who is the health of my countenance, and my God. —Psalm 43:5

When I was in second grade, I felt lost and alone. One afternoon, another child, LeeAnn Cheney, invited me to attend Primary. I didn't understand what Primary was. In the girl's eyes and smile, however, I sensed something special. My heart perceived it as well. I went with her. Looking back now, I realize LeeAnn had Christ's image engraven in her countenance.

In ensuing years, I sought the same sweet spirit I felt when I was in LeeAnn's presence. I often felt disheartened. I thought that since my family wasn't active in the Church—and since I wasn't perfect in every way—the best I could ever hope for was to feel the Spirit from others. I thought I would never be good enough. That I could never have—didn't deserve to have—a testimony of my own. Over time, I searched and pondered the scriptures. I issued fervent prayers. A wise and loving Heavenly Father balanced some quick answers to prayer with times when I had to struggle to navigate uncertainty and fear without His obvious assistance. I gradually came to know and understand why some of my prayers had not or should not have been answered immediately.

I'm thankful for LeeAnn, who even as a child emulated the Savior's example in word and deed. Her heartfelt invitation put my feet on the path to discovering my divine identity. I extend my heartfelt invitation to you to remember that when Christ issues the call, "Come unto me," He is speaking to everyone. Today join me in pondering ways to draw closer to Him.

JANUARY 4
The Gift of Prayer: Your Own EPS
Be thou humble; and the Lord thy God shall lead thee by the hand, and give thee answer to thy prayers. —D&C 112:10

GPS—the global positioning system—allows us to pinpoint our earthly location at any time. To successfully navigate mortality, we have another type of system at our disposal, one that can help us determine where to go and how to get there. It could be termed an EPS—an eternal positioning system—and is known as prayer.

We can talk to Heavenly Father about anything. No concern is too large or too small, no problem too complex or too trivial. There is no despair or discouragement or joy or triumph He doesn't want to hear about. An unfailing source of truth and knowledge who loves us, He is fully aware of perils that lie in wait. He will instruct us how to chart a course to safety.

While we should use words that reverence Deity, there is no need for sophisticated terms or phrasing. Prayers can be long or short and can be offered anytime and anywhere. Romans 8:26 bears the promise, "Likewise the Spirit also helpeth our infirmities: for we know not what we should pray for as we ought: but the Spirit itself maketh intercession for us with groanings which cannot be uttered."

Establish prayer as part of your daily routine. In days to come, as you kneel in faith and trust, with a sincere desire to receive His counsel, you will come to discover for a certainty that He is there and listening.

JANUARY 5
Seeking and Discerning Answers to Prayer
If ye would hearken unto the Spirit which teacheth a man to pray, ye would know that ye must pray. —2 Nephi 32:8

In the first stanza of her poem "Lord, We Know That Thou Art Near," English poetess Jane Fox Crewdson (1808–1863) writes about unanswered prayers:

> Lord, we know that Thou art near us,
> Though Thou seem'st to hide Thy face;
> And are sure that Thou dost hear us,
> Though no answer we embrace.

Many times I've commiserated over the unanswered. I wondered why Heavenly Father didn't realize how much I needed help. There was something more important than supplying me with what I wanted when I wanted it, however: the potential He provided me. My struggles with faith and circumstance helped me to learn and grow. As Jane so eloquently states in the third stanza of the poem:

> While withholding—Thou art giving
> In Thine own appointed way
> And while waiting we're receiving
> Blessings suited to our day.

Just because we don't readily obtain answers doesn't mean God has abandoned us. He is able to clearly ascertain what we require in order to help us cultivate resolve and strength of character and integrity, a belief in our own abilities that will help us be the best we can be. He allows us the privilege of problem solving. As Jane wrote, "Weaving blessings out of trials . . . answering prayer by wise denials."

JANUARY 6
A Year's Time . . . by the Moment
And ye shall seek me, and find me, when ye shall search for me with all your heart. —Jeremiah 29:13

Since we know the world makes judgments based on appearances, it can be tempting to try and conform to stereotypes. But time spent polishing and perfecting our exterior selves is a time-consuming, competitive endeavor. Clothing and hair styles change quickly, and one certainty of mortal life is that we age and our bodies change. When we can't keep up with the world's expectations of our appearance, we often feel unworthy of happiness.

As you look forward to the coming year, consider the benefits of spending an equal or greater amount of time on your inner self—your spiritual self, the things that make you who you really are—as you do on your exterior physical appearance. Just as when you shop for earthly cares, the gathering of spiritual necessities comes moment by moment, choice by choice, action by action.

Within a year's time, you can gain a testimony of your limitless capacity to succeed in the realms you are destined for—eternal realms where integrity and character will trump earthly fashion plays and vain aspirations. God isn't worried about trends in appearance, and unlike the things of the world, divine attributes never go out of style. Once you determine to incorporate them in your life, they only build and strengthen you as they continue to improve your inner beauty—a beauty that is enhanced by time and which need never fade.

JANUARY 7
Letters from Home
I did liken all scriptures unto us, that it might be for our profit and learning. —1 Nephi 19:23

Author C. S. Lewis observed that if he discovered in himself a desire which no experience in this world could satisfy, the most plausible explanation was that he was made for another world.[1] Indeed, this earth is not our first home. We may not possess distinct memories of the heavenly kingdom from which we came, but at times we feel inklings of remembrance and a trickle of the familiar. Like the caress of a gentle breeze or a shaft of sunlight that falls across our face, we are touched and warmed in ways that may be difficult to explain. We long for our premortal existence and all that was dear to us there. The good news is that staying in contact with our heavenly home is as easy as reading the scriptures—which are like letters from a wise and loving Father.

Daily scripture reading—even if only a few verses at a time—helps keep your focus on seeking and knowing God and His Son. Through stories and people and places that will become familiar to you, you'll learn about Heavenly Father's plan and purpose. You'll enjoy the companionship of the Holy Ghost. When your prayers are combined with scripture study, your ability to discern answers to problems and questions will be greatly enhanced. Through the scriptures, you can glean an understanding of who you are and what you need to do on the earth.

JANUARY 8
The ACT in Actually: Scripture Study
Do according to all that is written therein: for then thou shalt make thy way prosperous, and then thou shalt have good success. —Joshua 1:8

Though the scriptures—including the inspired words of living prophets—exist for our edification and enjoyment, the prospect of actually reading them can sometimes seem daunting. Concepts, ideas, and archaic wording and style may appear foreign and intimidating. Gleaning an understanding of scriptural texts can loom as unattainable. Finding time to study and ponder can also be difficult. All you need do, however, is take the first step: act.

If you have scriptures, find them—dust them off if necessary. If you don't, make plans to acquire a set. When you read, strive to enhance your comprehension. If there are verses that aren't clear, skip ahead to something you can relate to. Look for words that have special meaning to you, such as kindness, love, faith, hope, charity, or joy. Did you know there are sixty-nine references to the word *joy* in the Book of Mormon? Twenty-six of them are in Alma!

Keep a notebook. Record topics of interest. Post-it notes make great bookmarks and provide space to jot down impressions. Mark or code your scriptures so you can easily locate subjects for further study. Red can be used to mark passages that touch your heart or that provide insight you've been seeking. Gold or yellow could be used for scriptures about God and Christ. Light blue for the Holy Ghost and things of the Spirit. Purple for anything that applies to faith, peach for hope, green for forgiveness, pink for prayer, dark blue for the plan of salvation, etc. Make a key to insert at the front of your scriptures to remind you of which color refers to which subject.

The first step to getting acquainted with the scriptures is simply to act!

JANUARY 9
Strength: Our Part in God's Work
But when the Comforter is come, whom I will send unto you from the Father, even the Spirit of truth, which proceedeth from the Father, he shall testify of me. —John 15:26

The work of our Father in Heaven and our Lord and Savior Jesus Christ is to bring to pass the immortality and eternal life of man (see Moses 1:39)—and woman. They have no other agenda, no mortal cares such as stressing over debt, saving for a vacation in the south of France, or worrying about how they look. We, the human race, are their prime concern. To be anxiously engaged in God's cause is to serve Him by working toward being our personal best so we can touch hearts and lives, uplifting ourselves as well as others.

Elder M. Russell Ballard has counseled that piling all we own into a handcart or wagon and walking across the plains won't be expected of most of us.[2] Yet Heavenly Father will expect us to endure difficult situations that will ultimately reinforce our faith.

When we're engaged in our Father's work through simple acts of kindness and compassion, we become closer to Him. Our hearts fill with love.

Often fear of our own insufficiencies and weaknesses causes us to balk. Mother Teresa taught that if we give ourselves fully to God, He will use us to accomplish great things—on the condition we believe more in His love than in our own limitations.[3] In serving Him, we find our true selves. Our insufficiencies and weaknesses—whether perceived or real—become strengths.

JANUARY 10
Faith: What Does It Mean to Be a Disciple?
If ye continue in my word, then are ye my disciples. —John 8:31

The Lamanite woman Abish (see Alma 19:16–29) exemplified what it means to be a disciple of Christ. Abish was not only a servant to King Lamoni's queen—she was a faithful servant of God. Having acquired a testimony of her own, she was ready when the occasion presented itself to bear witness of His power. Verse 17 clearly indicates her state of mind. She surrendered fear of judgment and ran from house to house, spreading word of what she'd seen. Miracles unfolded. Many believed and were converted; they were baptized and became a righteous people—all due to the faithful witness of Abish, who was devoted to the cause of truth.

When we center or re-center our focus away from the world and toward our Father and Savior, there may be those who don't understand. We may be ridiculed for our beliefs. It's never easy when those we love try to persuade us, by withholding their respect or love, that we're wrong. If you encounter opposition in your quest to know you're a daughter of God, pray specifically for reassurance and strength. If the challenges that present themselves threaten to throw you off course, stand firm. Surrender fear of judgment in favor of what you know or what you are faithfully attempting to discern is true.

Sometimes, following in Christ's steps can feel like a lonely undertaking. He counsels us to not be troubled or afraid. Being His disciple bears the firm promise of peace and comfort as well as purpose and joy. Ultimately, your efforts to be a faithful witness will, like Abish's, be blessed.

JANUARY 11
In God's Eyes: Infinite Possibilities
For what shall it profit a man, if he shall gain the whole world, and lose his own soul? Or what shall a man give in exchange for his soul?
—Mark 8:36–37

Mortal life brings comparisons of physical appearances, material possessions, and skills. Harsh evaluations of ourselves and others can cause us to either become stressed in our pursuit of measuring up or withdraw into hurt, frustration, and disillusionment. We can fall into the habit of masking pain with pursuits and possessions, hiding what we fear is our inferiority. But where we see imperfections and deficiencies, God sees talents, abilities, and strengths just waiting to be discovered!

As God's daughters, none of us is inferior. While it's true we can learn from the example of the worthy achievements of others, we do not need to live in their shadows. Each of us has a noble, eternal purpose that is unique to us as individuals. If you're striving to do better each day, be proud of your progress. Have you recently finished something you've been putting off or added a special touch to something? Excellent! Have you smiled at someone who looked lost or sad, or were you kind when someone else was rude or difficult? Wonderful! Did you search for evidences of blessings in your life even though you might have felt lonely or downtrodden? Fantastic! Keep up the good work, and take pride in yourself and your accomplishments.

JANUARY 12

Enjoy: What's in a Word? Guilt-Free Journaling

I will impart unto you of my Spirit, which shall enlighten your mind,
which shall fill your soul with joy. —D&C 11:13

Mere mention of the word *journal* can send us into a tailspin of guilt. But journaling doesn't have to be tedious or intimidating, and it isn't merely for posterity. Writing down thoughts and impressions of difficult, forlorn, and anxious situations can serve as a release valve. Looking back on entries weeks or months later, we can see how far we've come. Observations of the good times will become all the sweeter.

Lengthy personal epistles aren't requisite to journaling. You can record ideas and tips on caring for self, home, and family. Jot down favorite quotes. Even write only one word! Singularly the words *hurt*, *afraid*, *alone*, *sorrow*, and *stress* bear deep meaning, as do the words *love*, *courage*, *smile*, *hope*, and *faith*. Try joy journaling—one-sentence slices of life that, like treasured photographs, capture moments of splendor and bliss. It's as easy as asking yourself what brings you joy. If you don't feel like writing, add photographs, cards and letters, event programs, recipes, lengths of ribbon, or pressed flowers.

By making friends with your journal, you're creating a safe haven within its pages where you don't feel pressured to make long, detailed entries or exact lively, creative prose. You'll be more likely to refer to it often. When you find yourself in need of a place to delve into deeper thought processes and analyze new ideas, discoveries, and inspiration, your journal will be ready and waiting for you—a dear friend as well as a treasured personal legacy.

JANUARY 13

A To-Live-By List to Live With

Ye pay tithe of mint and anise and cummin, and have omitted the
weightier matters of the law, judgment, mercy, and faith: these ought ye
to have done, and not to leave the other undone. —Matthew 23:23

In our day and age, opportunities for our want-to-do lists and possessions for our want-to-have lists are almost limitless. Most, however, do not come free of charge. When want-to-do and want-to-have lists grow long or are not within our budget, they create stress. With January comes increased pressure to make New Year's goals and resolutions. We can find ourselves wanting to do all and have all that we think will make us happier, wealthier, and more attractive or popular in the eyes of others. Yet worry over how we're going to do everything and pay for everything leads to spiritually debilitating discouragement.

Different from want-to-do and want-to-have lists, a to-live-by list keeps track of things that cost no money but can endow true happiness. It is a list of Christlike attributes we desire to attain and live by in the pursuit of becoming our best.

Do you want to become more faithful, humble, or compassionate? More honest, charitable, or loving? Having spent too much time mired in controversy, do you seek to become a peacemaker? The inside front cover of your journal is a great place to record the Christlike attributes you desire to attain. Refer to them often as you discover how to live them more fully.

JANUARY 14
Then Sings My Soul: The Power of Music
For my soul delighteth in the song of the heart; yea, the song of the righteous is a prayer unto me, and it shall be answered with a blessing upon their heads. —D&C 25:12

When I was in grade school, I began to attend sacrament meeting. I knew little or nothing about Jesus. It was while the congregation sang hymns that I first began to feel impressions of the Spirit. Sitting in the back of the chapel, I followed along, silently and intently reading from the hymnbook. My favorite hymn was "I Know That My Redeemer Lives." The sweet, confident words stirred my heart. I developed a deep yearning to know more about the Savior and His gospel.

While decorating, shopping, cooking, and celebrating, we tend to seek out and listen to inspirational melodies more during the holidays than at any other time of year. Yet music that praises, honors, and celebrates the inherent goodness of life and living can enrich our days all year long. Numerous inspirational and motivational artists offer selections in a wide variety of formats. You can get free music downloads for several personal music devices from LDS.org. With persistence we can find radio stations that offer programming that is toe-tappingly positive.

Bless and commemorate the days of January by listening to music that will invite the Spirit and uplift, strengthen, and inspire you. As you go about your day, you might even feel yourself wanting to sing along. Your singing voice doesn't need to be skillful, only heartfelt!

JANUARY 15
Growing: Nourish Your Faith
Yea, and how is it that ye have forgotten that the Lord is able to do all things according to his will, for the children of men, if it so be that they exercise faith in him? Wherefore, let us be faithful to him.
—1 Nephi 7:12

The chill winter landscape of January often causes a yearning for things green and growing. Planning and planting an indoor winter garden will add cheer to your home with its promise of new beginning and growth. Many varieties of vegetables, including early peas, chili peppers, and cauliflower, can be sown in washed yogurt or margarine containers. Small flowerpots or window boxes provide space to plant seeds for herbs and greens that will sprout quickly to provide tasty additions for salads and sandwiches.

Paperwhites (a relative of daffodils) can be started as well. In a shallow (three- to four-inch-deep) clear glass or plastic container, place a two-inch layer of glass beads, marbles, pebbles, or sandy soil. Place the paperwhite bulbs on the layer, pointed tip up, close to one another. Add a second layer of the same material to hold the bulbs in place, leaving the top third of each bulb exposed. Add sufficient water to reach only the base of the bulb—do not cover the entire bulb. Store paperwhites in a cool, dark place. Check them daily and ensure the water level is maintained. When roots develop, move the container to a sunny spot and watch them grow!

As you start and nourish bulbs or seeds, ponder ways you can sow seeds of faith in your heart that can be nourished by scripture study and prayer.

JANUARY 16
God's Love: Your Value as His Child

And the angel said unto me: Behold the Lamb of God, yea, even the Son of the Eternal Father! Knowest thou the meaning of the tree which thy father saw? And I answered him, saying: Yea, it is the love of God, which sheddeth itself abroad in the hearts of the children of men; wherefore, it is the most desirable above all things. And he spake unto me, saying: Yea, and the most joyous to the soul. —1 Nephi 11:21–23

The first time I knew God was real and mindful of me, I was a young teen. It was Father's Day. I knelt to say my prayers and suddenly realized I had never sincerely expressed my love to my Father in Heaven. I decided to wish Him a happy Father's Day. In a rush of warmth that wrapped me in joy and comfort, I felt the sure impression of His love for me.

Over the years it became easy for me to lose sight of the fact I was loved and valued. Acting on the example of one of my daughters, I began to record instances of God's influence in my life, and the confirmation of the Spirit of their truthfulness, in an M.O.M. journal—a Mindful of Me journal.

Spencer W. Kimball noted that we need to feel the love Father in Heaven has for us and understand the value He places on us as individuals.[4] Begin today to take notice of experiences and impressions that demonstrate God's love and concern for you. Record those experiences, both the small and the truly life-altering, in an M.O.M. journal, notebook, or your daily journal. In times to come, reading them will reinforce your testimony and fortify you when doubt and fear cast shadows on your life.

JANUARY 17

Overcoming Pride: Listen

*O that ye would listen unto the word of his commands, and let not this
pride of your hearts destroy your souls!* —Jacob 2:16

A few years ago, I was ill for several days. My body tried to get my
attention. I didn't listen. I coughed and sputtered but pretended
nothing was wrong. As part of a family outing, I hiked into the
depths of a canyon—knee-deep in snow. I quickly tired and became
chilled to the bone. Less than a week later, my fever shot up. I could
barely move, breathe, swallow, or walk. It took four days of being
bedridden before I regained some semblance of health.

The incident caused me to ponder all the times Heavenly Father
had tried to get my attention and I chose not to listen. I hadn't wanted
to bother Him with my problems. The word *pride* entered my mind.
In truth, when not paying heed to His voice I was convincing myself
I knew what was best. No wonder when I stubbornly fought to do
things without paying heed to His counsel, my efforts constantly fell
short of achieving what was required!

Today, if only for a few moments, practice tuning out the world
and tuning into the Spirit. After your prayers, remain on your knees,
and listen for counsel and comfort. Choose to have the courage to
follow the guidance you receive.

JANUARY 18

Embracing Gratitude

*When a person doesn't have gratitude, something is missing in his or her
humanity. A person can almost be defined by his or her attitude toward
gratitude.* —Elie Wiesel[5]

I love President Gordon B. Hinckley's nine Be's.[6] To me they are a
blueprint for who I want to become. Prayerful pondering increases
awareness of how and why I should implement them. None has
buoyed me more than the admonition to be grateful.

Gratitude was something that didn't always come automatically
for me. I wasn't in earnest search of it, and I had a difficult time

seeing the silver lining in life's clouds. A wise friend taught me there is indeed wisdom in counting our blessings. When she was having her worst days imaginable, she would enter the privacy of her closet and pour out her thanks. She thanked God for being able to breathe, see, hear, and taste. She thanked Him for the gifts of being able to chew and swallow and walk as well as other tasks often taken for granted. As I began to offer prayers similar to those of my friend, I was impressed by the numerous blessings I'd previously disregarded.

Rejoice in acknowledging your blessings by thanking Heavenly Father. Doing so will lead you to discover the splendor and goodness that is part of each day.

JANUARY 19
Your State of Heart: Showing Gratitude
O how you ought to thank your heavenly King! —Mosiah 2:19

On December 14, 2005, the *San Francisco Chronicle* carried the story of a female humpback whale that appeared to express thanks to divers who cut her free from crab trap lines. During her rescue, the creature remained placid. Had she thrashed and panicked, the event could have rapidly turned disastrous. When she was freed, the whale displayed what experts in marine biology termed as astonishing behavior for her species: she moved from diver to diver, gently nudging each in what seemed to be a gesture of goodwill and gratitude.

When we as a species are bound and pulled downward by forces out of our control, often the last thing we think to do is give thanks for our predicament. We fight against our circumstances. Our hearts may become hardened toward those around us—and toward God. We don't recall getting the memo that spelled out how difficult this life would be.

When we battle trials and challenges with anger, frustration, and anguish, refusing or neglecting to acknowledge the good in life, it becomes difficult for the Spirit to comfort and communicate with us. Giving thanks both during and after our trials enhances our ability to perceive the constant flow of blessings all around us. Though the situations we endure can be perilous, none are impossible to bear if the state of our heart is in harmony with God's.

A grateful heart continues to seek hope. It immerses itself in calm, holding tenaciously to joys past and future, even in the face of pain- and sorrow-filled circumstances of the present. President James E. Faust lovingly tutored that the beginning of greatness is a grateful heart.[7]

JANUARY 20

Witnessing for Yourself: Your Potential and Worth

O Lord, thou hast searched me, and known me. Thou knowest my downsitting and mine uprising, thou understandest my thought afar off. Thou compassest my path and my lying down, and art acquainted with all my ways. . . . I will praise thee; for I am fearfully and wonderfully made. —Psalm 139:1–3, 14

God knows you. He understands the demands of your life. Trials of hearth and home. Friends who aren't always friendly. Peers who are judgmental. He knows about time constraints. He's well acquainted with your innermost fears, your weaknesses and deficits, your worry over how others perceive you. He knows your name, face, and heart. He knows about giving up sleep for mothering and meetings, and about the mixed emotions and weariness you experience; He knows of the dreams and aspirations you put on hold.

He wants you to have life-sustaining blessings of happiness and self-assurance and testimony, to be able to distinguish your capacity to do good both as part of a group and as an individual. He wants you to recognize that you're part of a divine, royal family. He needs you to touch the lives and hearts of others as only you can. You are unique— remarkable in your ability to give. The marvelous, bounteous blessing and gift He will give to you is this: when you diligently work to help others develop and recognize their worth and potential, your ability to perceive your own worth and potential will be strengthened beyond measure.

JANUARY 21
Trusting God
Be still, and know that I am God. —Psalm 46:10

My Aunt Barbara was raised on a farm in eastern Idaho. Every fall she looked forward to the annual barley harvest. One day she was riding with her father on a combine, a piece of equipment that cuts and harvests grains. The terrain of the dry farm undulated, rising and falling in hills and valleys. As they advanced onto a steep slope, the combine tilted at a sharp angle. My aunt wondered if she would have the courage to jump should the machine begin to roll. With trust she watched my grandfather's face to see if worry or fear were etched there. He appeared steady and composed. She knew that if there was trouble he would tell her. When they got off the slope, he told her he'd been concerned but that he never perceived imminent danger.

To trust means to believe in and rely on the integrity, strength, or ability of someone else. You may not be able to see Heavenly Father's face, but you can find warnings in the words of His appointed leaders. You can watch and listen for His messages. When you do as He directs, your trust in Him will grow. Though you will encounter trials and hardship, pain and suffering on this earth as a result of your mortal state, He will not lead you into danger. President Henry B. Eyring teaches that trust in God is demonstrated by listening with intent to learn and repent and then do what He asks.[8] As you do so, your power to trust Him will grow and you will discover that He trusts you.

JANUARY 22
Will You Be Prepared to Return?
Ye cannot say, when ye are brought to that awful crisis, that I will repent, that I will return to my God. Nay, ye cannot say this; for that same spirit which doth possess your bodies at the time that ye go out of this life, that same spirit will have power to possess your body in that eternal world. —Alma 34:34

Imagine for a moment the following hypothetical scenario. There's a knock at the front door. The news you receive causes your heart to pound: it's your time to pass from this life to the next. You gasp and cast a frantic look around. Your mind races with could-haves and should-haves. Unspoken words of love and encouragement. Times you didn't listen with your heart or make an effort to understand. The many things you told yourself you'd be better at when you had time and energy. Loving, living, learning. Intentions stacked on shelves inside your head like books waiting to be read. All you planned but postponed slips from your reach.

Now consider another scene. There's a knock at the front door. The news you receive causes your heart to pound: it's your time to pass from this life to the next. You take a deep breath. You've done your best. You frequently expressed love. You showed kindness and concern, even when others didn't extend the same. You lived with compassion as you prayed for understanding of yourself and those around you. Sometimes others realized when you gave them your best. Often they didn't. But you knew, and so did God. You lived, doing all He asked in the best way you knew how. A sense of peace assures you your best was good enough.

Don't let life become too busy for the things that matter most. If you don't have time for the important stuff, the trivialities won't matter anyway.

Your choices establish your future.

JANUARY 23

Focus: Free Yourself from Technological Busyness
To be spiritually-minded is life eternal. —2 Nephi 9:39

Information and other sensory stimuli rush toward us at light speed from personal entertainment devices. Scientific studies have proven that focus becomes eroded when we remain in a perpetual state of technological busyness. The word *busy* is defined by active and attentive engagement in work or a pastime, yet busyness is characterized by meaningless activity. Or, as Jane Austen's character Fanny Price reflected, "Life can seem like . . . a quick succession of busy nothings."[9]

Technological busyness helps us feel like we're always in control, but it can occupy us to the extent that we lose sight of life's most important elements. Since busyness saps our time and energy, we're often left feeling exhausted, stressed, and unhappy—and wondering what more we can do to feel better.

Joy, contentment, and self-worth are not found in busyness. Accomplishing what you came to this world to do requires setting specific goals. Free yourself from the bondage of day-to-day technological busyness by slowing the stream of media consumption and superficial communication found in social media. Consciously elect to undertake the truly necessary with calm and purposeful intent. Sort truly necessary activities from those which are unnecessary so you have more time to listen to your heart and spirit and to focus on your dreams and destiny. Without constant distractions, the magnificent reality of you is only a whisper away.

JANUARY 24
Goals: Where Do You Want to Go?

Receive my instruction, and not silver; and knowledge rather than choice gold. For wisdom is better than rubies; and all the things that may be desired are not to be compared to it. —Proverbs 8:10–11

After you've set a goal, you still need to make decisions that will allow you to accomplish your desire. It's just like riding a bicycle. You need to keep focus, or steer, toward the objective. Your actions will determine your power and speed. The elements of prayer and scripture study—figuratively your properly inflated tires—will allow you to move forward in the most efficient manner. Faith is the foundation—or seat—that allows you to be in the right position to make it all work.

New York Times best-selling author Leslie Householder says that to reach a desired goal, we should set the intention—goal—for the future, act in the now, and be grateful. Simply put, since whatever you procrastinate becomes easier to procrastinate, you need to continue to advance toward your goal. If you look forward in faith, fix your sights on your objective, allow yourself to imagine how satisfying it will feel when you attain what you desire, and express gratitude along the way, your intended aspiration will be within your grasp.

As they become apparent to you, record decisions you need to make that will help you stay focused and keep progressing toward your goal of knowing you are a daughter of God, as well as other goals you have for the coming year. Plot a course for success. The most important element of both riding a bike and attaining a goal is you! Determination is the strength needed to get where you want to go.

JANUARY 25
Peace and Plenty: The Life God Has Given You
God is my strength and power: and he maketh my way perfect.
—2 Samuel 22:33

He is a wise man who does not grieve for the things which he has not,
but rejoices for those which he has. —Epictetus[10]

Keep on rollin'. —Meg Johnson[11]

A handsome husband, children who are bright, talented, and coop-erative. Travel to exotic destinations, a beautiful house, good health, lots of friends, ample money for needs and wants. Earth time radiat-ing with sublime, idyllic bliss. The "perfect" life is the stuff of dreams. But the reality is that life is far from perfect.

Before Meg Johnson fell off a cliff in southern Utah, she didn't let anything stand in her way. Suddenly faced with being a quadriplegic, she was unable to walk, sit up, eat, drink, or breathe without the aid of a machine. Despair hovered like a dark cloud. In her heart she began to express love for everything from tubes connected to her body, to her immovable legs, to empty visitor chairs. The combined power of love and gratitude for every element in her life created within her a feeling of happiness. She decided though she could no longer literally put her best foot forward, she could do it figuratively by choosing to find ways to continue to pursue the best life had in store for her. She was buoyed by the realization that she still had much to offer.

Often circumstances beyond our control prevent what we might have dreamed would be the perfect life, yet we can experience peace, plenty, and happiness by expressing appreciation and love for the life that is ours. Either in your journal or verbally, start and end each day by finding at least one thing for which to express love and gratitude.

JANUARY 26
A Light of Your Own: Developing a Testimony
If your eye be single to my glory, your whole bodies shall be filled with light, and there shall be no darkness in you. —D&C 88:67

The Light of Christ persuades us to seek and do good as it assists us in differentiating good from evil. If the power has ever gone out at your house during the night, you know how debilitating darkness can be. It's difficult to find your way from room to room. Walls and furniture turn up where you least expect them. You bump and stumble, feeling your way around for items usually taken for granted. With the aid of a lighted candle or a flashlight, dark spaces become illuminated. You're able to discern and avoid the obstacles that encumbered you in the darkness as well as find what is necessary.

Virginia U. Jensen, former first counselor in the Relief Society general presidency, noted the world contains many varieties of darkness including the darkness brought on by transgression, despair, aloneness, and thinking we don't measure up. She also stressed a simple truth: that when we exhibit faith in our Savior, striving always to seek and obey Him, the Light of Christ shines brighter than anything we must face.[12]

Gaining a testimony requires us to apply faith as an action verb. We are all blessed with the Light of Christ. If we ensure that it burns brightly by not allowing it to be diminished by the dampness of uncertainty and disillusionment or the bitter winds of sin, we are guaranteed essential light to dispel darkness. Guided by the Light of Christ, we will learn and grow and blossom as we discover the knowledge we need and desire.

JANUARY 27
Spiritual DNA: You Are Divine by Nature, Remarkable by Choice
Whereby are given unto us exceeding great and precious promises: that by these ye might be partakers of the divine nature. —2 Peter 1:4

You've seen them: remarkable women who hold their heads high. They exude confidence and radiate goodwill. They smile through both serenity and tempest; their laughter spills into the darkest of days like honey-golden rays of sunshine. You wonder, "How do they do it?" The daily demands of meals and laundry and carpools hover like dark clouds. Economic woes and social expectations howl in gales. Children who refuse to obey, relatives who don't understand, and unkind neighbors are lightning strikes within life storms already brimming and flooding with misery, suffering, and strife. Yet remarkable women maintain composure as well as harmony, sense of purpose as well as inner peace.

How do they do it?

They know their worth!

As daughters of God, our spiritual DNA is replete with inherited, infinite capabilities and strengths just waiting to be discovered and put into practice. With Heavenly Father's help, we can turn emotional weed patches into gardens, nourish withered hopes and dried-up reservoirs of faith, and transform the impossible into the possible, hurt into healing, and disaster into success. It starts with recognizing and tapping into our own worth.

Ask Heavenly Father to help you see innate abilities and qualities you may have overlooked in yourself. As His daughter you are divine by nature but remarkable by choice. Make a list of what you discover in your journal; refer and add to it often.

JANUARY 28
Situational Awareness: Spiritual Safety
Actions speak louder than words. —English Proverb

If you've held an umbrella in a rainstorm, you've made use of situational awareness. The term situational awareness means recognizing what's going on around you, comprehending your choices, evaluating that information, and taking action.

In any given situation, gathering the right information—the necessary information—is vital. For instance, if you're a hiker and you see a bear in the middle of the trail in front of you, there's no reason to count how many chipmunks might be on the trail!

Situational awareness can be broken down into four simple steps:

* Recognize
* Comprehend
* Predict the outcome
* Act—make a decision and do it

The same four steps can be applied to choices of a spiritual nature. Anything in our lives that persuades us to question, "Why does it matter if this harms me spiritually?" will rob us of our focus and impact our goals and objectives. Spiritual situational awareness can help us recognize what is going on in our lives, comprehend our circumstances and choices, and predict consequences so we can act as we make decisions that will keep us on track during our journey.

JANUARY 29
Clarity: A Place of Your Own
Come unto me, all ye that labour and are heavy laden, and I will give you rest. Take my yoke upon you, and learn of me; for I am meek and lowly in heart: and ye shall find rest unto your souls.
—Matthew 11:28–29

My grandparents' rural Idaho home served as a hub of family activities and as a hostel for relatives and friends. As a young teen, I quickly learned the value of solitude. With the house's few small rooms and one bathroom often over reasonable occupancy, I fled outdoors. During one visit from a gaggle of boisterous cousins, I sought sanctuary in the chicken coop. I was joined by one of my aunts and a cousin. Apart from the melee, we joked and smiled, relishing our special place of refuge. Now I retreat to the vacant bedroom that once belonged to one of our daughters, where I can discern the whisper of the Spirit as I pray and ponder. Invigorating solitude is mine.

Author Anne Morrow Lindbergh tells us that solitude is necessary in order for women to find the true essence of themselves.[13] Christ knew the value of being apart from the fray in order to seek guidance and inspiration as evidenced in Matthew 14:23: "He went up into a mountain apart to pray: and when the evening was come, he was there alone."

Do you have a quiet place where you can read, study, and pray? A place where you can feel in control, if only for the moment, and your thoughts can flow unfettered by confusion? You may not have a chicken coop or a spare bedroom, but you can find and designate your own special place or time. Early mornings before others arise provide a plethora of options. Honor your need for solitude. Don't feel guilty for treating yourself to the gift of time alone.

JANUARY 30
Gifts of the Spirit
Every good gift cometh of Christ. —Moroni 10:18

Spiritual gifts are given according to the Lord's will and time frame and are given not only for our own benefit, but also that the lives of others might be blessed. These gifts provide us with the things such as strength, confidence, and wisdom we need to succeed on our journey.

After we have received the gift of the Holy Ghost and are living in faithful harmony with God, these gifts, whether they be few or numerous, can become evident to us. They need to be humbly sought and pursued as we pray and seek to know the Father's will. Spiritual gifts include faith, hope, and charity, as well as the gift to teach, heal, or be healed, gifts of knowledge and testimony, and gifts of listening, forgiving, and caring as well as countless others.

Some women have the gift of calm during storms of calamity. Some have the skill of restorative communication, being able to provide crucial insights that help others. Some have been blessed by having acquired the art of listening. Some have the gift of being a loyal friend. Seek the gifts of the Spirit that are waiting for you. As Paul teaches in 1 Corinthians 12:31, "Covet earnestly the best gifts: and yet shew I unto you a more excellent way."

JANUARY 31
Charity

Verily I say unto you, Inasmuch as ye have done it unto one of the least of these my brethren, ye have done it unto me. —Matthew 25:40

The book of Esther tells a stirring account of how one woman's courage and charity changed history. Esther's selfless act saved the lives of her people.

Bob Votruba wants to change history as well. He's encouraging others to commit one million acts of kindness in their lifetime because he believes in the transformative power of kindness to make the world a better place.[14]

The 2010 movie *Letters to God* recounts the story of a young cancer patient whose letters ultimately convince several members of his community to improve their lives. In real life, Tyler Doughtie, the boy the story was based on, touched hearts and lives with his positive attitude and devotion to God.

When we exhibit charity, we can feel the exhilaration of what it means to be God's daughters. Alma was referring to charity when he spoke of "having the love of God always in your hearts." Just as a stone tossed into water sends out ripples, our acts of charity—as small and simple as a brief note expressing love, time taken to build a snowman with a child, hot cocoa and stories shared with family members—will radiate outward and make memorable and lasting differences. Indeed the restorative properties of charity provide healing that can't be obtained in any other way. How will you change history and make the world a better place? Find time today to set a goal for how many acts of kindness or charity you will commit each week.

January Recipes

Spice-It-Up January Salsa

1–2 jalapeño peppers, to taste
1–2 cloves garlic, smashed and chopped
1 (14.5 oz.) can diced tomatoes with fire-roasted green chilies
1 (14.5 oz.) can peeled whole tomatoes
2 green onions, chopped
¼–½ cup chopped fresh cilantro, chopped
1 lime, juiced
¼–½ teaspoon coarse sea salt

Wash the peppers and remove the stems. For a mild salsa, remove the ribs and seeds. Leave some of the ribs and seeds intact according to how hot you want it. Put the peppers and garlic in a food processor; pulse to blend. Add tomatoes, onions, cilantro, lime juice, and salt. For a chunky salsa, pulse only one or two times; more for a smoother salsa.

Party-Perfect Pico

10 fresh, ripe Roma tomatoes, coarsely chopped
½ medium white onion, diced
⅓ cup fresh cilantro, chopped
1–2 serrano peppers, diced
Dash salt
2 teaspoons fresh squeezed lime juice
2 teaspoons cider vinegar

Combine all ingredients and mix well. Chill.

Chunky, Not Spicy, Salsa

¾ cup fresh tomatoes, chopped	2 teaspoons fresh cilantro, chopped
½ cup sweet red onion, chopped	1 Tablespoon olive oil
1 teaspoon fresh garlic, minced	2 Tablespoons lime juice
1 green onion, very thinly sliced	1–2 teaspoons sugar

Combine tomatoes, red onion, garlic, green onion, and cilantro. Set aside. In a separate bowl, whisk together olive oil, lime juice, and sugar until sugar is dissolved. Pour over tomato mixture and stir gently to combine. Chill.

Creamy Hot Sausage Dip

1 pound uncooked spicy pork sausage	2 (8 oz.) packages Neufchatel cheese, cut into small cubes and softened
1 (15 oz.) can diced tomatoes with garlic	Optional: Tabasco or other hot sauce to taste
1 (4 oz.) can mild green chilies	

Cook sausage as directed. Drain. Crumble. Return to skillet and add tomatoes and chilies. Simmer 10–15 minutes. Reduce heat to medium-low, and stir in cream cheese until evenly blended. Add optional Tabasco or other hot sauce. Cook just until heated through. Serve warm.

Fiesta Guacamole

1 pound (about 7 medium) fresh tomatillos, quartered	1–2 Tablespoons lime juice
4–5 garlic cloves, roughly chopped	Dash Tabasco or other hot sauce
½ jalapeño pepper, quartered and seeds removed	Optional: 1 oz. cream cheese, softened
4 avocados, pits and seeds removed	Optional: 1–2 teaspoons Spice-It-Up January Salsa
¼ cup red onion, diced	
¼ teaspoon kosher salt	
½ cup fresh cilantro, chopped	

Preheat oven to 450 degrees. Remove husks from tomatillos and wash with warm water. On foil-lined baking sheet, place tomatillos, garlic, and pepper pieces, cut sides up, for 25–30 minutes. Turn the pieces halfway through the time. Allow to remain in oven until tomatillos and peppers are well browned and skins begin to blister. Do not burn. Cool. Add to food processor. Puree until smooth. Scoop avocado into tomatillo mixture. Pulse one or two times. Add onion, salt, cilantro, lime juice, and other optional ingredients if desired. Pulse just to mix.

FEBRUARY
Believe: You Can Do It!
Loving and Forgiving Yourself

THE SHORTEST MONTH OF THE year, February can nevertheless be long on blessings. In the United States, it is the month of hearts, and on National Wear Red Day, women wear that color to help save lives in support of the fight against heart disease. The United States and other countries celebrate Valentine's Day, a day for romantic love. In Finland the day is referred to as *Ystävänpäivä*—Friends Day, when well-wishes and sentiments of love and devotion celebrate friendship.

The Finnish word for February, *Helmikuu*, is said to mean "month of the pearl" because as ice droplets begin to melt and then refreeze, small pearls of ice form on tree branches. During this tranquil month of simple beauty, the pearls of wisdom you discover about yourself will bring life-sustaining blessings.

Making the Most of February

✱ Send e-mails, text messages, or letters expressing your love and devotion to your spouse or to other family members. Tell them how they make your life better and what you appreciate about them.

✱ Got Dickens? February 7 is Charles Dickens Day. If you don't have one of his classics to read by the fire, find one at the library or at a thrift shop. Also, make a list of books you want to read during the coming year. Add to it as you discover more.

✱ Visit an indoor garden or arboretum.

✱ Attend the symphony. Learn more about your favorite composer.

✱ Start planning for a vacation. Use an inexpensive spiral notebook as an organizer. Write down a list of possibilities for the coming year as well as dream destinations for years ahead. Clip photos from magazines and put them into the organizer. Send for or gather travel brochures.

✱ Clean the insides of your windows. You'll have a head start on spring cleaning.

✱ With your spouse or boyfriend, make a list of new date night ideas. They don't have to be costly or complicated. Enjoy simple pleasures like a theme dinner at home, roasting marshmallows over a stove burner for s'mores, or a fondue night.

✱ On February 14, 1853, ground was broken for the Salt Lake Temple by President Brigham Young. President Heber C. Kimball dedicated the site, and excavation began. Study temples. Learn more about your favorites. A few books to start with are *The Holy Temple* by Boyd K. Packer; *The Gate of Heaven: Insights on the Doctrines and Symbols of the Temple* by Matthew B. Brown; and *Holy Places: True Stories of Faith and Miracles from Latter-day Temples* by Chad Hawkins.

* Bring home fresh flowers, remove the lower leaves, and arrange them in an attractive container. Prepare the container ahead of time by filling it with a 50–50 solution of lemon lime soda and water. Add just a drop or two of bleach.

* Assemble your seed packets and figure out how long it takes each variety to sprout. Check the last frost date for your area and determine when to sow seeds.

* Cut out paper hearts; have family members write messages of kindness and love on them. Deliver the hearts in secret. Put them on plates, in drawers, shoes, or lunchboxes.

* Have a chocolate craving? Satisfy your literary sweet tooth with *Eating Chocolate and Dancing in the Kitchen* by Tom Plummer, or check out the delicious book *Chocolate Never Faileth* by Annette Lyon and Sarah M. Eden. Want to try your hand at a few chocolate delights? *Our Best Bites: Mormon Moms in the Kitchen* by Sara Wells and Kate Jones has a wonderful recipe for salted caramel cashews with dark chocolate. Or enjoy the recipes at the end of the section.

FEBRUARY 1

Your Destiny: Nurture Yourself Every Day
We are always getting ready to live, but never living.
—Ralph Waldo Emerson[15]

Those white slips of paper inside fortune cookies are said to contain wisdom. Whether or not their words truly bestow worthwhile insight is debatable. Something that can't be argued is that a sure foundation for happiness comes from fostering good emotional health. Having a stressed, fatigued mind depletes our ability to make sound decisions. Rather than reacting with frayed emotional responses, a calm and rested mind allows us to meet challenges and resolve problems efficiently. The health of our mind and spirit are every bit as crucial as the health of our physical body. Nurture of self is vital.

Today, cut twenty-eight strips of paper (twenty-nine if it's leap year) into the size of those found in fortune cookies. Sticky notes cut in thirds or fourths work great. On each slip, write a way to nurture yourself. Here are some ideas to get you started:

* Bring home fresh flowers.
* Sincerely compliment yourself.
* Emulate the joy of a happy child.
* Watch a movie that makes you laugh.
* Check out a fun children's book at the library.
* Get a pair of fuzzy socks to snuggle your feet into.
* Buy a stuffed animal to cuddle with.
* Have an unrushed breakfast by yourself.
* Buy the kind of chocolate you really love.
* See a good movie with friends.
* Get a houseplant to care for.

Fold the papers in half, and put them into a small jar. Tie a sparkly ribbon around the outside and keep your "fortunes" in a special place. Each day this month, take out a slip and follow what you've written.

How are you going to nurture yourself today?

FEBRUARY 2

Care of Self: To Wit's End and Back Again

For God hath not given us the spirit of fear; but of power, and of love, and of a sound mind. —2 Timothy 1:7

Psalm 107:23–29 tells of sailors on storm-tossed seas. Encountering conditions they cannot control, they reach a point of desperation. Their souls "melted because of trouble. They reel to and fro, and stagger like a drunken man, and are at their wit's end."

Where is your wit's end?

Is it at your in-laws, who won't stop criticizing you? Down the block at the neighbor's, whose child bullies yours? Or in your own home in the middle of the night when your teen consistently fails to meet curfew? Wherever, it can be challenging, painful, and, at worst, emotionally incapacitating.

The opposite of your wit's end is keeping your wits about you. Your capacity to stay alert and composed in life's stormy seas is a skill worth pursuing. The world may not change, but you can. The next time you find yourself heading toward your wit's end, take a deep breath. Sit down and focus.

Scottish minister Oswald Chambers said, "When a man is at his wit's end it is not a cowardly thing to pray."[16] Pray that, if it is God's will, the burden will be eased. Pray for knowledge of how to cope with your troubles, how to efficiently think through the steps you need to take. Pray to know what questions you should ask in order to find the answers you are seeking. Equally important, pray for peace of mind to accept what comes.

FEBRUARY 3

Time for You: Giving Guilt a Vacation

Guilt: The gift that keeps on giving. —Erma Bombeck[17]

Stress fluctuates from person to person. One woman's stress may be another woman's bliss. Stress can also be a byproduct of guilt. No matter the cause, the physical and emotional symptoms of stress range from mild to severe. Try to shove feelings of stress aside, and eventually they will resurface in the form of tension, illness, difficulty concentrating, relationship woes, and decreased ability to cope. Panic and anxiety attacks, crying, or compulsive behaviors may plague otherwise rational women when they feel overwhelmed.

Eliminating or at least easing stress is a fundamental aspect of caring for yourself. The less stress you have, the more efficiently you can manage your life. Replenishing yourself will rejuvenate your attitude and revitalize your emotions. Problems will seem more manageable when you take time away then revisit them. The same confusion you leave behind will patiently await your return. And a few peanut butter and jelly dinners—or breakfasts—will not hurt anyone!

Identify what brings you happiness and contentment. Putting yourself first isn't selfish. It ensures you will have sufficient energy to devote to loved ones. Give yourself permission to enjoy life. Don't underestimate the value of fun and laughter. Send guilt on a vacation, and toss stress out the window.

FEBRUARY 4
An Emotional Safety Net: A Joy Basket
When one door of happiness closes, another opens; but often we look so long at the closed door that we do not see the one which has been opened for us. —Helen Keller[18]

Remember your favorite toy or doll? Something you kept with you as a child to help you feel safe in the darkness of night or during the uncertainty of difficult times? Would it surprise you to know that many grown women still have their dolls or teddy bears? Objects from our childhood evoke pleasant memories of simplicity, serenity, and security.

As adults we need pick-me-ups to soothe us. A joy basket helps comfort threadbare nerves and emotions. An old basket or shoebox will work well. Line it with colorful fabric. Add items that appeal to your senses. Lotion, foot or hand cream, bath salts, scented candles and soaps, the chocolate you love or the exceptional, hard-to-find candy you're passionate about, fuzzy socks or slippers, hot chocolate, lavender spray or a lavender-filled eye pillow, perfume, gum, books, comforting music or movies, old cards and love letters, or keepsakes from loved ones who have passed on (like jewelry, embroidered handkerchiefs, doilies, dried flowers, swatches of ribbon, and cherished photographs). What about the cookies you crave (lemon-lavender shortbread for me) that everyone eats faster than you can get to them? Stash some in the box just for you. Don't forget childhood comfort toys like your teddy bear or stuffed bunny.

Next time your emotions need a boost, go to your joy basket and pamper yourself with something special.

FEBRUARY 5
Life Rhythm: Sing and Dance
A time to weep, and a time to laugh; a time to mourn, and a time to dance. —Ecclesiastes 3:4

Author and artist Vivian Green's admonition to dance in the rain instead of waiting for storms to pass is shrewd advice. Life's challenges seldom allow for a long break between rainy days. Music is a blessing that inspires and motivates us. President Spencer W. Kimball said he was comforted with the assurance that beautiful music would be present in heaven![19] When we let go of self-consciousness, music compels us to give blissful outward expressions of inner joy—to sing and dance and truly celebrate our existence.

How long has it been since you sang in the shower or danced just for the pleasure of it? Download music, find a favorite radio station, or organize a music swap. Get together with friends and trade CDs, old records, or tapes. Music that might be dated or lackluster for someone else may be just what you need to rejuvenate your spirit. Even if you think you can't carry a tune, singing and dancing is in your genes. Our ancestors used song and dance as means of worship, entertainment, and joyful self-expression.

This week cut loose and practice having fun. Sing in the car. Sing on your walk, run, or bike ride. Go ahead and sing in the shower or even on your front porch. Singing keeps you upbeat and chases away shadows. Dance with your two-year-old. Dance with your cat. Dance with your face heavenward and your arms spread wide. Dance for sunshine and rain. Dance for rainbows and snow. Make your heart and voice swell with the pure delight of being alive.

FEBRUARY 6

Imperfections: Seeing Your Own Inherent Beauty and Promise
And he said unto me, My grace is sufficient for thee: for my strength is made perfect in weakness. Most gladly therefore will I rather glory in my infirmities, that the power of Christ may rest upon me.
—2 Corinthians 12:9

The tale is told of an old Chinese woman who owned two large ceramic pots. The pots hung at the ends of a pole she carried on her shoulders. Every day she traveled to a stream for water. While one pot consistently carried its full measure, the other pot was cracked. Each time the woman returned home, it was only half full.

For years the woman made the trek to the stream. The perfect pot never failed to bear its load. The cracked pot was embarrassed of its imperfection, unhappy it was able to do only half of what the other pot did. Ashamed of its perceived failure, it confessed its sense of worthlessness to the woman. She, however, didn't view the pot as less valuable.

"Did you see the flowers on your side of the path? There are no flowers on the other side. I knew of your flaw, and so I planted flower seeds on your side of the path. Every day while I walk back I water them. Because of you being the way you are, I have beautiful flowers."

Like the cracked pot, we all have imperfections. It's those imperfections—those flaws—which make us unique. Often we find the good in others but overlook it in ourselves. We may perceive the lives of those around us as worthwhile, interesting, and admirable. Yet we view our own lives and selves as far less.

Embark on the adventure of seeing yourself as full of promise and beauty with unique characteristics and skills that can enrich your life and the lives of others.

FEBRUARY 7

Who You Are: Putting Your Best Foot Forward

And turn ye not aside: for then should ye go after vain things, which cannot profit nor deliver; for they are vain. —1 Samuel 12:21

It was prom night, and amid the clutter on my best friend's bedroom floor, the three-inch platform sandals shimmered like Cinderella's glass slippers. I wore a size 8; the sandals were size 6. But the exquisite footwear, my sixteen-year-old brain confirmed, would ensure I looked tall and glamorous. What did it matter if they fit?

Seconds before our dates arrived I managed to tug the sandals on. Before the dance, we went to eat. As I entered the restaurant, my feet throbbed. To make matters worse, our table was on the second floor. I clambered toward the stairway. As my long red and white gown draped the top of the second step, I tripped in front of what seemed to be the entire world. I was too embarrassed to make eye contact with my date. I couldn't eat my expensive dinner. On the verge of tears, I asked to be taken home. We never made it to the dance.

I've often reflected on my prom night experience. In wearing too-small shoes, I sacrificed common sense. In asking to be taken home, I was consumed with the fear that others would judge me. The world is always ready to let us know how inferior we are—never pretty enough, thin enough, popular enough, rich enough, and the list goes on. But trying to be someone we're not almost always ends up hurting.

Embrace yourself and all your humanness. Strive to love yourself the way God does—without regard for appearances and without judgment of flaws and idiosyncrasies. It will help you to put your best foot forward.

FEBRUARY 8

Bloom: Finding Yourself

In me he shall have glory, and not of himself, whether in weakness or in strength, whether in bonds or free. —D&C 24:11

Consistently doing the right thing amid opposition can be challenging. Critics abound, especially, it seems, when we're striving to do our best. The closer we draw to our Father in Heaven and Savior, the more Satan uses all his available means to discourage and dissuade us. When painful comments or ridicule are received from others—especially those we want to love and value us—it can be tempting to give up. Despair can cause us to question ourselves and what we believe in. We can come to fear failure, fear getting hurt, or fear being judged to such a great extent it blocks out the light we have as children of God. So much so, sometimes, that we forget it's even there.

When it comes to those who seek to drag us down, it's helpful to remember that what they say about us actually says more about them. In other words, negative emotions come from inherently negative sources, just as positive things flow from a source of truth and light. We only have to watch or read the news to see that the world seeks out complaining and faultfinding. We all know those who have the ability to make even bad situations more difficult. Recognize that people who work hard to keep others down are fighting within themselves a bitter, lonely battle. We can learn from them what we don't want to become. We have within ourselves power—a choice to bloom wherever we are planted.

FEBRUARY 9
A Good Night's Sleep: Stop Counting Worries
Remember the worth of souls is great in the sight of God.
—D&C 18:10

A few years ago, researchers at Oxford University debunked the myth that counting imaginary sheep helps us fall asleep. In fact, it was discovered that sheep counters stayed awake longer![20] It turns out that counting sheep is too boring to keep most folks' minds off life's stresses and trials.

If you're among the one in ten adults who find their minds frequently struggling to cope with nerve-racking concerns when you'd rather be sleeping, write down your worries. Several hours before your scheduled bedtime, find a sheet of paper. Divide the page into two columns. The left side is for worries and problems. On the right hand side of the page, briefly state possible resolutions. Tuck the paper away and give yourself the night off. If you wake up early and find yourself stressing again, locate the paper and jot down additional concerns and solutions.

The Oxford researchers who discredited the sheep/sleep method also discovered that creating an interesting scene in your mind, perhaps envisioning your dream home or a hoped-for vacation, can be an effective tool to take your attention off worries. And don't underestimate the power of prayer in preparing for a good night's rest; the Lord is ever mindful of us and always willing to listen.

Try these ideas and let yourself—and the sheep—get a good night's sleep.

FEBRUARY 10
Live: Letting Go
But lay up for yourselves treasures in heaven, where neither moth nor rust doth corrupt, and where thieves do not break through nor steal.
—3 Nephi 13:20

There are attributes I've cultivated and convictions I hold fast to because I know they're right. There are qualities and practices I wish to ingrain in myself because I want to strive to do my very best. There are also superfluous traits and habits—like worrying about being judged for how I look, act, and sound (I do not like my singing voice)—I've acquired because of my own vanity or because others urged me to adopt them.

What are some of the least important elements in your life? Emotional disarray caused by worrying about the negative opinions of others? Waiting for your life to begin and not really living the gift of it each day? Or perhaps clutter caused by material possessions you don't really need or rarely use? You can add greater depth to living by eliminating unnecessary elements, which will in turn allow you to spend more time on things that really matter. Discover and develop attributes and habits that will help you attain the promises of your heavenly birthright as well as blessings that will bring true joy.

FEBRUARY 11

Overcoming Procrastination

And now, my brethren, I wish from the inmost part of my heart, yea, with great anxiety even unto pain, that ye would hearken unto my words, and cast off your sins, and not procrastinate the day of your repentance. —Alma 13:27

Time can slip away from us. In spite of good intentions, we don't accomplish what we set out to do. But if day after day, week after week, the same stuff on our to-do lists never seems to go away, we're probably avoiding it. Procrastination plagues all of us at some point in our lives, but it's a habit we can choose to overcome.

One reason we balk at certain tasks is that we've never done them before, or that we believe we didn't do them well enough the last time. We might not know how to get started or how to do a particular thing with proficiency. But we can learn how by seeking the advice of others who have completed similar tasks. Then, after studying our options— and not over analyzing them—we need to compel ourselves to action. If we're afraid of failure, we can pray with sincerity for the guidance and courage necessary to allow us to press forth. Making mistakes is part of life. With God's help we can always go back to the drawing board and learn the best way to efficiently accomplish whatever it is we need to do.

What are some of the things you put off doing? Do you know why? Record your responses in your journal along with thoughts and ideas you'd like to implement to keep yourself on track and prevent procrastination from robbing you of time and opportunities.

FEBRUARY 12

The Way You Touch Lives

I will make a man [woman] more precious than fine gold. —Isaiah 13:12

A baby knows a mother's voice; a mother can soothe and comfort her child in ways no one else can. Similarly, you can do things like no other that will give depth and meaning to the lives of those around you. Maybe it's the inflection of your voice as you teach a lesson to busy adults or read nursery rhymes to restless children, something about the warmth of your tone or strength of your spirit that resonates with their needs. Maybe it's the compassion you extend—like an artist exploring composition and color as you find new ways to touch the hearts of others. Maybe it's the depth of understanding you alone are able to offer to relieve distress and reassure someone who has lost their way; you've trodden similar ground and fought your way back— you have a unique perspective that is your gift of hope.

Just as your fingerprints are unlike any other, your spiritual imprint is one of a kind. You are exclusive in your ability to express yourself in word and deed. Take notice of the things that make you special, and embrace them as gifts of hope. The way you see yourself can give new meaning to the way you live.

FEBRUARY 13
The Stuff of Dreams: A Life Collage
Life is what you make it. Always has been, always will be.
—Grandma Moses[21]

We grow great by dreams. . . . Some of us let these great dreams die, but others nourish and protect them, nurse them through bad days till they bring them to the sunshine and light which come always to those who sincerely hope that their dreams will come true. —James Frances Dwyer[22]

When we focus on who we want to become and how we'd like our life to be, we move closer toward that which we desire. President Brigham Young taught that when we learn to master our feelings, we become able to master our thoughts, and thus stay on track in the pursuit of what we are seeking. He further noted that the more we apply our thoughts to any correct purpose, the quicker we benefit from an increase of knowledge and truth.[23]

When chaos and strife abound, it's difficult to focus on where we'd like to go, difficult to remember our journey was meant to be joyous. Having the assurance of tomorrow—the promise of a new day—can pull us through the complexities of today. Creating a bulletin board or magnet board where you can display images relevant to your goals will help you visualize what you're working toward.

Do you dream of returning to the ocean-side cottage you visited years ago? Put up photographs of your last vacation there. Pictures of sea stars, sunshine, and smiles. Do you yearn to finish your art degree? Display a class schedule that will motivate you to take action. Do you want to make a better cheesecake? Put up the new recipe you found.

Quotes, short stories, articles, travel brochures, mementos, business cards—what is your life collage going to look like?

FEBRUARY 14
Valentine's Day: Queen of Hearts
Love one another, as I have loved you. —John 15:12

Hearts and flowers and candy, lacey valentines decorated with ribbons and bows, affectionate couples with stars in their eyes and their heads in the clouds. The romantic sentiments associated with Valentine's Day can stir the hopes and dreams of some and evoke dismay and an accentuated sense of aloneness in others. Love yet to be expressed, lost love, broken hearts, and dashed expectations still exist even with Cupid fluttering around like a dazed butterfly.

If the romantic nuances of the day are enough to send you into hibernation with the shades pulled down, celebrate with the people of Finland. Commemoration of friendship on this day pays homage to the love we feel for dear friends. Send cards, make phone calls, and express thanks. Scrapbook special pages. Display photos of those you love—both friends and family—on the front of the refrigerator or even on the front door. Don't forget to add photographs of yourself. Intermingle cards you've received, notes and expressions of kindness, or favorite lines of poetry.

Remember that romance isn't the only thing deserving of accolades of flowers and candy—your favorite old auntie, lonely next door neighbor, or new friend who just moved to town will appreciate you remembering them.

Today search for the magic the day can bring, common threads of beauty and joy in all your relationships: love that is, love that has been, and love that is to come.

FEBRUARY 15
Ten Ways to Give Yourself Daily Gifts of Peace
The Lord lift up his countenance upon thee, and give thee peace.
—Numbers 6:26

Slow down, but don't be late. Awareness of deadlines is good, but rushing at them with lack of regard for your health and well-being causes stress. Being late is a stressor as well. Give yourself ample time for tasks at hand.

Catch up on rest. You'll function better when your mind and body are well rested. If you don't have time for added slumber, take precious minutes to retreat to a tranquil place where you can close your eyes and still the pace of your heart and mind.

Pray for comfort. Trust that it will come and allow yourself to find respite in the Spirit's embrace.

Don't deliberately start disputes. When you look for contention, you'll find it. When you seek harmony, you'll find that as well.

List your favorite joys. Remember those one-sentence slices of life that capture splendor and bliss? Remember to look for and record them. Read and savor them when you're blue.

Don't do things you know you'll regret later. Enough said.

Edit the information that comes into your life. Whether pessimistic input comes from outside sources or from within your own tendency to look for clouds, make it a habit to sift out and discard the negative.

Be patient with yourself. Allow yourself time to learn, to heal, to grow, to know, to weep, to smile, to stomp, to stride. Soak in life's tender, precious moments and revel in them.

Seek encouragement. When your heart and mind are weary, be willing to seek support from trusted family members, friends, or leaders. If everyone else seems to fail you, strive more diligently to seek God.

Expect miracles. When they come, gather their evidences like beautiful, delicate blossoms.

Gifts of peace are forever yours to enjoy!

FEBRUARY 16
The Perfecting Qualities of Imperfection
Condemn me not because of mine imperfection, neither my father,
because of his imperfection, neither them who have written before him;
but rather give thanks unto God that he hath made manifest unto you
our imperfections, that ye may learn to be more wise than we have been.
—Mormon 9:31

Imperfection. The longer we live—the more we live—the more our faults, blunders, mistakes, and errors in judgment rise up to greet us. If we let them, they will taunt us with reminders that we are far from perfect, attempt to convince us our goals and dreams are unattainable, and chide us into fear as we come to believe life is not worth living to its fullest. But imperfection is not our enemy. The fact is God views perfection differently than we do.

While we might gaze in horror at the sight of a raspberry jam–covered child (with an equally jam-covered terrier by his side) opening the front door to unanticipated company, we perceive fault: we can't keep our child clean. Heavenly Father sees a child loved by a mother who cares enough to make and feed him jam on warm slices of bread.

Where we see the dent in a car's fender as evidence of our ineptitude, He sees our desire to be honest as we wait for the car's owner to come out of the grocery store.

After we say something in haste that unintentionally hurts or offends, Heavenly Father sees the state of our heart when we bear responsibility for the comment, showing we are humble and willing to learn.

When we don't fear it, imperfection can teach us to think in new and different ways that yield positive emotions and outcomes.

FEBRUARY 17
Extending Forgiveness to Yourself
For God sent not his Son into the world to condemn the world; but that the world . . . might be saved. —John 3:17

Jewel Adams had a childhood riddled with sorrow and pain. The daughter of an alcoholic mother and a stepfather who abused her, she had no self-worth as a teen and no idea of who she really was. To escape her situation, she married young and, following a tragic accident, was widowed by age eighteen. She fell into drugs and alcohol, her way of self-medicating, but realized that regardless of her childhood, the choices she made as an adult were hers alone. If she was going to turn her life around and not be like her mother, she had to make decisions that would lead to change.

"I wanted better," she says. "It took me a long time to love myself because of all the poor choices I made in the past. I didn't know if I would ever be worthy." It took a blessing from her new husband to ease Jewel's mind and let her know she had been forgiven. "It was then that I truly began to know my worth. After that, I never looked back." As Jewel eagerly attests, Heavenly Father loves us, and the Savior knows our hearts because he suffered and experienced everything we feel. "We are never too far gone to change. God sees what we can become and wants to help us reach our full potential. I will forever be a work in progress in this life, but I know that as long as I am trying to do what is right, I'm getting a little closer each day to being the daughter He knows I can be."[24]

In what areas might you need to extend forgiveness to yourself?

FEBRUARY 18
Healing through the Atonement
And the world, because of their iniquity, shall judge him to be a thing of naught; wherefore they scourge him, and he suffereth it; and they smite him, and he suffereth it. Yea, they spit upon him, and he suffereth it, because of his loving kindness and his long-suffering towards the children of men. —1 Nephi 19:9

If we have been the recipients of unkind words, gossip, rumors, or backbiting, we may believe we are inferior. If we have been ostracized, given the silent treatment, or if others have acted in a manner that has emotionally or physically injured us, we may feel too inadequate to matter. Even tiny mistakes can become proof to us of our lack of worth. If we adopt and practice behaviors that are not in harmony with Christ's teachings, we will ultimately experience an abiding sense of hopelessness. That hopelessness can be compounded by anger and dislike for ourselves when we become accustomed to thinking that no matter what we do we will fail. As a result, we find ourselves drifting farther and farther away from our divine selves. We become convinced that God does not love us because we are not worth being loved.

The Atonement, Christ's suffering the penalty for our sins and bearing our sorrows, avails us of the opportunity to heal not only from the offenses of others but also from the burdens we have placed upon ourselves. Studying the Atonement reassures us of our infinite eternal value and that we are dearly loved as individuals. Our Savior did not offer himself up only to forsake us in our mortal life.

In the topical guide in your scriptures, look up "Jesus Christ, Atonement through." Choose a few scriptures to prayerfully study.

FEBRUARY 19

Positive Thinking Is Faith in Action: Do You Expect to Succeed?
Train up a child in the way he should go: and when he is old, he will not depart from it. —Proverbs 22:6

It's a proven fact that how we view our own abilities or limitations can impact our view of a child's ability to succeed. When our expectations are diminished, their expectations of themselves will generally follow suit. The same principle applies when it comes to ourselves.

Sometimes benign comments from others can seem like unsympathetic criticism. Add those supposed censures to judgments we make about ourselves, and we find a growing burden of limiting beliefs that weigh us down and prevent us from achieving our full potential.

Setbacks and obstacles are normal, mistakes inevitable. But when we make a conscious choice to channel our thoughts into a positive flow, the results can help us in incredible ways. Make realistic expectations of yourself. Positive thinking doesn't mean you'll avoid life's realities, just that you'll be able to cultivate courage to face problems head on. Positive thinking is faith in action. Even if your earthly parents never cheered you on, your Heavenly Father and Elder Brother will support and encourage you.

FEBRUARY 20
Juggling Responsibilities
Grace and peace be multiplied unto you through the knowledge of God, and of Jesus our Lord. —2 Peter 1:2

Elder Dallin H. Oaks lovingly counsels that as we contemplate our choices in life, we need to recognize that while some decisions are good, the value of others are better or even best.[25] How do we weigh our choices so that we benefit from the best?

Attempting to do too much, multitasking to the point of exhaustion, sets us up for letdowns. Our thoughts and attention become divided and divided again until we have little to nothing left to offer ourselves or others. Inconsequential concerns crowd out those that are most important. We need to ensure our lives don't become so out of balance that we falter and fall from mental, emotional, or physical fatigue.

Of all the tasks we're accountable for each day, our responsibilities to God, ourselves, and our families are most significant. Prayerfully strive to find the balance between responsibilities, work, service, and leisure time. If you find yourself constantly overwhelmed and frustrated—out of balance—reexamine the true and lasting value of life's and love's most important elements. Determine which, as Elder Oaks terms, are good, better, and best.

FEBRUARY 21
Your State of Heart: A Plan for Healing
Search me, O God, and know my heart: try me, and know my thoughts.
—Psalm 139:23

At one time it was believed that our emotions were merely expressions generated by our perception of the world—the brain acting all on its own. But in recent years, studies have explored the connection between the heart, mind, body, and spirit. We can learn to manage our state of heart—our attitude and emotions. If we retain ill will, we cannot be in harmony with God's will. If our heart has become scarred by past hurts and offenses, we have the choice to begin to take the steps to heal it:

* Take a few minutes each day to process sorrow or anger by writing or talking through issues. Letting go of pent-up emotion increases energy. Be quick to acknowledge and express delight and joy. Meditation, relaxation, yoga, and expressions of gratitude are becoming increasingly heralded as means to heal the body, mind, heart, and spirit.

* Pray for the help and guidance and strength the Atonement can bring.

* Increase your awareness of your feelings. Are you angry, sad, or lonely? These emotions are important to recognize and acknowledge. Do you consciously recognize the circumstances that cause you to feel certain emotions? How could you react differently to those circumstances?

* Express your emotions in constructive ways. Write the cookbook you've been wanting to write; paint a room a color you love; run; bike; sing at the top of your lungs; dance; create; clean the house from top to bottom; cultivate a garden, flowers, or indoor plants to care for; love a pet; do temple work or genealogy; initiate positive communication with those who have offended you in addition to conversations with those you trust.

* Serve others. Find someone who has more troubles than you and write to them, call them, or visit them. Step out of your comfort zone and get to know their needs. Volunteer to help children learn to read, or read to the elderly.

✳ Forgive those who have wronged you. It is a sublime expression of faith and courage to put into practice the Lord's admonition from the Sermon on the Mount, "But I say unto you, Love your enemies, bless them that curse you, do good to them that hate you, and pray for them which despitefully use you, and persecute you" (Matthew 5:44).

FEBRUARY 22
A Road Map

Counsel with the Lord in all thy doings, and he will direct thee for good; yea, when thou liest down at night lie down unto the Lord, that he may watch over you in your sleep; and when thou risest in the morning let thy heart be full of thanks unto God; and if ye do these things, ye shall be lifted up at the last day. —Alma 37:37

Our perceptions of ourselves can be most tender. If someone says or does something that strikes a sensitive cord, we can become particularly wounded. We might feel tempted to carry the pain of our past into the present and even into the future. If the depth of our past pain causes us to avoid interaction with our Father in Heaven, we need to ask ourselves why, and we may need to seek assistance.

We wouldn't set out to travel to another country without any preparation. If we spun ourselves around, pointed our feet in a wanton direction, then took off walking, we could end up anywhere! We need to know the right direction, the estimated distance, and the provisions we'll need. For the same reasons we consult a road map, consulting our bishop is the best place to begin if we've lost touch with God. A bishop's job is to provide us with direction that will aid us in exploring our options to help us reach the destination Heavenly Father knows is best for us.

FEBRUARY 23
Focus on Now

Judge not, and ye shall not be judged: condemn not, and ye shall not be condemned: forgive, and ye shall be forgiven. —Luke 6:37

Once a week I drive across a stretch of road that is uncomfortable for me to travel. In the past several years, two of my close friends and three girls I knew in high school have died on that highway. Knowing exactly where each of them died is unsettling. When I first started driving the road, I often found myself stressing over other vehicles—especially those in my rearview mirror. How many were behind me? How fast were they driving? Were they following too closely?

The Spirit whispered to me that the way I was making the weekly trip didn't make sense. I had no control over what I saw in the rearview mirror. Spending so much time looking back made it difficult for me to concentrate. The more time I spent stressing over what was behind me—cars and memories—the less able I was to focus on the most important aspect of my travel: what was directly in front of me. With prayer and faith, I was able to refocus my attention on the road ahead to ensure I did the best possible job of moving forward.

Don't keep looking back. Today, make a mental list of all the things you're doing right and that are going right, right now. Are you reading even a few scriptures each day? Are you striving to pray and seek the Spirit? Are you curbing your desire to criticize others? Are you being kind and loving to yourself and looking for the best in you? How important it is to do so! In the days and months ahead, make a habit of adding to your list as you consciously and consistently move forward.

FEBRUARY 24
Loving Yourself: Respect
Reproach hath broken my heart; and I am full of heaviness: and I looked for some to take pity, but there was none; and for comforters, but I found none. —Psalm 69:20

R—Realize you're not like everyone else and that God didn't intend you to be. Believe in yourself and your abilities. Be friends with yourself!

E—Expect the best from yourself. Be proud when you attain your best. Don't quit when you don't quite measure up to where you desire to be; don't be too hard on yourself.

S—Self-worth is demonstrated by your actions and attitudes toward life. Treating others with love and regard helps you cultivate respect for yourself. Those who mistreat or put themselves or others down don't understand respect. Misery might love company, but enthusiasm is contagious and draws a crowd. Surround yourself with positive people who respect themselves; good character is of immeasurable worth.

P—Protect yourself from harm. Staying close to God nurtures spiritual well-being. Not overextending yourself on credit cards or loans builds sound financial health. Not insulting yourself fosters emotional and mental well-being. Staying away from harmful substances helps ensure physical health. Always being honest with yourself promotes a healthy outlook on life.

E—Eternal potential and possibilities come first. Don't let others talk you into doing something your conscience tells you you shouldn't. Don't change to please others; don't conform to standards you know are false.

C—Courageously face criticism. The opinions of others don't define you unless you allow them to. Value your own insights. If criticisms are justified, use them to better yourself.

T—Trust in your values and don't forget what's important to you. Just because others expect you to act in a certain way doesn't mean you have to. When you're doing what you know is right, you don't need the approval of others. Father in Heaven's opinion is the only one that matters.

FEBRUARY 25
Fitting In: Your Positive Attributes and Strengths
The Lord is the strength of my life; of whom shall I be afraid?
—Psalm 27:1

Have you ever felt the sting of not fitting in? Felt like an outsider because you were different? Consider this: what if your difference is really your unique strength? A distinctive dissimilarity that can change hearts and lives?

Whether what makes you different causes you to confront your past, change your present, or work toward a brighter future, you can serve as an example to others. Women who confront abuse and injustice lend courage to those who are fearful. Women who choose to adopt because they are unable to bear children of their own pave a path of love. The determination of women who battle disease gives hope to those desperately seeking relief from the burden of hopelessness. Women who pattern their lives after the Savior's, extending forgiveness and compassion despite devastating challenges, are role models worthy of emulating.

Perseverance leads us to excel in ways we may have never dreamed possible. What are some limitations or disadvantages in your life that may actually be positive attributes and strengths waiting to be discovered?

FEBRUARY 26
Authentic Self: Expressions of the Heart
If you don't find yourself, you'll always wonder who you are.

What we do and how we act can be shaped by a competitive desire to appear flawless. Competitive drive compels us to meet or exceed milestones set by others.

Our expression of self comes from heartfelt yearning to communicate our deeply held convictions. If we believe having a meticulously clean house is important, we feel we have failed if others view it in a less than ideal state.

Often our actions are a mixture of both competitive urge and the need to put forth the essence of self. Maintaining equilibrium is essential. If what you set out to do in a day ends up evoking stress, you may need to reexamine your motivations. Trying too hard to match the efforts of others can leave you feeling empty. Unreasonable expectations of self can cause anguish. Do you really need to explain disorder to unexpected visitors? What would their home look like if you showed up unannounced? A house is not a home unless it is used by the people who live there; disarray is normal!

Tapping into realistic expectations will ease anxiety. There are women who bake perfectly risen bread. It's okay if you're not one of them. If your family wants homemade bread, trade a jar of your delectable apricot jam or some of your special tamales for a loaf. Think outside the box as you consider how noncompetitive expressions of self can bring an abiding sense of peace and fulfillment.

FEBRUARY 27
A Love Letter to Yourself
It's not who you are that holds you back; it's who you think you are.
—Author unknown

Notebook paper, flower-embossed stationery, bright circles and stars— choose paper that speaks to the real you. Find a quiet spot alone where you know you won't be disturbed. Take a deep breath. You're about to write one of the most important letters you'll ever pen.

A love letter to yourself.

Think. Reflect. Laugh. Get a box of tissues and cry. For some of us this is hard work! Start by writing about how proud you are to be you. Without all you've been through, how would you have gained strength and courage? Every experience you've had, mistakes and victories alike, propelled you closer to finding who you are. Write about your triumphs and achievements. Tell yourself about your best qualities. Your great sense of humor. Your patience under pressure. Your compassion. Extol your talents. The fabulous dinner you made. The wonderful lesson you taught. A new piece you learned for the piano. The room you redecorated. The beautiful quilt you tied. The powerful poem you wrote. Tell yourself what a superb job you did.

Write of secret aspirations and heartfelt desires. Laugh. Cry some more. Start a second sheet, a third—you're that wonderful! Seal the letter in a beautiful envelope. Have a stamp ready because, yes, you need to mail the letter to yourself. Better yet, give it to a close friend to hold onto for when she knows you're having a tough time.

FEBRUARY 28

Savor the Moment: Experiencing Joy
In the world ye shall have tribulation: but be of good cheer.
—John 16:33

When did you start to take joy for granted? Was it when you grew up and decided you needed to act a certain way to meet the expectations of others? Was it when you stopped looking at the bright side because the glare was too intense? Was it when you stopped doing things that brought you delight because you felt you didn't deserve to be happy? How did the joy of plain and simple moments get lost?

Watch a young child eat an ice cream cone. Their eyes wide with excitement. A grin punctuated by sweet, creamy goodness that runs down their chin. They don't care if their faces and hands—or your kitchen floor—get sticky. The very picture of rapture, they savor the moment.

We get so caught up in sprinting toward the future where we hope happiness can be found that we forget the present used to be the future. There is joy waiting in every day. Eat your meals slowly; relish the taste. Feel the warmth of water on your hands and face. Watch the bubbles form when you lather bath soap or dish soap. Put your hand on your stomach and feel yourself breathe. Be aware of the comfort of the pillow under your head, the softness of the blanket that covers you, the crisp touch of fresh, clean sheets. Close your eyes and listen to the voices and laughter of your loved ones. Breathe in the sweet smells of babies and newborn puppies, flowers and food, the scent of rain and the mouthwatering aromas from the bakery.

Practice living in the moment. Savor it as the blessing it is. Glean joy, and experience the thrill of letting it flow through you.

FEBRUARY 29

The Power of Believing
With God all things are possible. —Matthew 19:26

Both my grandmothers have passed away, but rarely a day goes by that I don't think of them. Etched in my memory are evidences of their character—their kind words to strangers, patience in listening to woes and concerns of loved ones, hugs, smiles, and laughter lent an air of wonder to time spent in their presence. From them I gained respect for the art of finding the lighter side of life. I observed with reverence the skill of meeting challenges with grace. The fine nuances of grieving with gratitude. Finding courage to move forward when there was no apparent path. But it was their belief in me—their confidence—that I would do my best and be my best that was and is the glue that holds my life together.

Still there are bleak days when I simply cannot comprehend my worth. I have to struggle through self-doubt and labor to call to mind the words of my grandmothers: exchanges of thoughts and ideas, cards and letters written to me when my faith was at an ebb. Loving words sustained me and taught me the confidence to know I was capable of thriving. It then becomes my responsibility to choose to follow their example and believe in myself.

Do you have someone who believes in you? Count them as a rich personal blessing. When you look in the mirror, tell yourself that you believe in you too.

February Recipes

Quadruple Chocolate Trifle

1 (19.8 oz.) package brownie mix
1 (19.8 oz.) package chocolate fudge cake mix
1 (14 oz.) can sweetened condensed milk
1 ⅓ cups milk
1 (6 oz.) package instant chocolate pudding

¼ cup whipped topping
1 (8 oz.) container whipped topping
1 dozen Oreo cookies, crushed*
2 dozen fresh whole strawberries, halved

Bake the brownie and cake mixes according to package directions. Cool. Cut into ¾-inch squares.

To a large bowl, add the milks. Whisk in chocolate pudding. Chill for 5 minutes. Blend in the ¼ cup whipped topping.

Layer the bottom of the trifle bowl with half of the brownie squares. Spread ½ of the pudding mixture on the squares. Cover with half of the cake squares. Add a layer of whipped topping. Sprinkle with crushed Oreos. Repeat layers. Refrigerate several hours or overnight. Top with strawberries.

*To crush the Oreos, put them in a Ziploc and roll with a rolling pin.

Chocolate Raspberry Tart Cookies

½ cup unsalted butter
1 cup granulated sugar
1 egg, beaten
2 teaspoons vanilla extract
1 ½ cups flour

½ cup unsweetened cocoa powder
¼ teaspoon baking soda
¼ teaspoon baking powder
2 dozen raspberries
Fudge sauce

Preheat oven to 350 degrees. Cream butter and sugar, adding egg and vanilla. Beat until combined. Blend in flour, cocoa, soda, and baking powder. Stir until smooth. Roll the dough into teaspoon-sized balls. Put on ungreased cookie sheet. Depress the center of each cookie with a melon baller. Add a raspberry to each cookie. Bake for 10 minutes. Drizzle with fudge sauce.

Heavenly Chocolate Cake

1 cup brown sugar
1 cup granulated sugar
⅔ cup shortening
2 eggs
2 cups flour

½ cup sour milk
½ cup cocoa
1 teaspoon vanilla
1 cup boiling water
1 teaspoon baking soda

Cream sugars, shortening, and eggs. Sift flour and add alternately with sour milk to the first mixture. Add cocoa and vanilla and beat well. Add the water and soda last; blend well. Bake at 350 degrees for 30 to 35 minutes or until a toothpick inserted in the center comes out clean.

Marshmallow Chocolate Frosting

2 ½ cups granulated sugar
1 cup evaporated milk
6 oz. chocolate chips

1 cup marshmallow cream
1 stick butter

Cook sugar and milk to soft ball stage. Add chocolate chips, marshmallow cream, and butter. Stir until well combined. Cool to room temperature before frosting cake.

Marvel Young's Fudge

2 cups granulated sugar	¾ cup milk
2 Tablespoons butter, melted	1 teaspoon vanilla
Dash of salt	Nuts (optional)
2 Tablespoons cocoa	

Using a plastic spatula, blend the first five ingredients in a medium saucepan. Stirring constantly over medium heat, bring to a boil. Cover the pan to steam the sides (so the mixture won't stick) for about two minutes. Meanwhile, rinse and dry the spatula so sugar crystals don't develop. Boil the fudge to a soft ball stage (230 degrees), stirring constantly. Add vanilla (and nuts if desired). Pour onto a large, chilled platter and allow to cool. Fudge cannot be warm when you beat it. When cooled, beat the fudge with a fork until it starts to set. Divide into equal portions. Put the portions onto waxed paper and roll up jelly-roll style. When completely cooled and set, unroll the waxed paper and cut the fudge into pieces.

MARCH
Determination: Moving Forward
Trials and Strengthening Your Faith

IN THE AFTERMATH OF THE tsunami that devastated the city of Rikuzentakata, Japan, on March 11, 2011, a pine tree became a symbol of hope. Buildings, homes, and lives were destroyed; the massive surge of water left at least 1,000 people dead and more than that number missing. The sole survivor of a centuries-old forest of over 70,000 trees, the towering pine's lower branches were torn off, yet the top portion of the tree seemed to be thriving.

Amid loss and despair, the scarred tree attracted worldwide attention as residents fought to rebuild their community and begin to heal. The tree became a symbol of hope.

Months later, however, anticipation of the tree's survival dimmed. The ground was saturated with saltwater. The pine showed signs it was losing its battle to survive. Some lamented the prospect, and implications, of its loss. Others took action and preserved cuttings from the tree that were grafted onto similar trees in anticipation of one day recreating the forest. The grand pine finally succumbed, however, and an exact replica—a towering sculpture that serves as a monument—has since been erected.

The ultimate miracle for the city of Rikuzentakata may well have been the resiliency of its people as they decided, despite all odds, to press forward. During March the memory of winter's hold is stirred by flurries of persistent snowflakes, yet the first tender evidences of earth's reawakening allow us to bask in the promise of miracles and the welcome renewal of hope.

Making the Most of March

✳ March 10 is Harriett Tubman Day. Harriett escaped slavery and followed the North Star to freedom in Pennsylvania. She helped over 300 people gain their freedom from slavery. This month learn more about one of your female ancestors who made a difference in the lives of others. Teach what you learn to your family.

✳ The Relief Society was organized March 17, 1842. Celebrate by attending your ward or stake's annual Relief Society birthday party. Invite nonmember or less-active friends to go with you.

✳ Reexamine your exercise plan. Schedule specific exercise days and times each week. Plan for fun workout sessions with friends. Designate a specific spot for your workout gear with socks, shoes, and exercise clothes ready and in plain sight. Make sure gear—like your yoga mat—is readily accessible as well. Reassess what you eat and make plans to eat more healthy foods.

✳ Dust the cobwebs off your gardening tools. If you didn't clean them before winter, take time to wash and organize them. Seal the handles of trowels, spades, or hand rakes with wood sealer or paint them in bright colors. Look for watering cans on sale or at thrift stores. Draft a garden plan by determining how much space you have and what you're going to plant.

✳ It's said March comes in like a lion. Winter clutter can cause your home to look like one's been living with you! Tame disorder by dividing the house into zones. Pick one zone a week to work on. Choose whether you're going to work in areas of worst disarray first or last.

✳ Welcome new neighbors who may have moved in during blustery winter months by taking them a batch of warm muffins.

✳ Bring freshness into your home with delicately scented air fresheners. Make your own with dried lavender. Make potpourri to simmer on the stove with crushed cloves and cinnamon sticks.

Add drops of lemon extract or vanilla. Try fruit slices like apple, lemon, and orange, or herbs like mint. Continue to add water to your simmering potpourri as it evaporates so the pot doesn't go dry. Lavender dryer sheets can be folded under heat registers or placed around the house to lend an air of freshness as well.

* It's maple sugar season in Vermont. The sap usually starts running in early March. Make one of the syrup recipes at the end of this section and enjoy! The delectable cookbook *Our Best Bites: Mormon Moms in the Kitchen* by Sara Wells and Kate Jones contains a wonderful recipe for puffed French toast. The book also contains recipes for banana chocolate chip pancakes, peanut butter syrup, and buttermilk caramel syrup.

* *Life's Lessons Learned* by Dallin H. Oaks deals with some of life's tough experiences. Elder Oaks draws conclusions to illuminate major principles of the gospel in a universal and meaningful way. *Angels to Bear You Up* by Judy C. Olsen is a collection of true stories from ordinary members of the Church. *Sunset: On the Passing of Those We Love* by S. Michael Wilcox deals with finding hope after loss.

MARCH 1
Growing Conditions: Life in the Zone
Choose to thrive.

Last summer, the six potato plants I purchased from a local nursery struggled to survive. Heat and grasshoppers took their toll. In the fall, I moved the plants into the garage to try and winter them over. I didn't hold out much hope. In warm climates, a sweet potato vine is considered a perennial. In colder climes like mine, it's expected to last only one growing season. And while the vines tolerate short periods of drought, when left for too long without water, the leaves wilt and brown.

After only a few days in the garage, the plants drooped. Even with watering, they shrank to withered stems. I gave up and forgot about them. Almost six months later—after lows that had dipped to around zero and no water—I saw a miracle. A single, tiny green leaf thrust itself up out of the parched potting soil in one of the planters.

I tugged the cumbersome planter out to the driveway. I pulled and pushed it toward the reach of the hose, soaked the soil with water, and situated it in a sunny spot. Within a few days, the little sprout—a single potato vine—grew and spread and flourished. Its lime-green leaves spiraled out of the planter and spilled onto the front porch.

As women we experience extremes in highs and lows of happiness and grief as well as droughts of loss, frustration, and anxiety. But it is our trials that allow us to grow strong. We can choose to thrive no matter our conditions; spiritual nourishment is always available.

In what ways can you fortify your process of growth?

MARCH 2
Becoming
Whosoever shall put their trust in God shall be supported in their trials, and their troubles, and their afflictions, and shall be lifted up at the last day. —Alma 36:3

One frantic day a few springs ago, I realized I'd lost sight of the woman I was trying to become. It started out with a few simple things—silly things, really, one right after the other in rapid succession—which began to cause me a great deal of frustration. When my computer refused to work, a temporary cap popped off my tooth, a swarm of hornets battled me for rights to the mailbox, and a wild bird flew through the house leaving little evidences of its presence—even on me—I became distraught. I'd accomplished nothing of obvious significance. Was I marked for disaster?

My faith, courage, and commitment to doing my best were definitely waning.

I knew the bout of complaining I felt inclined to embark on would not serve me well. I wanted more than just a transitory fix. I urged a smile onto my face, wiped the bird droppings off my hand, and started over.

Even little bumps in the road of life can become daunting obstacles if we allow them to. Take a minute to smile and laugh off the little stuff as you focus on the kind of woman you desire to become.

MARCH 3
Asking for Blessings
The woods are lovely, dark, and deep, but I have promises to keep, and miles to go before I sleep, and miles to go before I sleep. —Robert Frost[26]

Jodi Wilding's son, Skyler, died from cystic fibrosis at the age of seventeen. "When my son passed away, it was a great challenge for our family," Jodi says. "We missed him terribly. There was a huge hole missing in each of our hearts . . . a part that would always be with him. But we found great comfort in knowing that he was wrapped in the arms of the Savior. He would have no more pain, no more treatments, no more hospital stays. He was whole."

Instead of focusing on the fact that Skyler was no longer with them, Jodi says the family made a conscious choice to focus on being grateful for the seventeen years they'd had together and for the precious memories they were able to create. "It wasn't always easy to do, but we knew deep down in our hearts that we would see him and be with him again. We knew this because of our testimony of the Savior."

Jodi says her testimony came over many years of dedicated scripture study and church attendance. It also came from serious meditation and prayer. "Because of my knowledge and faith I am able to carry on with my life with the reassurance that we will be together again. I have learned through my study of the gospel and the Savior's life that I am truly a daughter of a God. A God that loves me and knows me by name. A God that I can call Father. And one that hears and answers my prayers. Prayers can't be answered if they aren't said. If I want the blessings, I must ask for them first."

What blessings do you need? Ask.

MARCH 4

Life: A Little Farther Each Day

Running is the greatest metaphor for life, because you get out of it what you put into it. —Oprah Winfrey[27]

Around the time Skyler passed away, Jodi Wilding began to run. "I would spot a tree and run to it, and then walk, and then run to a telephone pole, and walk, and repeat it until I was eventually running up to a mile. . . . I kept going a little farther each day until I made it up to three miles!"

After a 4.7-mile race, a 5K where she won medals in her age category, a 10K, and then a half marathon, Jody decided to run a full marathon. Twenty-six miles, she says, seemed like an insurmountable task, an unreachable goal. She began training in earnest. When the day of the marathon arrived, she did well . . . until mile 21.5. Her calves started to cramp. The pain was almost debilitating. "It was also very emotional at that point," she says. "I have never experienced anything like it. I wanted to quit so desperately, yet at the same time, I knew I wanted to cross that finish line more desperately. I had to. I prayed for strength. I pleaded. I begged. My answers came in the form of many angels along those last 4.5 miles. The feeling of crossing that finish line was like none other. I had to reach deeper than I've ever reached to pull out from inside what I needed."

In your journey, you may encounter challenges and obstacles that seem insurmountable and goals that appear unreachable. Don't quit. Whether running the distance, finding hope after loss, courage in the face of fear, or faith instead of doubt, resolve to keep going. Do a little more each day. Search deep inside yourself. You'll discover strengths you never knew you had.

MARCH 5
Keeping Spiritually Fit
For behold, this life is the time for men to prepare to meet God; yea, behold the day of this life is the day for men to perform their labors.
—Alma 34:32

For several months in advance of a marathon, runners train four to five days a week. They tailor their diet to meet the demands placed on their body. They load on carbs the night before a long run and consume protein afterward. Water is essential. Mental preparation involves continued focus on the end goal. Setting and attaining daily, short-term goals provides needed stamina.

Spiritual preparation enables us to meet the demands of life in much the same way as a runner prepares for a marathon. On earth, our spiritual fitness is constantly tried and tested. We must be ready. Being in sound spiritual shape enhances our reserves of resilience when difficult trials occur. There is power in prayer, strength to be found in the scriptures. One step of faith leads to another. Faithfully attending meetings and partaking of the sacrament revitalizes us and provides fortification. Heeding the direction of the Spirit is vital to reaching our destiny.

What preparation do you need to undertake to enhance your spiritual fitness?

MARCH 6
Choice: What If?
A good man out of the good treasure of the heart bringeth forth good things. —Matthew 12:35

Nearly twenty years ago, I decided to stop asking *Why me?* and instead start asking *What if?* One by one, in an often slow and painful process,

I replaced negative emotions with positive ones. I stopped wondering why I couldn't make everyone around me happy. I stopped becoming despondent when nothing I did seemed to change others or their opinions. I instead started asking things like, "What if happiness really is a choice? What if it can be my choice, no matter what anyone else thinks or feels?"

Instead of commiserating over why my extended family couldn't accept me for who I was and what I believed in, I asked myself, "What if I could choose my own thoughts and emotions based on what I know in my heart is right and true?" In short, "What if I accept myself for who I really am?"

How can changing your *why me*'s to *what if*s change your life? Today celebrate your choice to do so.

MARCH 7

Breathe: Living with Determination
And, if you keep my commandments and endure to the end you shall have eternal life, which gift is the greatest of all the gifts of God.
—D&C 14:7

It was my maternal grandmother who told me the story of my birth. My delivery was complex. When I finally arrived, I was near unresponsive. I'd been held upside down and given a healthy swat on the derriere. "Breathe, you little stinker," the doctor urged as he repeatedly flipped the bottoms of my feet with his fingers. Due to his persistence, I finally "pinked" up and began to breathe.

Sometimes life wears us down to the point that we lose sight of our purpose. We may feel as though we are barely existing, merely surviving. In times of struggle and self-doubt, we need to hold on and make choices with the firm hope and belief that tomorrow— or even the next day—will arrive full of renewed opportunities and blessings. We need to shake off unresponsiveness so we can live with determination.

Woven into the fabric of each second is at least one small miracle in our vicinity, more, many more, if we look outside ourselves and our immediate circumstances. Seek to enjoy even the tiniest of life's miracles. The small and simple joys we discover can become stepping stones to carry us across times of despair. Often the best things in life come whispered on a gentle breeze or breath. The power of the still, small voice is great, and breathing is a gift that should never be taken for granted.

MARCH 8
Life: Triage
But seek ye first the kingdom of God, and his righteousness; and all these things shall be added unto you. —Matthew 6:33

Triage is a French word that means "to sort." The term originated in World War I and was used by French doctors endeavoring to prioritize the severity of the patients' injuries so they could decide which to treat first. Triage can also mean to determine priorities for action.

Often we have many difficult decisions to make in a relatively short amount of time. All may impact our lives to varying degrees. When pressures mount, we can use life triage to prioritize what is most important. Look at the decisions you are faced with. Choose:

What is most important and needs to be done right away.

What is less important and can be put off for a while.

What is least important and least likely to impact your health (spiritual, physical, mental, or emotional).

You can also use triage to help make decisions on goal setting. Determine:

What's going right in your life that you should continue to do or improve upon.

What hasn't worked to help you meet your spiritual and emotional needs.

What the insignificant things are that have little or no bearing on your life and dreams.

Life triage makes decisions easier to tackle and helps to keep positive, forward momentum in your life.

MARCH 9

Self-Inflicted Trials: Self-Doubt

Always be a first-rate version of yourself, instead of a second-rate version of somebody else. —Judy Garland[28]

In grade school, I entered a poster contest. It took a painstaking effort to complete. A group of sixth graders served as judges. Their reaction to my poster was that it was good—too good. "You cheated," one girl asserted. "You traced it from a book."

I wanted to disappear, never return to school. I didn't understand that other kids thinking my drawings had been traced was—though they didn't realize it—a compliment. In my young mind, I was stupid for trying.

Those grade-school feelings of inferiority still sometimes rustle through me. Even having illustrated an award-winning picture book, I hesitate a moment when I start to do anything artistic. Am I good enough? I suppose the point could be argued. As one woman at a book signing told me, one woman's art is another woman's, well, not so much art. Yet I've had the privilege of meeting lots of children whose faces light up when they see the illustrations. "You're the illustrator?" they ask with awe in their voice. To them I'm okay. And the fact is I love to draw.

Eugene Delacroix said, "Artists who seek perfection in everything are those who cannot attain it in anything." Life is the same way. By succumbing to misgivings about ourselves, we impose limitations and self-inflicted trials.

Today, pray for help in rising above self-doubt.

MARCH 10

Putting Your Faith in the Lord

First, faith in the Lord Jesus Christ. —Article of Faith 4

Canadian teacher Mary H. Brown wrote:

> It may not be on the mountain's height, or over the stormy sea;
> It may not be at the battle's front my Lord will have need of me;
> But if by a still, small voice He calls to paths I do not know,

I'll answer, dear Lord, with my hand in Thine,
I'll go where You want me to go.[29]

Life takes us many places we do not initially intend to travel. We may enjoy grand landscapes of opportunity, abundant fields of friendship, sweeping panoramas of romance, and pleasant valleys of motherhood. We're also likely, however, to experience rocky hillsides of misunderstanding, thorny grounds of discontent, barren wastelands of isolation and loneliness, deserts of despair, and steep canyons of physical and emotional crisis.

Elder Dallin H. Oaks teaches that our confidence both that the Lord knows all things and that He will respond to our prayers in the most beneficial way are a necessary component of our faith in Him.[30]

Mary H. Brown wrote of answering the Lord's call, of trusting that He knows what is best. Wherever our journey takes us, we can figuratively put our hand in that of the Lord's, trusting ourselves to His good care.

MARCH 11
How to Be Brave
Courage doesn't always roar. Sometimes courage is the little voice at the end of the day saying, "I will try again tomorrow."
—Mary Anne Radmacher[31]

How to be brave:
Believe in Him and what He says.
Rely on Him; He will not lead you astray.
Acknowledge that His way is the only way.
Vow to follow Him and do His will.
Earnestly serve Him.

MARCH 12
Taking Action: Face Doubts and Fears
Inaction breeds doubt and fear. Action breeds confidence and courage. If you want to conquer the negative elements in your life, do not sit home and think about it. Go out and get busy. —Dale Carnegie[32]

Extending patience, long-suffering, and other Christlike virtues toward ourselves is equally as important as extending them to others. Condemning ourselves and labeling ourselves as worthless or not good enough damages our self-worth, spiritual growth, and progression. Dwelling on our shortcomings is a fast track to misery. If, however, we look for our strengths and talents we will find them. With Heavenly Father's help, they can be magnified.

God's plan is to help us grow and progress. Mistakes do not mean we are doomed to fail; they are temporary actions, not our true identity of promise and potential. If circumstances in your life are holding you back from goals and aspirations, commit to developing the courage to live up to your full capabilities. Repent if necessary, and move on. The list of Christlike attributes you are developing, your To-Live-By list, will help you.

MARCH 13
Words of Wisdom: Helps for Facing Trials
The greater the difficulty, the more glory in surmounting it. Skillful pilots gain their reputation from storms and tempests. —Epictetus[33]

Some days are just plain difficult. Despite prayer and hard work, patience and goodwill, a cheerful attitude that perseveres, sometimes we reach a point where we want to cry.

And we do.

The juice stain won't come out of the new carpet, nor will the muddy footprints. A friend refuses to listen to reason. A loved one succumbs to illness. We've paid tithing in full, but there's not yet enough money to pay bills. Our sincere love isn't sufficient to heal the pain of a child. We are tired, tattered, and torn between self, family, and future.

Blessings can come through the words of others, those who have passed the same way and endured similar trials. Their stories provide hope and courage. Here are some to start with:

★ *No Doubt About It*; *No One Can Take Your Place*; and *If Life Were Easy, It Wouldn't be Hard*, by Sheri L. Dew

* *Standing For Something: Ten Neglected Virtues that Will Heal Your Heart and Home* and *One Bright Shining Hope* by President Gordon B. Hinckley
* *21 Days Closer to Christ* by Emily Freeman
* *Believing Christ: The Parable of the Bicycle and Other Good News* by Stephen E. Robinson
* *I Am a Mother* by Jane Clayson Johnson
* *Counting Blessings: Wit and Wisdom for Women* by Kerry Blair
* *Change Your Questions, Change Your Life* by Wendy Watson Nelson

MARCH 14

Regular Scripture Reading: Promise and Blessings

The Bible gives me a deep, comforting sense that "things seen are temporal, and things unseen are eternal." —Helen Keller[34]

In 2005, President Hinckley issued a challenge: read or reread the Book of Mormon before the end of the year. For me the quest brought great blessings. Never had I realized the extent of the power that comes from diligent and attentive scripture reading. Never had I felt the presence of the Spirit with such magnitude. Never had I grasped the concepts in the pages of the Book of Mormon with such clarity. Precepts came into sharp focus. Regarding the necessity of regular scripture reading, I remember standing in the kitchen one night and telling one of my daughters, "I get it!"

Reading the scriptures invites the Spirit into our lives. They are filled with countless answers, assurances, guidance, and promises that will lift us up and sustain us on our journey.

Today, commit or recommit yourself to reading the scriptures daily so you can fully enjoy their promises and blessings.

MARCH 15

Healing: A Spiritual Medicine Cabinet

And we had obtained the records which the Lord had commanded us, and searched them and found that they were desirable; yea, even of great worth unto us. —1 Nephi 5:21

In our homes, we all have a place for medicines that help ease pain and enhance health. The scriptures can be considered a spiritual medicine chest, providing relief and healing.

* For peace and comfort, read Philippians 4:7, Isaiah 66:13, Alma 17:10, and 2 Corinthians 1:4.
* For help in overcoming fear or loneliness, study Isaiah 41:10, Psalm 27:1, Joshua 1:5, and D&C 112:10.
* For help in times of trial and challenge, ponder Psalm 40:1, Psalm 27:5, Psalm 46:1, Psalm 34:18, and Lamentations 3:22.
* For hope, courage, and healing, read Romans 8:24, Joshua 1:9, Luke 9:11, and Matthew 11:28.
* When you seek miracles, consider the words in Mormon 9:19 and Alma 37:40.
* For assurance of love, review John 15:9, Ephesians 2:4, and 1 John 4:18.

As you read the scriptures, discover verses that contain the healing properties you seek. Choose a color and mark them.

MARCH 16
Courage for Life
Wait on the Lord: be of good courage, and he shall strengthen thine heart. —Psalm 27:14

Some days we need "big" courage—a mix of nerve and valor that propels us to stand up for what we believe in. Once in a while, we need "little" courage—a smidgen of daring in order to accomplish something others might take for granted, like squashing a bug. Sometimes, our courage needs to last a long time—when a friend or loved one is ill or dying. Often we need courage that lasts for only a relatively short amount of time—like when we have to talk in church.

The world brims with turmoil, illness, and economic woes. Some days it feels like there has never been more to be fearful of. Yet choosing courage illuminates all the reasons to look forward with hope. Being able to get out of bed in the morning is a blessing. So is seeing the sun rise triumphantly over misted mountaintops, smelling the fragrance of flowers, the sense of joy that is yours when you serve others in the Lord's name, and knowing—despite fear—that you've done your best to have courage, be it big, little, long, or short.

Discover courage by facing your fears. Have you always wanted to try ballroom dancing? Take a class. Would you like to learn how to fly an airplane? Find out where lessons are taught in your area. Do you want to learn to speak with more ease in front of others? Explore the options offered by books, classes, and seminars that can teach you how.

What else can courage do for you?

MARCH 17
Stacey Day: Celebrating Life's Journey
The world is upheld by the veracity of good men: they make the earth wholesome. They who lived with them found life glad.
—Ralph Waldo Emerson[35]

On December 17, 2007, my friend Stacey Eyre died after having battled leukemia for four years. Despite her own suffering, it was important to her to continue to nurture friendships and let others know they were valued. Undergoing chemo, losing her hair, and coming back repeatedly from the brink of death during the harrowing course of both disease and treatments, she taught me that whether you're living or dying, life is what you make of it.

Now, each month, I strive to observe the seventeenth with gusto. It is my Stacey Day. A time to remember, to reflect, and, most importantly, to enjoy life's journey to the fullest. Sometimes I hike up a mountain I never thought I could climb. Or I enjoy the company of close friends and family, rejoicing in each. I eat foods I love and don't feel guilty for doing so!

Choose one day each month to really celebrate your life. Go all out, and enjoy it.

MARCH 18

Faithful Problem Solving

Do what you can, where you are, with what you've got.
—Squire Bill Widener[36]

In 1 Nephi 16 we read the account of Nephi's broken bow: "And it came to pass that as I, Nephi, went forth to slay food, behold, I did break my bow, which was made of fine steel; and after I did break my bow, behold, my brethren were angry with me because of the loss of my bow, for we did obtain no food." Laman and Lemuel and the sons of Ishmael grumbled. Even Lehi began to murmur. Nephi kept his composure. He set out to solve the problem. He made a new bow and arrow. He also armed himself with a sling and stones. When he was ready, he asked his father, "Whither shall I go to obtain food?" He was ultimately directed to the top of a mountain where he was able to acquire enough food to feed everyone.

The story of Nephi's broken bow is a prime example of faithful problem solving. Had Nephi chosen to invest his time in complaining like the others, the outcome may well have been dire. When he made the decision to press forward and find a solution, his life and the lives of others were blessed. "And it came to pass that I did return to our tents, bearing the beasts which I had slain; and now when they beheld that I had obtained food, how great was their joy!"

Henry Ford noted, "It is failure that is easy. Success is always hard."[37] How can Nephi's example of faithful problem solving help you overcome obstacles in your life?

MARCH 19

Opportunities to Learn: Key Experiences

Verily, verily, I say unto you, ye are little children, and ye have not as yet understood how great blessings the Father hath in his own hands and prepared for you; And ye cannot bear all things now; nevertheless, be of good cheer, for I will lead you along. The kingdom is yours and the blessings thereof are yours, and the riches of eternity are yours.
—D&C 78:17–18

When Ann Oliver Rice crossed the plains in 1866 at the age of thirteen, she was blind; an accident had claimed her sight. Her sister and mother both died on the trek west. Arriving in Utah, Ann worked boxing matches. She married and bore eight children. Three died in infancy. Despite hardships, Ann chose to persevere in faith and good cheer. She loved to sing, recite poems, and tell jokes. She scrubbed the floor on her hands and knees, going over some places twice to ensure they were clean. She milked cows, gathered eggs, and raised and fed chickens. She knit stockings, sweaters, mittens, and slippers. In her later years, she knit a pair of slippers for each member of her Relief Society in Pleasant View, Utah—four hundred large pairs and three hundred small pairs and pin cushions.

When we view problems as learning opportunities instead of punishments, setbacks as possibilities instead of roadblocks, and mistakes as education instead of failure, we unlock the way to living fully. Norman Vincent Peale aptly stated that how we think about problems is more important than the problem itself. "Believe that problems do have answers. Believe that they can be overcome. Believe that they can be handled. And finally, believe that you can solve them."[38]

Holocaust survivor Viktor E. Frankl stated, "Everything can be taken from a man but one thing: the last of human freedoms— to choose one's attitude in any given set of circumstances, to choose one's own way."[39]

How can changing your attitude toward problems, trials, and challenges change your destiny?

MARCH 20
Waiting upon the Lord
But they that wait upon the Lord shall renew their strength; they shall mount up with wings as eagles; they shall run, and not be weary; and they shall walk, and not faint. —Isaiah 40:31

How is your year going? What joys and triumphs have unfolded thus far? What unexpected trials have taken you by surprise? In January, we talked about our state of heart. How gratitude, expressed abundantly both during and after trials, enhances our ability to perceive the constant flow of blessings and good all around us. How, even though the situations we endure can be perilous, none are impossible to bear if our heart is in harmony with God's. No matter our past, current, or future circumstances, faithfully waiting upon the Lord strengthens us and enables us to endure.

Elder Robert D. Hales asks us to consider what it means to wait upon the Lord.[40] He clarifies that we must hope and trust in Him in faith and patience, humility and meekness, as we strive to endure to the end. Are you enduring in your commitment to draw closer to God? To renew or repair your relationship with Him? Remember to record your thoughts and impressions in your journal. When you look back, you will see evidence of how far you have come.

MARCH 21

Positive Thinking: Take a Hike

Thou wilt shew me the path of life: in thy presence is fullness of joy; at thy right hand there are pleasures for evermore. —Psalm 16:11

Do you ever wake up and know it's going to be the best day ever— and it really is? Such days are priceless. What about when it's not the best day ever even though you thought it was going to be? Even though you perhaps desperately needed it to be? It's easy to become discouraged, but how you react makes all the difference.

According to a recent study by the U.S. Centers for Disease Control and Prevention, antidepressants are the most commonly prescribed drugs in the United States.[41] They are more often prescribed than drugs used to treat high blood pressure, high cholesterol, asthma, or headaches. As a child, when I was bored or disillusioned, my Grandma Esther had her own brand of medicine: take a hike. She said it literally but in the kindest possible way. A walk to the pond worked wonders for clearing the senses. A hike up a nearby mountain was a surefire remedy and quickly put things into perspective. How good it felt to get back home and soak my aching feet in a bucket of warm water.

The world is a place where negativism abounds; talk of things positive seems to be the exception rather than the rule. Yet we have a choice in how to respond to trials and heartaches. Our reaction has a direct bearing on how the day turns out. A brisk walk around the block, a hike up the mountainside, or training to participate in an organized walk or run can help clarify muddled thoughts, distill anguish, and put disappointment into proper perspective.

MARCH 22

Living: The Way You Spend Each Day
Do not fear death, but rather the unlived life. You don't have to live forever. You just have to live. —Natalie Babbitt, *Tuck Everlasting*[42]

The Unlived Life

An unlived life
Is not the sum
Of lack of worldly ways.
Pursuit of gold
Feats reckless bold,
Lend mindless, hapless haze.
An unlived life
Is not accrued
By overlooking fad.
Waxes or wanes
Of fashion gains,
Clothes never bought or had.
An unlived life
Is not the loss
Of popularity.
The human mind,
Not always kind,
Molds things we should not be.
Open the gift
Of life and live.
Days build your destiny.

In word and deed
In thought and creed.
Love of God sets you free.

Today, spend some time contemplating your eternal nature. Record your thoughts in your journal.

MARCH 23
Blossoming amid the World: Faith and Courage
If ye were of the world, the world would love his own: but . . . ye are not of the world, but I have chosen you out of the world. —John 15:19

If you feel lost, disappointed, hesitant, or weak, return to yourself, to who you are, here and now. And when you get there, you will discover yourself, like a lotus flower in full bloom, even in a muddy pond, beautiful and strong. —Masaru Emoto[43]

Held in high regard for its ability to thrive amid harsh, uninviting conditions, the lotus blooms in beauty and grace. A symbol of purity and understanding, the flower flourishes even in muck-filled swamps. From mud and mire, the determined flower pushes its way upward to find the sun. Delicate petals open at dawn and close at dusk. The next day the cycle is repeated, bringing stark contrast between brilliant blossom and dire environment.

Like the lotus, the conditions we live in might be far from perfect; the opposition from mortal opinion and worldly cares may live just around the block or reside in our very own home. The warmth of God's love, however, draws us upward. We work our way toward Him in faith and courage. We fight to overcome. Destined for full bloom, we can fulfill our life's purpose under His guidance and care.

What opposition do you need to overcome? What's your plan for doing so?

MARCH 24
In the Lord's Hands: Trust
I can do all things through Christ which strengtheneth me.
—Philippians 4:13

When we pray for Heavenly Father's will to be made known to us, when we humbly acknowledge our willingness to accept it, we are exhibiting great trust in Him. Sacrificing personal ambitions to more fully follow God is difficult, yet His help will surely come. While we cannot change His wisdom and will, the power we have to effect good, the promise of our purpose here, will be made manifest to us. We will be given courage to press on.

In whatever challenges you are facing, assess your level of trust in the Lord. Pray for help in increasing your spiritual reliance on Him in accordance with His will.

MARCH 25
Calm amid Life's Storms
I am not afraid of storms, for I am learning how to sail my ship.
—Louisa May Alcott[44]

Idaho native Elder John H. Groberg recounts his missionary experiences in Tonga in his book *In the Eye of the Storm*. The book and subsequent movie, *The Other Side of Heaven*, detail the perils of his journey to Tonga. After much difficulty, he arrives on the remote island of Niuatoputapu. Life on the island is a challenge for the young missionary. Mosquitoes, a tropical storm, near starvation, rats that eat away the bottoms of his feet, and exhaustion are among the hardships he endures.

During one of the most poignant parts of the movie, Elder Groberg and his two counselors are lost at sea. Thrown overboard during a storm, they swim to safety, finding it by God's mercy. Realizing they have survived near drowning, one of the counselors offers, "Sometimes God calms the storm. Sometimes He calms the sailor." Elder Groberg then adds, "And sometimes He makes us swim."

Do you sometimes feel as though you've been swept overboard? That you're swimming alone in the middle of the ocean, storm surging on all sides? Hang on—help will come, sometimes through means you expect but often in ways you never dreamed of. Hold tight to the safety of the gospel. Pray for Heavenly Father's assistance.

How can you help calm someone else's storm today?

MARCH 26
When Lost, Find the Temple
The way to love anything is to realize that it might be lost.
—G. K. Chesterton[45]

A few years ago, Elder Gary E. Stevenson told a story in general conference about driving through Logan, Utah, with his father and two young sons. When they came to a place where they had never before been, Elder Stevenson's father asked the boys if they thought they were lost. The youngsters looked across the valley. Pointing at the spires of the Logan temple, one child stated his belief that one can never be lost if the temple is in sight.[46]

The story caused me to think of experiences I've had traveling in large cities: chaos and confusion, traffic, hurry and worry. I knew approximately where I was. Yet, for all intents and purposes, I was lost. In each city, one thing stood resolute, a beacon of hope: the temple.

Locating temples in the hustle and bustle of large cities not only helps me get my physical bearings but secures me to spiritual moorings. The things I need to do to find myself, temporally or spiritually, come into sharp focus. The same is true when I'm at home. Temple photos and paintings evoke peace and sense of purpose.

Elder Stevenson counseled that, indeed, we are never lost when the temple is in our sight. A beacon of eternal light and direction, it can guide us to where we need to be.

Can you see the temple from where you are in life?

MARCH 27
Joyful Living
Be strong and of a good courage; be not afraid, neither be thou dismayed: For the Lord thy God is with thee whithersoever thou goest.
—Joshua 1:9

I used to be bad at crisis. When calamity occurred in multiples, I was particularly inept at keeping my head above water. Merely surviving, definitely not living. At some point I began to notice how others coped with disasters of health, heart, and home. Those who looked for the worst found it. Those who looked for the silver lining in dark clouds found the best.

When my family was adrift in challenges, fair-weather friends and family bemoaned, "Life isn't fair—is it? Why you? How are you ever going to handle this?" Those I admired most, however, issued words of support and encouragement: "We're praying for you. You can do it. You're strong. Hang in there. Think positive." I learned to cherish and admire those people. In their own lives, they'd experienced much more heartache and tragedy than those who lamented life was unfair. With faith and optimism, they rose above their own trials to lift others.

Study the example of those who maintain faith and composure during hard times. Find what they have to teach. Strive to implement what you learn into your own life. A few books to get you started are *The Hiding Place* by Corrie Ten Boom; *As I Have Loved You* by Kitty de Ruyter-Bons; and Helen Keller's autobiography. Also the movie *Delivered by Hope: The True Story of Mariama Kallon.*

MARCH 28
The Help You Need
He hath said, I will never leave thee, nor forsake thee. . . . The Lord is my helper. —Hebrews 13:5–6

In Doctrine and Covenants 50:27, we learn "all things are subject unto him, both in heaven and on the earth." In Luke's words we know "for with God nothing shall be impossible" (Luke 1:37). Illness, pain, and suffering, injustice, poverty, and bias, feelings of abandonment, loneliness, and fear. No matter our circumstances and their temporal consequences, we can received needed help.

The world presses in around us with frightening calamities and challenges, leaving us, at times, feeling powerless. We need our Lord and Savior. Through Him we can focus our state of heart on gratitude and hope.

This week ponder the help you need. Search LDS.org to find Elder Richard G. Scott's October 1991 general conference address

"Obtaining Help from The Lord" to discover how to better ask for divine assistance.

MARCH 29
Why Not? The Inherent Wonder of You
We are not human beings on a spiritual journey. We are spiritual beings on a human journey. —Pierre Teilhard de Chardin[47]

Recently, my youngest daughter received a calling that surprised her. She wondered, with so many other capable young women in the ward, why she'd been chosen. "Why me?" she asked. "Why not you?" I responded.

Self-doubt can become ingrained in our psyche. Perceived inadequacies are fertilized with self-deprecating views of our own abilities. But we are daughters of God. Marvelous opportunities await! Opportunities to give and serve with our unique talents and gifts. Chances to move mountains with our love. The prospect of changing hearts and lives for the best with our kindness and compassion.

In her book *A Return To Love: Reflections on the Principles of a Course in Miracles*, author Marianne Williamson proffers, "We ask ourselves, Who am I to be brilliant, gorgeous, talented, fabulous? Actually, who are you not to be? You are a child of God. Your playing small does not serve the world. There is nothing enlightened about shrinking so that other people won't feel insecure around you. We are all meant to shine, as children do. We were born to make manifest the glory of God that is within us. It's not just in some of us; it's in everyone."[48]

Abandon self-inflicted trials of fear, self-doubt, or perceived inadequacy. Celebrate the wonder of you!

MARCH 30
Direction from the Spirit
But there is a spirit in man: and the inspiration of the Almighty giveth them understanding. —Job 32:8

All around us are directions telling us what to do, where to go, and how to do things. Sometimes we pay attention. Sometimes we try to take matters into our own hands. When we end up with a cake that doesn't rise, traveling on the wrong road, or having assembled something that doesn't work quite right, we realize we need to pay more heed to directions.

When we need guidance for life's dilemmas, both temporal and spiritual, the Spirit gives us direction. We may receive gentle promptings for what actions to take or what words to speak; we may receive warnings. Practice listening with intent to the direction of the Spirit. The Lord promises in John 14:16–18, "And I will pray the Father, and he shall give you another Comforter, that he may abide with you for ever; Even the Spirit of truth; whom the world cannot receive, because it seeth him not, neither knoweth him: but ye know him; for he dwelleth with you, and shall be in you. I will not leave you comfortless: I will come to you."

MARCH 31

The Miracle of the Hail: Nourished and Strengthened by Hardship
Yea, they shall not be beaten down by the storm at the last day; yea, neither shall they be harrowed up by the whirlwinds; but when the storm cometh they shall be gathered together in their place, that the storm cannot penetrate to them; yea, neither shall they be driven with fierce winds whithersoever the enemy listeth to carry them.
—Alma 26:6

Yesterday it hailed. Pellets of ice pummeled the ground. Shoots of newborn grass bent under the burden of what looked like heaven's frozen tears. My split-second first impression was of the injustice of it all. To understand the lesson the hailstones had to teach, however, I needed to consider more than just the passing hardship endured by my lawn.

After a long winter, spring was doing its best to breathe life into my barren backyard. Blades of grass sprouted upward with faith and zeal. Under darkened skies, they stood, at first, steadfast, little green soldiers resolute in maintaining their position despite the storm. In seconds, the weight of the hail became too much. Hardened capsules of ice glistened triumphant.

But then the storm, as all storms do, moved on.

The sun shone. The hailstones melted. A perilous trial minutes before, the stones now lent life-giving water that would nourish and strengthen the grass, allowing it to continue to grow.

Challenging life storms that bring the weight of icy doubt and fear crashing down on us only have the power to smother our convictions and determination if we allow them to. When, like the blades of grass, we are driven to our knees in despair, we need but to endure trials in faith. When the storm has passed and once more we are able see the light of hope and truth—finding, as always, that it was always there—we will find ourselves growing once again, nourished and strengthened by hardship.

March Recipes

Berry Blueberry Sauce

1 ½ cups frozen blueberries   Juice from half a lemon
3 Tablespoons granulated sugar

Combine berries, sugar, and lemon juice in a saucepan and bring to a simmer; simmer 10 minutes. Mash some of the berries with a fork to release juices. Serve warm.

Orange Syrup

1 cup granulated sugar
2 teaspoons freshly grated orange
     rind
½ cup bottled orange juice

1 Tablespoon lemon juice, fresh
     or bottled
1 Tablespoon white corn syrup
½ teaspoon vanilla extract
1 Tablespoon orange extract

Combine all ingredients in a heavy saucepan. Over medium heat, bring mixture to a boil. Reduce heat. Simmer for 5 minutes, stirring until sugar dissolves. Great on vanilla ice cream!

Lavender Lemon Syrup

1 cup water
¼ cup fresh-squeezed lemon juice
1 cup granulated sugar

3 Tablespoons dried lavender flowers
Optional: ½–1 drop yellow food coloring

Combine all ingredients in a small saucepan. Bring to a low boil; boil 5 minutes, stirring occasionally until sugar is dissolved. Simmer for 5 minutes over low heat. Remove from heat and cool. If desired, strain syrup to remove the lavender flowers. Use on fresh fruit, crepes, thin waffles, or lemon pound cake.

Easy Peach Syrup

1 ½ cups sugar
½ cup water

3 cups pureed fresh or canned peaches
1 Tablespoon lemon

Combine sugar and water in a medium saucepan. Stirring constantly, bring to a boil over medium heat. Boil 1 minute. Add peach puree. Return to low boil and boil for 5 minutes; continue stirring. Remove from heat. Add lemon juice. Store in refrigerator in tightly sealed container.

APRIL
Travel Plans
Goals and Dreams

DOROTHY HAD TO TRAVEL OVER the rainbow to discover she had the answers to her problems all along. She wasn't happy in what she perceived as the dry, barren landscape of Kansas. She dreamed of something better. When she saw the tornado coming, she ran to the cellar to hide; she didn't make it. Transported to another land, she wanted only to get back to Kansas where she was loved and valued. She wanted a quick fix. There was no easy way. She learned how strong she really was. When she finally returns home, life has new meaning because of what she's learned about herself and the new way in which she sees her world.

In life's journey, storms challenge our resolve; we want to hide. We long for home. There is no easy way back. Dreams may not turn out as wonderful as we anticipate. Answers to problems are not in the places we hope. By facing our challenges and fears, we gain confidence in setting and attaining goals. Our minds become attuned to truth. We rejoice over milestones we thought we'd never have stamina to reach. Those milestones will be all the sweeter when we finally return to our heavenly home and reflect on all we've learned.

What are your travel plans?

Making the Most of April

* Buy everyone in the family a small, inexpensive notebook in which to record their thoughts and impressions of specific topics from general conference. Encourage them to jot down quotes and sketch pictures that are related to the talks. Gather the conference notebooks for use in future family home evenings and to use next conference. Store them in a special place.

* Open windows and let some fresh air in. Put the rugs outside. Mist them with lavender spray or a mixture of water with a few drops of vanilla or lemon oil and let them air in the sun.

* Organize the coat rack or closet. Dry-clean winter coats and sweaters; pack them away for next year. Gather winter socks, mittens, gloves, hats, and scarves. Sort, clean, and store them in your winter gear box. Clean and condition winter boots. Buff up spring and summer footwear so you'll be ready for fun in the sun. Olive oil mixed with a few drops of lemon oil can be used as shoe polish. Compile ideas for shortcuts to cleaning. Learn how to make nontoxic homemade cleaning products for your house.

* Write notes to children in your family, ward, or stake who have recently been baptized. Bear your testimony to them and congratulate them on their desire to become members of the Church.

* Commemorate Take Our Daughters and Sons to Work Day. Check the Internet for more information and the date. Take your children to your workplace and acquaint them with what you do. Denote the important work done in your home with a special family home evening. Tell your children about your decision to be a parent and what it means to you.

* Get gardening. Pump up your mood and your muscles by cleaning up fall leaves and winter debris. Turn over the soil so it can breathe. Finish diagramming your garden. Plan for a few new veggies this year. What are some you'd like to try?

* Soak up some sun. On warm days, begin taking longer walks. Sit on the porch with a book and enjoy the day. Plant spring bulbs that will bloom in the fall: calla lilies, begonias, gladiolas, and lilies are some to start with. Check with your local gardening store for more ideas.

* Look for the first ten varieties of flowers you see blossoming. Take photos of your favorites and tape them into your journal. Write about why you like the flowers, what they remind you of, etc.

* Clip coupons. *Savvy Saving: Couponing Secrets from the Stockpiling Moms* by Melissa Jennings and Shelley King-Steimer provides expert coupon strategies as well as menu planning and other household management skills.

* Research Easter traditions of your ancestors; discover how the holiday is celebrated in the country where they originated. Try the spring recipes following this section.

APRIL 1

Who You Are in Twenty-Five Words or Less

If you have built castles in the air, your work need not be lost; that is where they should be. Now put the foundations under them. —Henry David Thoreau[49]

In the past few months, we've discussed how it's possible to gain faith that you are a daughter of God. You've learned about the implications of that relationship—wonderful possibilities and limitless opportunities as well as sacred responsibilities. I'm confident that you've refined and practiced the Christlike attributes of integrity, honesty, and kindness. As spring begins to blossom with the promise of new life, begin to explore what you need and want to accomplish on earth.

In all conditions and circumstances, beautiful hopes and dreams can flourish. Many more await being sown. Nurture your dreams by having a personal mission statement of who you are, how you intend to live, and the goals you aspire to attain. It might be something like *I am a child of God. I can accomplish anything I set my mind to as long as it is in accordance with His will,* or *I want to use my talents and abilities to create a better world. I will use my gift of life to bring joy to others,* or perhaps *I want to live life to the fullest. The expression of who I am will be evident in all I do and say.* Here's mine: *My decisions define who I am. I will use my ability to choose wisely and with integrity, always giving thanks to God.*

In your journal, define yourself, your life intentions and goals, in twenty-five words or less. Use your personal mission statement to direct you as you navigate your future. Read it often.

APRIL 2

Be the Hero of Your Own Story

Life is either a daring adventure or nothing. —Helen Keller[50]

Often we cruise through life like we're taking a scenic drive. We might ooh and ah at the sights, stop to eat once in a while, and pull over and stretch our legs, but then it's back behind the wheel. There's an earthly destination we feel we have to reach. Days merge into days. We increase our speed, driving on and on toward a distant yet somehow perpetually out-of-reach horizon. Brilliant landscapes that once captivated us become commonplace. In our peripheral vision, our surroundings blur. Years go by. We're older, our children grown. We've still not managed to reach the place we intended to travel. Landscapes of missed opportunities and experiences have passed by.

To enrich means to improve or enhance. If our lives are to be enhanced, each day, each moment, we must live consciously and decisively. Not doing so can result in sorrow and bitter disappointment. Living consciously in the moment requires us to think things through so we can understand how each decision impacts our lives. Situational awareness is broken down into four steps: recognize, comprehend, predict the outcome, and act.

Every choice you make determines your future. This month practice making decisions with faith, confidence, and determination as you learn to live fully and without fear. Don't keep traveling aimlessly.

APRIL 3
Setting Goals
You are never too old to set a new goal or to dream a new dream.
—Author unknown

The Latter-day Saint Woman: Basic Manual for Women describes a goal as "a standard, a skill, an ideal, or a destination that is to be achieved." The manual further states, "We set a goal when we decide to accomplish a particular thing. Some goals, such as cleaning a room or reading a book, may take a short time to accomplish. Other goals, such as saving money to buy a new home or doing things to improve the love and peace within the family, may take months or years. Goals that will help us become worthy to dwell eternally with our Heavenly Father may take an entire lifetime. Some goals may not even be attained during a lifetime on earth but may require additional effort in the hereafter" (271–81).

Goals allow us to make steady progression in our journey. If you haven't already done so, begin to ponder your goals and aspirations.

APRIL 4
You Are What You Believe
Dreams are the touchstones of our characters. —Henry David Thoreau[51]

In January, we talked about the fact that our spiritual DNA is replete with inherited, infinite capabilities and strengths waiting to be discovered and put into practice. Attaining our best—spiritually and secularly—requires us to know what we believe about ourselves. Eleanor Roosevelt aptly pointed out that our beliefs are best expressed through our choices and that the choices we make are our responsibility. The sheer number of choices we face can be staggering. The choice of what to do about our choices compounds the difficulty even more. When we keep in mind, however, the simple truth that our choices have eternal implications, the way becomes clearer.

Since your to-live-by list already contains goals regarding the kind of woman you want to be, it's a helpful guide for planning and preparing to make life choices. Review the list, and add any additional Christlike attributes you desire to attain, characteristics that will prepare you to make sound temporal and eternal decisions.

Next, use a page in your journal to begin a life list—a list of hopes, goals, and dreams. These might include becoming a mother, revisiting educational pursuits, planning for a vacation or a garden, starting a business, planning for a career, helping a young woman complete her Personal Progress program, or working on it yourself.

Think about the choices you make. Are they in line with your infinite potential? You can do whatever you set your mind to.

APRIL 5
Life Tapestry: Threads of Hope and Persistence
There's no such word as can't. —H. L. Wiese[52]

The eldest son of a desperately poor farm family, my grandfather became a self-made man who forged his life with hard work and determination.

Attaining his ambitions took years of planning and hard work. His stern German father forbade him to pursue his dream of attending flight school. However, after seeing a photo of an ice plane, Grandpa decided to build a plane of his own. For years, he scavenged parts from old, abandoned aircrafts. He finally came up with enough components to create a sno-plane.

Grandpa's sno-planes (he built nearly ninety of them) were tri-skied vehicles powered by an airplane engine and propeller. The speeds they were capable of reaching enabled him to "fly" over snow and ice. With each subsequent model, he added improvements that allowed him to go farther and faster. He became one of the first men to enter Yellowstone during the winter via mechanical means. In later years, he spoke to school children about his life. The farm boy who tried and never gave up told them, "There's no such word as can't."

Grandpa's sno-planes weren't built in a day but rather by moments of trial and error, weeks of learning, and years of trying again and again. Though he had no formal engineering or aviation mechanic training, his dreams were threaded together with hope and persistence. His life became a patchwork quilt of sorts that, piece by piece, became his legend.

Today, determine that whatever tapestry you choose to create, you will use the essential threads of hope and persistence.

APRIL 6
Persistence, Perseverance: Press On
I was so grateful to the Lord for preserving me, for bringing the gospel into my life, and for allowing me to serve a mission. I knew that His angels truly had been round about me, to bear me up.
—Miriama Kallon[53]

Wisconsin native Libby Riddles sought adventure. She grew up loving animals and chose to race sled dogs. In Alaska, she sold fish and raised her own dogs. In 1985, she entered the Iditarod as an unknown. During the race from Anchorage to Nome—twelve hundred miles— she endured savage blizzards, deadly cold, and debilitating fatigue. Yet, when she and her dogs passed over a last section of sea ice, she was miles ahead of her nearest competitor. Realization hit home. Not only would she win the race, but she'd be the first woman ever to do so.

While perseverance can be used as a definition for persistence—which is to have continued determination—the deeper meaning is one of firm resolve. Whether blizzards of distraction threaten to blind and bind you, the bitter cold of popular opinion stings, or the inherent fatigue of travel sets in, persist in perseverance. Run the race. Complete the task. Go the extra mile. Finish the job. Press on. As with the season, just when we think hope for warmer weather is fading, spring bursts forth with the warmth of new and beautiful promises.

APRIL 7
Whatever You Want Has a Price
All our dreams can come true—if we have the courage to pursue them.
—Walt Disney[54]

I love planting a garden. The monetary investment is the cost of seeds and seedlings. The greater investment—fertilizing soil, pulling weeds, and watering and harvesting my crops of herbs and vegetables—is paid for with my time.

Whatever is desired—fresh produce; learning to quilt, dance, or practice medicine; pursuing a degree; running a marathon; becoming a successful musician; traveling to exotic destinations—every available mortal option has its price. Usually, the monetary price of a desire is considered first. However, the price paid with time and energy as well as emotional, physical, and spiritual health should weigh equally in decision making.

Will the time you spend pursuing your passion for art or writing rob you of vital sleep? Perhaps you'll find that a crucial replenishment of esteem is worth lost hours of slumber. Does the emotional boost from twice-a-week yoga enable you to have more patience with your family? Do the monetary benefits of holding down a full-time job or the educational benefits of carrying a full course load outweigh not seeing your children as much as you'd like?

Know the price you're willing to pay for your dreams. Prayerfully seeking inspiration from the Spirit will help you discern the answers that are right for you.

APRIL 8
The Rhyme Scheme of Life
I like rhyme because it is memorable. I like form because having to work to a pattern gives me original ideas. —Anne Stevenson[55]

A rhyme scheme is the pattern of rhyme between lines of a poetry or a song. It is commonly referred to using letters (A, B, C, D, etc.) to designate which lines in a poem or song rhyme. It provides a standard blueprint of rhyming words. A pattern. Structure or form. As we problem solve, the necessity of working to fit a form or pattern can help foster creative ideas. Likewise, the structure of marriage and family can be as limiting or enabling as we decide and express through our own creative efforts.

How to adequately care for our own needs and those of a husband and children and make it all work and still wake up feeling happy and fulfilled each morning is complex. It is another royal privilege to problem solve, given us by a wise Father.

Maybe nothing in your life seems to rhyme right now. Maybe you've considered marriage and motherhood as obstacles that hold you back. Work to balance caring for loved ones with taking good care of yourself. You might have to write and revise during the entirety of your life to get things right, but the rhyme of how to reach your potential can be patterned as easily and naturally as you are willing to allow God to help. The life poems written within the walls of your home are where true greatness and joy will be found.

APRIL 9
Realizing Who You Are
Many of life's failures are people who did not realize how close they were to success when they gave up. —Thomas Alva Edison[56]

In his book *The Remarkable Soul of a Woman*, President Dieter F. Uchtdorf tells us that the process of creating yields a sense of accomplishment. God, he reminds us, is the most creative Being in the universe. As His daughters, it is our right and heritage to create things of beauty and take joy in our efforts. Just as cultivating a garden, painting a sunset, or writing a book are ways we can express ourselves, so generating peace in our homes and relationships and bringing smiles to the faces of those who need our love and friendship are ways we can employ our divine ability to create.

What would you like to create today?

APRIL 10
Becoming: Write It Down
By recording your dreams and goals on paper, you set in motion the process of becoming the person you most want to be.
—Mark Victor Hansen[57]

In her book *Write It Down, Make It Happen*, Henriette Anne Klauser, PhD, tells us that the action of writing down goals is the first step to achieving them. The basic act of putting pen to paper helps us understand what we want out of life. "What is the 'it' in 'write it down'?" she asks. "When you don't have an answer to that question, when you don't know what your goals are, you can use your writing to point you in the right direction. If you don't know what you want, start writing . . . let your writing help point you to the path you were meant to follow."[58]

A few days ago, you added hopes, goals, and dreams to your life list. Today, take a few minutes and select one or two of the things you wrote down to expand on. For instance, if you listed scuba diving, write down exactly what you want to do: I want to go scuba diving in Hawaii. This month I'm going to find out where I can take lessons and how much they cost, make a plan for saving, decide when I want to start, and then plan an itinerary.

Then write a vivid description of your dream as you imagine it already happening. Incorporate your senses. What will you see, feel, taste, touch, or hear?

Henriette advises, "Educate yourself; get some brochures or books showing pictures of what you want looks like; talk to those who have done what you want to do; then write about some practical aspect of it to get grounded."

Congratulations. You're on your way!

APRIL 11
Talents and Gifts: Our Spiritual Destiny
Behold I say unto you, that by small and simple things are great things brought to pass. —Alma 37:6

Depending on what you were raised to believe about yourself and the beliefs you are now trying to define, getting in touch and staying in touch with your spiritual self can seem odd, uncomfortable, and at times, unattainable. But continue to give yourself a chance. Fully embracing our spiritual selves can lead us to experience a metamorphosis that has the power to take us from who we believe we are to who we are capable of becoming.

Consider which talents and gifts you'd like to discover.

APRIL 12
Just Be!
Obstacles are those frightful things you see when you take your eyes off your goal. —Henry Ford[59]

President Hinckley taught that as the result of our presence, the world must be a better place; and that we need to rise above mediocrity and indifference and speak up for that which is right.[60] In his book *Way to Be!,* he gives us nine ways to be happy and make something of our lives. The Be's are a practical guide for women of all ages: Be grateful, Be smart, Be involved, Be clean, Be true, Be positive, Be humble, Be still, and Be prayerful.

As women, most of us are multitaskers. Being still can be difficult. President Hinckley counsels that it's okay to spend some time by ourselves. And we need to do so in nature where we can think and breathe deeply. Most often the technological noise and opinions we are constantly barraged with do nothing to enrich our lives. He adds that we need to spend time reading and thinking and simply being still: taking time to think about the kind of women we want to become.

Contemplate President Hinckley's Be's. Study them in the topical guide of the scriptures or with relevant resources at LDS.org. Consider ways to implement them.

APRIL 13
This Is Your Brain on Multitasking
The brain is a lot like a computer. You may have several screens open on your desktop, but you're able to think about only one at a time.
—William Stixrud, PhD, Neuropsychologist[61]

You're on a two-lane highway in heavy, rush-hour traffic. You know you shouldn't use your cell phone, but you convince yourself a call or two won't hurt a thing. Wrong. Research has proven that your capacity to drive safely is lowered when you use your cell phone. Even using a head set, your response time is inhibited. When a pedestrian darts in front of you, the car ahead slows dramatically, or a piece of debris falls into the road, you want to be fully on your game to avoid a catastrophe. And what about all those vehicles in the other lane? Would you prefer their drivers keep their full attention on driving? Or that they be driving while texting while trying to find a radio station while sipping on a drink while they drive full speed toward you?

As with driving, truly productive time that yields solid results is not gained when we're attempting to multitask two, three, or maybe more activities. Quality comes from giving things our full attention. Whether in mothering, learning, working, or simply finding joy in a particular season or circumstance in your life, as you set goals to carry you toward your dreams, prioritize. Use an expanded form of life-triage to determine

* Things that are totally essential and have to be done right away.
* Things that need to be done but not immediately.
* Things you'd like to do at least in small measure.

* Things someone else can to do help you.
* Things that don't matter at all.

Attempting to switch from task to task in minutes or milliseconds robs mental energy. What things do you need to prioritize so you can more efficiently focus?

APRIL 14
Lights, Camera, Focus

Focus and simplicity. Simple can be harder than complex: You have to work hard to get your thinking clean to make it simple. But it's worth it in the end because once you get there, you can move mountains.
—Steve Jobs[62]

Face fears; learn from failures. Make the best of difficulty. When things don't go as planned, look for what there is to be learned. Apply what you learn to your next try. Don't give up.

Optimism is key. Don't let your past define you. Even if you didn't do well at math in high school, college math could be your forte. Even if you didn't understand elements of art or the perspective that would make your images appear three dimensional, it doesn't mean you can't learn techniques now that will make you a great artist.

Confidence comes from taking small, simple steps. Start with something you know you already have natural talent for. Set uncomplicated goals and mini-goals. Your self-confidence will improve with each accomplishment. Celebrate and build on every achievement.

Use positive thinking. Tell yourself you know you're going to succeed. Give yourself psychological pats on the back. Good work. Great job. You can do it.

Stay on course.

APRIL 15
What's on Your List?

Act as if what you do makes a difference. It does. —William James[63]

Most of us keep temporal bucket lists, a wish list of things to experience, do, or see before we die. Mine includes traveling to Ireland, relearning how to ski, finishing a book about my grandfather's life, and participating in a sled dog race with my Siberian Huskies. I also dream of eating at restaurants I've read good reviews on, hiking dozens of trails, meeting several people who I think are fascinating, and having a *New York Times* best-selling novel.

Recently, it occurred to me that I should also be keeping a spiritual bucket list—a wish list of things that will help me not only do more, but be more. I've included items like attending the temple more often. I'd love to visit my favorite temples: the Cardston Alberta Temple and The Hague Netherlands Temple. I want to do genealogical research on a couple of lines in my family and prepare more names for baptism. I've also set a goal to read or reread the conference talks and writings of several general authorities and to learn all I can about the lives and teachings of the prophets. Oh, and I'd like to memorize many more verses of scripture than I have and even learn to sing!

How about you? What's on your list?

APRIL 16

Impossible Dreams

Never, never, never, never, in nothing great or small, large or petty, never give in except to convictions of honour and good sense.
—Winston Churchill[64]

Muriel is not just any airplane. A Lockheed Electra L-10E, she came off the assembly line in 1935 and is a sister plane to the craft Amelia Earhart flew in 1937 when she attempted to become the first female pilot to fly around the world. Grace McGuire is not just any pilot. She owns *Muriel*—named after Amelia's younger sister—and she intends to fly the plane on the same route the legendary aviatrix took when she vanished.

Amelia disappeared on the last leg of her flight to Howland Island—a remote location in the Pacific. To date, no trace of her, her plane, or her navigator has been found. Speculation abounds. When she undertakes her own flight, Grace intends to prove Amelia was the victim of faulty coordinates. "This is my dream," Grace says, "to do this as a tribute to Amelia."

Not long after she rescued *Muriel* in 1984, Grace discovered she had Lyme disease. The illness took its toll. She spent years weakened and near physical incapacitation. Only recently has she felt well enough to continue to pursue her dream. Plan by plan, part by part, ensuring *Muriel* is restored accurately, Grace presses on.

What is your impossible dream? How do you plan to attain it?

APRIL 17
Living Defined
We live in deeds, not years: in thoughts, not breaths; In feelings, not in figures on a dial. We should count time by heart-throbs. He most lives Who thinks most, feels the noblest, acts the best. —Philip James Bailey[65]

Living means having life, being active or functioning, full of life or vigor. The definition of living a good life is more subjective. As Latter-day Saints we enjoy the blessing of knowing why we are here. We have responsibilities, covenants to keep. Yet the car we drive, the house we live in, the color of our bedroom, how many trees and flowers are in our yard, etc., etc., is up to us. There is no patent definition of a materially meaningful life we must adhere to. Though stereotypes press in, it's up to us to decide what's important.

If your happiness or security is entirely dependent on things of a transitory nature, then happiness will be transitory as well. What is your definition of living? In a world brimming with innumerable distractions, options, and choices, what do you find necessary and unnecessary to a life that is active, functioning, and full of vigor? Record your thoughts in your journal.

APRIL 18
The Organized Life
Organize your life around your dreams and watch them come true.
—Author unknown

The living room—pillows, chairs, couch. The kitchen—dishes, glasses, silverware. The family room—toys and games, television remotes, magazines and newspapers. The office—"in" pile, "out" pile, "to-be-filed" pile. The bedroom—clothes, shoes, miscellanea. The bathroom—towels, toiletries, toothpaste. What can you rearrange to bring clarity, balance, and stability to your life and purpose?

Today, rethink your most crucial living areas—those you spend the most time in—and create a plan to make them more functional. When your home is organized, your life will follow suit.

APRIL 19

Joy: Living with Confidence
No one concerns himself with how well he should live, only how long: while none can count upon living long, all have the chance of living well. —Author unknown

Thinking of the latter days can cause anxiety—storm and famine, earthquake and disease, war and wickedness. When we see such things play out in movies, it's a little unnerving. But to anticipate being right in the midst of suffering and calamity is downright scary. Our faith must prevail. In a fireside in September 2004, Elder Jeffrey R. Holland instructs that we should not become paralyzed with fear and cease living. Rather, we need to live life more completely than ever before.

No matter what comes, as long as we are here, we must continue to hope and have dreams. Even as prophecies are realized and the world itself becomes darkened with despair, we have the assurance that joy can be ours. Elder Holland reminds us that we can look forward to a happy future. While times may be hard, if we have built our lives on the firm foundation of the gospel, we will prevail.

Live in confidence; dream with joy!

APRIL 20

Listening: The Right Path at the Right Time
Rivers know this: there is no hurry. We shall get there some day.
—Winnie the Pooh[66]

Alone, my daughter and I wound our way through rounded outcroppings of red rock. Within an hour, we'd moved away from the well-beaten path. Other hikers thinned to a trickle. A slight tingling in my stomach told me to go back to the trailhead. The forms of the boulders we'd already hiked were shrouded with dusk-gray shadows. On the edge of an overhanging cliff, a not-so-distant silhouette stood out clearly against the rapidly advancing sunset. A man. "He's been following us," my daughter whispered.

I knew we had to immediately return to the trail even though it passed directly beneath the ominous figure. Retracing not more than a dozen paces took us back around a ten-foot-high by fifteen-foot-wide boulder. There, another man waited. Placing my full trust in the Spirit, I boldly walked past him and excitedly began to chatter to my daughter. I spoke in loud, clear tones about soon meeting up with her dad. I babbled as if I didn't have a care in the world. Darkness fell as we made it, safe and sound, back to our vehicle.

One day we'll return. It wasn't the place but the timing that could have led to peril. There were clues I should've heeded. Common sense and the tingling in my stomach. If I would've stopped to listen intently or pray, I could have discerned guidance long before I did.

Safely traveling the right paths at the right time is a skill honed by listening to the Spirit. Pacing yourself, being aware of your surroundings, and keeping your perspective will aid you in getting safely where you need and want to go.

APRIL 21
A Travel Companion
To the soul there is hardly anything more healing than friendship.
—Thomas Moore[67]

I've hiked numerous trails in three countries and in several states. Both expected and unexpected hazards and thrills were made more meaningful because I traveled with family or friends. My husband and children are my most frequent hiking companions. With their encouragement, I've conquered fears of heights in Zion National

Park. I've gotten up and continued on after having fallen, slipped, and slid during a terrifying ride down an avalanche chute in northern Utah's Wellsville Range. I've persisted in meeting goals on trails known to be frequented by bears in Canada and the Tetons—bears are not my favorite animal. I've expressed thankfulness for health and safety after almost disastrous missteps, rattlesnakes, cougars, and the near drowning of my middle daughter following a rock slide. Each experience, each trail, made us stronger, wiser, and more grateful for our lives.

When journeying through life, a travel companion lightens burden and hardship. Miles become shorter, landmarks clearer, paths more discernible, vistas more exhilarating. Who is your trusted travel companion? Your husband? A member of your family? A dear friend? God? Share with them your dreams. Talk and plan with them. Smile with them. Thrill with them over ascent into lofty mountain peaks. Cry with them when the way seems blocked. Confide in them when the altitude renders you fearful. Ask them for bandages for your blisters and water to hydrate you. Rejoice with them when grand vistas finally come into view.

APRIL 22
Using What You Have
The thing always happens that you really believe in; and the belief in a thing makes it happen. —Frank Lloyd Wright[68]

In John 6, we read of the miracle of the loaves and fishes. Sometimes, you may feel you figuratively have only five loaves and two small fishes—not enough to reach your goals. You may worry you're not smart enough or worthy enough to attain your dreams or perhaps even to have dreams. Money may be scarce, time in short supply. Self-confidence may wane. Illness can slow you physically, mentally, and emotionally. Circumstances, even ego and pride, may bind you where you are.

In such cases, you must begin. Begin to believe in yourself and your abilities, gifts, and talents. Begin to think and act in faith. Begin to expect that possibilities will present themselves. Begin to trust that help will come. Begin where you are with what you have.

If having a happy, blissful family life seems out of reach, begin by doing what you can to change the environment of your home from one of discord to one of harmony. Pray for and with family members. Search for ways you can improve your own attitude and example. Cultivate patience and kindness.

Miracles will begin when you do. Gather the crumbs and fragments of what you currently have and get going. Heavenly Father will bless and magnify your efforts.

APRIL 23
Your Legacy: An Ethical Will
No legacy is so rich as honesty. —William Shakespeare[69]

Personal historian Katie Shepherd teaches the art of making an ethical will: a method of passing down our values to posterity. "An ethical will," she says, "can be written by people of all ages to people of all ages . . . Whether our stories are funny, silly, embarrassing, or tragic, they create who we are and give us strength to move forward . . . They hold the potential to change lives when shared and passed on."[70]

An ethical will can be addressed to a child or grandchild or to posterity in general. It can express love and concern, life lessons learned, reflections on the purpose of life, struggles overcome, wise counsel, and dearly held moral values and beliefs accompanied by stories of how we came to adopt them. An ethical will can also include accomplishments, turning points, decisions, and consequences of choices. Gratitude is an important element that Katie says can cement loving relationships and allow us to reach out in reconciliation and forgiveness to those we may have hurt. It is an opportunity to let grudges go.

Continue to refer to the personal mission statement you wrote at the first of the month. As part of your travel plans, begin to contemplate what you want to include in an ethical will.

APRIL 24
Your Love of Life Will Bring a Life of Love
True joy is an earnest thing. —Author unknown

Just as the lens on a camera zeros in on an object, when you're working diligently toward achieving something, focus can get you there. Yet you are a woman with needs beyond spiritual and secular achievement. You need to feel loved and valued. To receive both, you must give both.

Remember to express love. Say it out loud and often. Send notes expressing love to your family members and friends. Love without the expectation of being loved or pleased or praised in return. Realize everyone has different ways of showing love. Help fellow travelers. Extend empathy. Give respect. Be kind and considerate, not demanding. Be ready and willing to receive love from others.

Work to maintain your emotional equilibrium as well. Celebrate each day by waking with a positive attitude. Watch the sun rise. Commit to seeking and choosing happiness. Plan the night before for a breakfast you can make with minimal effort and maximum enjoyment. Enjoy the tranquility of evening. Watch the sunset. Read a bedtime story to older kids or even to your husband. Get plenty of rest. Always count your blessings, and store your knowledge of them within ready access.

APRIL 25
Prepare: Enduring Adversity
As part of Heavenly Father's plan of redemption, all people experience adversity during their lifetime. Trials, disappointments, sadness, sickness, and heartache are a difficult part of life, but with the help of the Lord they can lead to spiritual growth, refinement, and progress.
—Gospel Topics, "Adversity," Gospel Library, LDS.org

Frequently, even when we're on the right track, we get derailed by adversity. Yet if our lives and faith are centered on Christ and the gospel, all things lead to hope. That doesn't mean we'll be immune from adversity—only that we are best prepared to face and endure it well.

Today, research the subject of adversity in the topical guide in your scriptures. Ponder and pray to learn about ways adversity can be overcome.

APRIL 26
First and Foremost a Daughter of God
O that cunning plan of the evil one! O the vainness, and the frailties, and the foolishness of men! When they are learned they think they are wise, and they hearken not unto the counsel of God, for they set it aside, supposing they know of themselves, wherefore, their wisdom is foolishness and it profiteth them not. And they shall perish. —2 Nephi 9:28

Satan doesn't want you to see or realize your greatness and infinite capabilities. He will try and convince you that spiritual necessities like regular church attendance, scripture study, and prayer are insignificant. He makes it his profession to deceive. Thus we must be on our guard so we are not misled. The adversary wants us to think the world's way is best, that obedience to God is foolhardy.

No matter what happens to you in life, no matter the wrong turns you may take or the missteps you chance to make, no matter what others may try to convince you of, you are still and always—first and foremost—a daughter of God, a child of royal birthright. For all your travels, pack, maintain, and guard spiritual necessities. Use them as they were intended to be used, and they will sustain you. Never lose or discard them.

APRIL 27
Patience: Hand in Hand with Success
It is strange that the years teach us patience; that the shorter our time, the greater our capacity for waiting. —Elizabeth Taylor[71]

As women we tend to be inherently hard on ourselves. Self-judgments are riddled with self-inflicted pressure to do better—now. The gravy doesn't taste quite right; we need to add more salt or toss it out and start over. The house isn't tidy enough; we should push ourselves to do more. We can't seem to finish everything we'd like to do in a day; we should work faster.

Impatience sets in like a plague.

I find comfort in the words of President James E. Faust, who counseled that we should not become discouraged if we perceive no apparent victories in our lives. Indeed, some things cannot be measured. If we continue to do our personal best each day to use our time and energy wisely, we can be satisfied that our best is good enough.[72]

This week, practice having patience with yourself.

APRIL 28

Milestones: Enjoy Each Accomplishment
Celebrate what you want to see more of. —Thomas J. Peters[73]

Milestones are markers on a road that are placed at mile intervals or at parts of a mile. They serve as reference points to show the distance traveled. In life, milestones designate an event or a stage in one's progress. When a baby first crawls, utters her first word, or takes her first steps, she is said to have reached a milestone. There is much joy and rejoicing. Photos are taken; the date is recorded and remembered for years to come. Marriage and birth are major milestones in our lives, as are graduating from high school and college. We send out invitations to request others to witness the special event. Other important points in a woman's life are birthdays and anniversaries, both of which are accorded special commemoration.

Life milestones can come in any increments we choose. They don't have to be understood or embraced by others. Every day we face and overcome obstacles others don't comprehend. Only Heavenly Father knows the full measure of our true victories.

In his novel *The Looking Glass*, Richard Paul Evans's character Hunter Bell tells us, "I have learned a great truth of life. We do not succeed in spite of our challenges and difficulties, but rather, precisely because of them."

Goals and dreams are reached though plain, old-fashioned hard work. Each one is worthy of celebration. No matter the size, enjoy and celebrate the milestones in your life.

APRIL 29

Tips for Enjoyable Travel

The past, I think, has helped me appreciate the present, and I don't want to spoil any of it by fretting about the future. —Audrey Hepburn[74]

Face your fears. What are you afraid of? Examine your fears and their implications. Would you rather go through the pain of overcoming your fears or the pain of regret later?

Cry when you need to. Life is hard. Anguish inevitable. A good cry washes away clouds so the sun can shine once again. Feel the pain, grieve, and then move through it.

Live purposefully. To take in optimum joy, slow down. Chew slowly: enjoy texture and flavor. Listen carefully: hear things you've been too busy to hear before. Watch closely: see the world through new eyes.

Learn from older people. Learn from their wisdom. Soak up their wealth of stories and experiences.

Take the day off. Relax: enjoy seclusion and silence.

Think outside the box. When something doesn't seem to be working, consider new perspectives. Often we already have what we need to help us keep going.

Be in the moment. Rather than worrying or dwelling on things you need to do tomorrow or the next day, consider what you're doing now. Seek beauty, goodness, promise, and hope in the moment.

Laugh. Find humor, and take pleasure in it.

Be positive. Recognize and quell negative thoughts and self-doubt. Don't take to heart complaints and criticism from others.

APRIL 30

Time: Savoring Life

Happiness is a miracle that happens inside you, no matter what else is going on.

Taking pleasure in life comes from simple, conscious acts. What's your passion? Reading, sewing, singing, baking, backpacking? Whatever it is, love and do it well.

Make healthy food choices. Foods impact your mood.

Spend time out of doors. Don't let the cold or the rain stop you. Optimism soars when you're outside. Enjoy sunny days. Play a sport for enjoyment. Walk through the grass in your bare feet. Watch birds or other creatures. Capture them with a sketch pad or camera. Seek adventure. It doesn't have to be costly or complex, just something new.

Move away from the television or computer. Quit checking e-mail, news, and chat groups. Real life is happening right now; you can be a part of it. Don't let time slip from your grasp. Get adequate exercise. Start with small goals, and work up to going farther or faster. Being active will make you feel alive and replenished.

April Recipes

Minnie's Eggs Mornay with Ham Sauce

6 eggs, hard-boiled and peeled
1 teaspoon lemon juice
½ teaspoon white onion, finely chopped

¼ teaspoon salt (optional)
⅛ teaspoon pepper
Half and half

Cut cooked eggs in half lengthwise. Reserve the whites, and mash the yolks with a fork. Mix in the lemon juice, onion, salt, and pepper into the mashed yolks. If the mixture seems stiff, add a little half and half to soften. Carefully fill the eggs whites with the yolk mixture. Place the twelve stuffed egg halves in a well-buttered casserole dish.

Ham Sauce

3 Tablespoons butter
3 Tablespoons flour
¾ cup chicken broth
¾ cup half and half
2 raw egg yolks

⅓ cup Parmesan cheese
1 teaspoon butter, softened
2 cups finely diced ham
Optional: buttered bread crumbs

Melt the butter over low heat. Whisk in the flour. Gradually add the chicken broth. Add the half and half, and bring to a boil, stirring constantly. Cook 1 to 2 minutes, then remove from heat. Beat

3 Tablespoons of the sauce mixture into 2 raw egg yolks. Add to the remaining sauce, and return to heat. Add the Parmesan cheese and butter. Mix until smooth. Fold in the ham pieces until well blended. Pour the sauce over the eggs, and heat for 30 minutes at 325 degrees or until center is set.

Breakfast Eggs a La King

1 cup celery, chopped	½ cup milk
¼ cup green bell pepper, chopped	1 cup American cheese, cubed
¼ cup white onion, finely chopped	4 hard cooked eggs, chopped
2 Tablespoons light olive oil	6 stuffed green olives, sliced
1 can cream of celery soup	Optional: hardboiled egg slices

In a large frying pan, sauté the celery, green pepper, and onion in oil until tender. Add the soup, milk, and cheese; heat and stir until the cheese melts. Add the chopped eggs and olives; heat through. Spoon over hot, buttered toast. If desired, garnish with egg slices. Makes 4 servings.

Ham and Eggs Quiche

1 8-inch pie pastry shell	1 cup Parmesan cheese
2 sliced hard-boiled eggs	4 raw eggs, slightly beaten
1 ½ cups diced ham	1 cup half and half
½ cup onion, chopped	3 Tablespoons flour
½ cup swiss cheese, shredded	Dash cayenne pepper
½ cup cheddar, shredded	

Prepare the pastry shell by baking at 375 degrees for 10 minutes. Remove; cool slightly. Spread sliced hardboiled eggs onto the crust. Layer ham, onion, and cheeses. In a bowl, combine the raw eggs, half and half, flour, and pepper. Blend well. Pour the mixture over the ingredients in the pie shell. Bake at 375 degrees for 30 minutes or until a knife inserted in the center comes out clean.

Ham-Stuffed Peaches

From *Peachy: A Harvest of Fruity Goodness*

2 ham slices, finely chopped
2 green onions, thinly sliced
2 oz. cream cheese
Salt and pepper to taste

1 (29 oz.) canned peach halves, drained
Buttered bread crumbs

Preheat oven to 350 degrees. Combine ham, onions, cream cheese, salt, and pepper. Place peach halves in shallow, greased baking dish. Fill centers of peaches with a scoop of the ham mixture, and top with bread crumbs. Bake for 10 to 12 minutes or until heated through.

MAY

Dancing along the Way
Friendship, Sisterhood, and Joy

FROM REALITY TV AND TALENT programs to televised competitions, from dancing their way through theatrical and cinematic productions to music videos, Latter-day Saint dancers are making their mark in the dance world. Their talent and enthusiasm have earned national and international awards. Their examples of faith and determination have earned respect.

President Brigham Young advised that if we want to dance—we should! Recreation and diversion are integral to our happiness and well-being.[75]

Maya Angelou teaches that everything in the universe has a rhythm and that everything dances. Moving to the pulse of the season, May's flowers burst forth in glorious, colorful blossoms to sway to a melody of gentle spring breezes. Follow their example of expression. Dancing to your own inner symphony of faith and determination is a gift in which you will find great joy and purpose.

Making the Most of May

* Books to read and share with your friends: *Women of Character* by Susan Easton Black and Mary Jane Woodger; *When Life Gets Hard* by Meg Johnson; *Women of Christ* by Toni Sorenson; and the *Butterfly Box Trilogy* by Michele Ashman Bell.

* Remember the strength of women united. Volunteer with friends and family members. Attend the temple with them. Take cooking, decorating, or flower-arranging classes together. Discover new outdoor activities and sports.

* Get your bicycles out and ready for summer; air up the tires.

* Take a photo of your home. Import it into your photo enhancement software. Use the text feature to add your family's surname and the date you moved in. Add the names of each family member if desired. Frame and hang the photo.

* Cinco de Mayo is celebrated in commemoration of Mexican heritage and to commemorate the Mexican defeat of French troops at the Battle of Puebla in 1862. Use Google Earth to visit the countries where your ancestors are from, or check out books from the library and research certain areas.

* Plan an end-of-school party with family and neighbors. Go potluck. Invite and honor your children's teachers.

* Schedule a party for stargazing. Give earrings or other trinkets with stars to commemorate the event.

* Plan a special lunch for your mom to honor her for Mother's Day. Make a photo book with current photos of you and your children. Or create a Mother's Day memory book and include special memories from your childhood and what they taught you. Tell your mother how her example, determination, or spirituality touched your life. If your mother has passed on, plan a tribute. Family members can gather for a meal or get together to share memories and photos.

* Random acts of kindness are as good for friends as they are for strangers. Send flowers to a friend. Or buy or sew matching aprons for all your girlfriends.

* Visit flea markets or yard sales to find summer treasures like outdoor chairs, tables, and candleholders—anything you can buy for pennies that will enhance your outdoor decor.

* Be nice when you don't have to be; be the first to apologize.

* Make a gift basket for a woman in need: a runner, mother, chef, gardener, crafter, quilter, yoga, business woman, blogger, reader, or stuffed animal lover. Find cute specialty items, key chains, old photos, postcards, and mementos. Give the basket as a special surprise.

* Initiate a cobbler night with the recipes following this section.

MAY 1

Dance!

If thou art merry, praise the Lord with singing, with music, with dancing, and with a prayer of praise and thanksgiving.
—D&C 136:28

You can dance anywhere, even if only in your heart. —Author unknown

Our ancestors knew the importance of dance. In the northwest of Bulgaria, the Magura Cave contains paintings dating back to the Stone Age that depict dancing women and men. Throughout history, dance has bonded, healed, and transformed. It has allowed personal journeys to be enriched with self-discovery, inspired peoples to stand for what they believe in, and moved cultures to live more fully in love and harmony as the shackles of the past and drudgery of life were shaken off.

There is a quote said to have its origins as an Indian proverb: "To watch us dance is to hear our hearts speak."

What does your heart yearn to say?

Will your dance bond, heal, or transform? Will it inspire others to learn and grow and strive to be all they can be? Can you teach of overcoming despair? Will finding just the right words strengthen and fortify others against life storms? Can you emulate the light of joy so others can find their way out of darkness? Does the happy dance inside your head show in your smile?

If you wish to dance, dance!

MAY 2

Simple Things: The Power of One Heart to Touch Another
A merry heart maketh a cheerful countenance. —Proverbs 15:13

I don't remember her name, but I'll never forget her face.

Framed by amber ringlets, that little face was marked with great anguish. Her small chin trembled. Her eyes were wet with tears. Crouched on the blue tumbling mat in the gymnasium, she cast furtive glances at the throng of children gathered for a birthday party.

A mother of four, I recognized what was wrong: the child felt overwhelmed and out of place. Before I could cross the room to help, I watched, spellbound, as a rosy-cheeked, blonde eight-year-old made her way to the mat and bent over the crying girl. I could see a brief exchange of words and smiles. Immediately, the countenance of the curly-headed child was transformed. She straightened and rose to her feet. Radiant joy broke through the shadows of her tears. Her face glowed as she went to join the others in play.

Amazing how easy it is for one heart to touch another.

How can you bless the lives of others with something simple today? A friendly wave or pleasant smile can work wonders!

MAY 3
The Alphabet of Sisterhood
A sister is a gift to the heart, a friend to the spirit, a golden thread to the meaning of life. —Isadora James[76]

As women we lead, mentor, teach, love, encourage, and uplift one another. Gifts inherent to each of us, unique in our individual expression, make up the alphabet of sisterhood:

Authentic and Adept
Brave and Brilliant
Courageous and Competent
Delightful and Determined
Enthusiastic and Enduring
Fantastic and Funny
Gentle and Gifted
Happy and Hopeful
Inspiring and Important
Jubilant and Jovial
Kind and Keen
Loving and Long-suffering
Magnanimous and Merciful
Nurturing and Noble

Outstanding and Optimistic
Philosophical and Passionate
Queenly and Qualified
Resilient and Resourceful
Splendid and Spirited
Tenacious and Trustworthy
Unselfish and Uncompromising
Vivacious and Virtuous
Witty and Whimsical
Xenial (hospitable) and Xenodochial (friendly)
Yearning and Youthful
Zany and Zealous

Express thanks to the women in your life for the characteristics they have that make the world a better place.

MAY 4
The Fun of Friendship
A friend is a gift you give yourself. —Robert Louis Stevenson[77]

I love to shop. I love shoes. I love boots. I love coats—my husband jokes I have one for every day of the week. He's right; I'm a bargain hunter, and most were found at sales. I especially love to shop with friends. I love the enthusiasm of a sisterhood of shoppers, enthusiastic to buy what we think will make us look better or feel younger. Trying on and recommending and laughing over both the ridiculous and sublime!

Vanity in action? Perhaps.

Frivolous fun? Yes!

Even if no one spends a dime, the blithe errand of shopping or window shopping for clothing or home decor with adored friends lightens our mood. Taking a break from everyday pressures that could cripple emotionally, we become more pleasant when we engage in a bit of dreamy, girlish togetherness.

Shopping or eating or enjoying. Find a purse. See a movie. Girls' night. Fancy restaurant, downtown café, uptown gourmet. Upscale chic or dollar store. Road trip. Concert. Conversation. Kindness. Makeovers. Surprise party. Paint your toenails. Scavenger hunt. Craft project.

What sounds fun?

Make plans. Start friend traditions monthly or yearly. Invite those you love as well as those you'd like to get to know and those who need a friend.

MAY 5

No Matter the Season, Live and Grow with the Spirit
Women are flowers growing in the garden of God. —Author unknown

In the tender, budding season of girlhood, the full blossom of womanhood, or the aging grace of senior years, Christlike attributes flow through you, waiting to be expressed in the beauty of your words and deeds: mercy, truth, love, compassion, peace, patience. When you live and grow in harmony with the Spirit, peace of presence and refinement of soul are yours. Guard and treasure them. They provide you power to evoke good in a world filled with pain, anguish, and iniquity as you persuade everyone around you to be more. More faithful. More hopeful. More humble. More diligent. More obedient. Wiser. Kinder. Gentler. All by simply being yourself.

No matter your season, thrive. Drink in the nourishing words of the scriptures. Humble yourself in prayer. Seek God's will. Heed His call to serve and obey. Yours is a life of divine possibility. Lead the way for others with your depth of faith and unbreakable spirit. You can because you were born to do so.

MAY 6

Lead: Peace, Purpose, and Possibilities
A lot of us go through phases where we think we have to be, act, and look like everyone else in order to fit in. I tried it, and it didn't work. I let go of the status quo and decided just to be me. —Suzy Toronto[78]

Mortality comes with every shape and size of enticement to walk the walk and talk the talk of what is termed popular. The car we should

...ouse we should live in. The colors and styles we should embrace each season. Your true self, your divine nature, doesn't demand the mortal approbation of fitting in.

In the peace of early morning, what comes fluttering like an airy butterfly to your mind? When the deepness of night arrives, what do your heart and soul whisper? What do you yearn for? Peace and purpose, possibilities forged by your conscience rather than impossibilities imposed by conformance to the code of the world?

The longing for authentic destiny is assuaged by addressing the underpinnings of your divine need to act in a manner attuned to heaven. Don't wait for someone else to fill the stomachs of starving children. Don't wait for another to organize an effort to help the homeless. Don't postpone your contributions of time and talent for a Relief Society activity. You don't need a degree, position of authority, wealth, or recognition to make a true and lasting difference for good. All that's required is time and a loving, willing heart—a willing heart unafraid to be different from worldly norms.

Lead out, and address issues you feel passionate about. Just be you!

MAY 7
The Power of Sisterhood United
Efforts and courage are not enough without purpose and direction.
—John F. Kennedy[79]

Women have the unique ability to support and empower one another to do the impossible. The power of sisterhood united—women working together for a common purpose—changes lives. Decide on a purpose, a cause that needs the love and attention of the power of sisterhood. Organize women you know and those you don't know. Plan a life-changing activity:

* Make a quilt for a homeless woman or a blanket for an infant with no family.

* Plan a wedding or baby shower for a woman who has no else to do it for them.

* Hold a tribute dinner for a woman not yet recognized for her contributions.
* Plan a birthday party for an elderly woman who has no family.
* Organize a balloon launch in memory of a friend who has passed away.
* Collect money to buy a headstone for a woman's grave that doesn't have one.
* Shop for clothes for a needy woman.
* Prepare a special breakfast for someone who is a shut-in.
* Collect money to give to a widow.
* Buy phone cards for service women and men.
* Buy gas cards for a single mom trying to care for her family alone.
* Help provide for a family that has a parent in the military.
* Help with a Special Olympics activity, or organize a run or walk for a charitable cause.
* Visit the children's ward of a hospital or an assisted living center and sing or play musical instruments for the patients.
* Arrange with a tree farm to provide Christmas trees for the needy next December.
* Make care packages for women and children in hospitals or homeless shelters.
* Provide housecleaning for a woman who is ill.

MAY 8
Wishes: Lives Changed

Ye will not suffer that the beggar putteth up his petition to you in vain . . . Perhaps thou shalt say: The man has brought upon himself his misery; therefore I will stay my hand . . . for his punishments are just . . . whosoever doeth this the same hath great cause to repent; and except he repenteth of that which he hath done he perisheth forever, and hath no interest in the kingdom of God. For behold, are we not all beggars?
—Mosiah 4:16–19

Every wish is like a prayer—with God. —Elizabeth Barrett Browning[80]

What if you could grant wishes?

Written in 1905, the novel *The Little Princess* by Frances Hodgson Burnett takes place in Victorian-era England. Young Sara Crewe is living in a London boarding school. Her mother dead, her father believed dead, Sara is subjected to the cruel whims of the headmistress. In the dark, drab chill of the school's old attic, she awakens one night to find her room transformed. A benefactor has provided food, and the attic is warm and cheerful.

What if you could do something similar? What if the homeless person on the corner really does need help? What would Christ do? What if you took the person a hot meal? A real meal, not unlike Thanksgiving dinner itself? What would you lose? What could you gain?

What if you "adopted" a needy child in your area for an entire year? If you spent time learning the child's needs from caregivers, social workers, or clergy? What their dreams and aspirations are? You could plan and prepare, involve friends and family members in your ideas, even if only to write letters of encouragement or send birthday cards.

What if?

MAY 9
Miracles of Friendship
Friendship is born at that moment when one person says to another, "What! You too? I thought I was the only one." —C. S. Lewis[81]

When you look at an apple, do you think of it as bearing wonder? If you cut it in half horizontally, you'll find a beautiful five-pointed star. Twigs from cottonwood trees hold the same marvel: a tiny, delicate star within.

Friends can come in the same way, not always readily apparent but someone who is suddenly viewed with new perspective. The neighbor you've met only once in two years approaches you in the grocery store. In the produce section, she pours out her heart to you. You discover you have more in common than you could ever have imagined. The woman you've seen dozens of times at church but never talked to. You decide to take her a batch of cookies. It turns out she needs a friend as much as you do. The beautiful new ward member you convinced yourself had a life of ease. When you chance to meet at the hospital, you find her life is actually difficult and complex. Both your child and hers have asthma; she becomes an ally and confidant to share the trials of childhood illness with.

Look for and celebrate the miracles of friendship.

MAY 10

Blessings: Friends
A friend is one who knows you and loves you just the same.
—Elbert Hubbard[82]

The women in our lives—daughters, grandmothers, mothers, biological sisters, sisters in the gospel, aunts, cousins, friends, teachers—enrich and sustain us. Because of them we find strength to smile, to resolve to dry our tears and move on, and to laugh about bad hair days, white laundry that somehow turned pink, and silly things we said without thinking.

Today, write down the names of women in your life, past and present, all ages, who have touched your heart and lifted you higher.

* A woman to whom you are indebted to for an act of service or who forgave you.
* A woman who taught you to be valiant and stand up for what you believe.
* A woman who showed you how good it is to laugh.
* A woman who loved you even when you didn't feel you were worth loving.
* A woman who showed you mountains can be moved with a strong heart and gentle voice.
* A woman who helped you find the gift of yourself and showed you it was okay to be you.
* A woman whose testimony strengthened yours.
* A woman who taught you about the joy of service.
* A woman you've admired from afar.

* A woman whose gentle smile filled the world with love.
* A woman who calls you friend because of and despite all you have
  been through together.

   Pick one from your list. Take the time to express sincere appreciation for how she has made your life better. Write her a thank-you note, call her, or take her out to lunch.

MAY 11

Making a Difference: Remembering
*And when he cometh home, he calleth together his friends and
neighbours, saying unto them, Rejoice with me; for I have found my
sheep which was lost.* —Luke 15:6

Ours was the kind of friendship that unfortunately, over the years, dissolved into what could be termed as only a mere acquaintanceship. I left the neighborhood but vowed to return to see Julie. I never did. Through the grapevine, I heard she moved. I didn't think of her again for years until an obituary caught my eye—Julie's young son. A little voice told me I should go see Julie. It wasn't just the kind of voice that prompts you to return home to check and see if the iron's on. It was the kind of voice that shouted, "Go home. The house is going to burn down!" But life was busy. I ignored the prompting.

   A month passed. The local newspaper in my hands, that same little voice, as if in a reprimand, told me to turn to the obituaries. Julie. I trembled with remorse. Would it have mattered if I had paid my respects when her son died? Put my arms around her? My mind told me I'd never know for certain, yet my heart whispered the truth: even our smallest efforts, if sincere and heartfelt, can lend needed hope. I'd been so busy trying to be a good person in the eyes of the world I forgot the world is comprised of individuals.

   When the sun sets on each of our yesterdays, they become engraven in the past. In our todays and tomorrows, we can choose to search our hearts as well as all the faces we might otherwise pass by. We can commit ourselves to remembering and serving—even if time permits it only through prayer.

MAY 12

Erasing the Sum: Inner Accounting
It is more blessed to give than to receive. —Acts 20:35

Adding hurt upon hurt because we feel neglected, tallying up inconsequential actions that disappoint us, a friend doesn't thank us when we send a card, another doesn't return our wave, and someone else fails to buy an item from the home decor catalog we dropped off. What's more, she never brings the catalog back!

The sum of inner accounting, keeping track of what we feel we're due, depletes our energy and emotions, leaving us in a state of forever trying to calculate injustices. The more people we associate with, the more chance we have of feeling let down or disappointed. When we insist on compounding the notion that we are treated with disregard, we open the door to self-limiting beliefs. We become frustrated when it seems no one will sympathize with us. We resign ourselves to continue the process of adding to our grievances. Joy and the Spirit flee.

We almost always neglect to factor in that others may not even be aware of expectations we set up for them! Or, due to circumstances beyond their control, they may simply not be able to meet what we expect of them. Within their hearts they may hold us in high regard, even if we believe their actions fall short.

With the help of the power of the Atonement, we can free ourselves from the effects of inner accounting. We can choose to erase the feeling that we are constantly owed something from friends, loved ones, or those we serve.

MAY 13

Cherish: Appreciating Friends Who Are Dear to Us
Worship God, in whatsoever place ye may be in, in spirit and in truth; . . . live in thanksgiving daily, for the many mercies and blessings which he doth bestow upon you. —Alma 34:38

We sat on her sofa, vintage needlepoint pillows tucked behind our backs. She sat on the love seat, bent slightly forward with age and intent. On the coffee table at our knees was a small wooden bust of an African woman. Her soulful eyes looked out at us as from carved bondage as our hostess told of Kenya in 1996. She saw animals too numerous for her camera to capture. She and her second husband had stayed at a place owned by William Holden. Clocks ticked off the seconds of our stay, grains of sand slipping through the fingers of time. She served us a delicacy of jazz saxophone and honey-smooth vocals, favorite tunes shimmering on the last rays of summer afternoon. Then she led us outside.

A creek bed that once fed a waterfall was dry and withered. It reminded me of the woman herself; the dearth seemed to pulse with its desire to be full and alive once more. Native grasses and new bursts of sagebrush erupted in the higher terraces, nature reclaiming what the woman had, in her younger years, borrowed for her own to carefully tend as flower beds. I studied her smile-worn face, the wind blowing short wisp-curls of silver-grey hair around her forehead. She was as beautiful as her pictures of Kenyan gazelle, and, like the photos, fading. The tender lover, world traveler, gentle gardener had aged gracefully, but, just like the moment, I knew she would slip away all too soon.

Today, cherish friends who are dear to you.

MAY 14
Visiting Teaching: The Ripple Effect of Love
Everyone is kneaded out of the same dough but not baked in the same oven. —Yiddish Proverb

In being visiting taught by sisters from your ward, you've doubtless met one or two who left you feeling puzzled. Maybe they never came. Maybe they came too often and stayed too long. Maybe you felt you were being judged instead of ministered to. I once had a visiting teacher who expressed, in so many words, that it was not worth her time to visit me. Her "teaching" consisted of an occasional smile, wave, or casual comment at church. I agonized over her demeanor.

I asked myself what Jesus would do. I became impressed with the fact that if we are instructed to love our enemies, bless them that curse us, do good to them that hate us, and pray for them who despitefully use and persecute us, it follows that we should also love, bless, do good for, and pray for those who are seemingly austere or simply inattentive. Surely, I admitted to myself, I had unknowingly disappointed those I visit taught at one time or another.

While adhering to the Savior's example, you will recognize ways you can improve your stewardship. You will be blessed with the strength to cope with challenges in the form of misunderstandings with, miscommunication with, or misperceptions of the sisters with whom you attend church. Your efforts to do your best will have a ripple effect. One day, perhaps years down the road, those you have visit taught or otherwise associated with will remember how you reached out to them in sincerity and love. Then they, in turn, will choose to more fully minister to the needs of those whom they serve.

MAY 15

Creating a Memory Box
So long as the memory of certain beloved friends lives in my heart, I shall say that life is good. —Helen Keller[83]

In a square, pink satin box, I store special keepsakes. When days are long and hard and I need a boost from good times with my grandmother—who was as much mother to me as grandmother—I open my dresser drawer. In reverence, I lift out the box. Pink was her favorite color. When I lift the ribbon latch and open the lid, my nose is greeted by the scent of a rose sachet. My fingers touch handkerchiefs with delicate edges crocheted by loving hands. One is embroidered with a rose and three brilliant buds; my diminutive grandmother cherished roses. She loved their scent and the meaning of their blossoms: red for beauty, perfection, and deep, abiding love. Pink for grace, elegance, admiration, appreciation, and joy.

Inside a small white envelope are family photos that remind me how far I've come and how far I need yet travel. Other mementoes remind me that the travel need be done with my head held high and my heart in the right place so that my hands might work miracles. I want my grandmother to be proud of me. Grandma Minnie's script, her own font of sculpted, cursive letters with b's that loop in elegance and jaunty lower case y's, brings tears to my eyes. Her love of quotes, Browning and Rice and Dickinson and others too numerous to count, gave me my love of words. Her stories, family and faith, mystery and magic, gave me the passion to tell tales.

Near the bottom of the box, old perfume samples and more rose sachets; the Avon lady was Grandma's most devoted friend. If I hold them, I can breathe remembrance of Grandma into my soul. All innocence and goodness and hope and joy and laughter.

My fingers locate a silver and azure necklace, faux gems and stones. I never actually saw her wear the choker. I wish I had. She saved it for best occasions. I wore the necklace and matching earrings to church once. Even though I managed to lose one of the earrings, I don't think she minds. Memories aren't dimmed by one lost earring and love not diminished by death.

Today, make a box in memory of a woman who made a difference in your life. Add dried flowers, photos, cards, letters. When days grow long and hard, revisit and add to the box. Let it give you strength and reconnect you to your purpose. Let it help you remember all you know she expects of you.

MAY 16
The Strength of Those Gone Before
In all of us there is a hunger, marrow deep, to know our heritage—to know who we are and where we came from. Without this enriching knowledge, there is a hollow yearning. No matter what our attainments in life, there is still a vacuum, an emptiness, and the most disquieting loneliness. —Alex Haley[84]

On our old upright piano are photos representing eight generations: a photographic history from my three-greats grandmother, Jesse, down to my first granddaughter, Abby. Jesse arrived in this country with only her doll and her name. Purportedly left in the care of a ship's captain, she sailed from Wales when she was only four or five years old. Through scant pieces of oral history, I learned she once saved vital records from a burning courthouse in West Virginia.

In another tintype photograph, Jesse sits with her daughter, Mary. Etched in the tin on the chests of both Jesse and Mary is scratched an X, a practice undertaken when a loved one passed. When I look at those Xs, I feel a sharp sense of pain. Their faces tell of hardship, yet their eyes show firm resolve and faith. Other photos on the piano include Mary's daughter, my great-grandmother, and her daughter, my grandmother—the one who loved roses. When I pass by the photos, I do so in reverence for women who lived and loved, struggled and survived, so that I could be who I am and where I am today.

Research the life of one of your female ancestors. Find out all you can about her: her favorite color, food, or hobbies, the place she lived, her accomplishments, her heartaches and joys. Determine if her temple work has been done, and if the temple work for her parents, siblings, or children needs to be done. In your journal, write down your thoughts and impressions about the woman. Explain what her story or example has taught you.

MAY 17
Your Story: Think Grand, Live Grand
Arise and shine forth, that thy light may be a standard for the nations.
—D&C 115:5

When I think of my grandmothers, I can't help but think of myself: perhaps someday captured in the stillness of a photograph in a frame on a descendant's piano. No matter when the photo is taken, I hope they will see faith in my eyes. If I am elderly, I hope they will see smile and laughter lines instead of wrinkles. Perhaps they will look at me and wonder, "Hmm, I wonder what her story is?" I pray they will take the time to find out. Until then, my story is still one in the making.

I am human—achingly so. I make mistakes on a daily, sometimes hourly basis. I am impatient, prone to being irritable when I am tired, and I do not always keep up on caring for my home and family as I should. But I am trying to be stronger, more patient, more loving, more an example of the happiness and serenity which I seek. Beyond the tangible evidences of undone laundry and all my human frailties, I love my Father in Heaven and His gospel. I pray the way I live my life will be a testament to that love. Within the gospel, my family, and my life, I find great satisfaction. I am endeavoring to make my story better each day. I want my descendants to be able to look at my photo and discern my faith, joy, and strength.

What will your story be? What will your progenitors know of you? In your journal or ethical will, record what you love and what brings you joy.

MAY 18

The Qualities of Friendship

I never considered a difference of opinion in politics, in religion, in philosophy, as cause for withdrawing from a friend. —Thomas Jefferson[85]

Friendship is both a noun and a verb: a friendship is a valued relationship; to friendship is to befriend. A friendship is a unique and extraordinary opportunity to enjoy the company of another human being. It provides the opportunity to interact and serve on a deeply personal level as we learn about our friends and about ourselves. Through friendship we can lighten burdens and encourage others to believe in themselves, to excel.

Friendshipping, offering a relationship of friendship, brings many responsibilities and necessary traits: respect, patience, kindness, honesty, compassion, understanding, cooperation, humility, reliability, sensitivity, trust, dependability, thoughtfulness, sincerity, forgiveness, optimism, politeness, integrity, encouragement, supportiveness, caring, and loyalty.

Can you think of other qualities necessary to friendship? Which do you need to work on? Which are you already good at extending? Ponder and practice the qualities of friendship.

MAY 19

Angel-friends: The Blessings of a Positive Outlook
*Remember faith, virtue, knowledge, temperance, patience, brotherly
kindness, godliness, charity, humility, diligence. —D&C 4:6*

As a young mother, I felt lonely and depressed. In our ward, there
were no sisters my age. An elderly neighbor, Phyllis Valentine, tried to
friendship me, but I wasn't receptive. I'd prayed to find friends with
similar interests who could provide compassion and support. Why
hadn't my prayers been answered?

One particularly difficult day, I needed a few minutes respite.
I went to Phyllis's home and found myself gently urged to stay. I
let myself relax and enjoy being in her company. I marveled that—
despite the fact she was nearly fifty years my senior—we were very
much alike. We shared common interests in crafting, gardening,
family history, and old photographs as well as in handiwork and
canning. Sheepishly, I realized my prayers had been answered.

In days to come, I learned that despite challenges of health and
family, Phyllis maintained a positive outlook as well as a bottomless
reserve of unconditional love and optimism. Her unwavering
righteous example taught me I had the power to overcome adversity.

Though other women my age eventually moved into the ward
and became my friends, dearest of all was my association with
Phyllis. We attended Relief Society together, crafted and canned and
gardened together, laughed and cried together—all as she taught me
the blessings of maintaining a faithful, optimistic mind-set and about
how Heavenly Father answers our prayers, sending angel-friends,
who—no matter their age—change our lives.

MAY 20

The Personal Touch: Strengthening Friendships
*A friend is one who walks in when others walk out. —*Walter Winchell[86]

Things were not going well. Consumed by both headache and heartache, I was a less-than-picturesque picture of what a mother should
be. My seven-year-old argued incessantly. My teenage son challenged

me on a curfew restriction. A relative seemed intent on picking apart everything I did. My house was a disaster. Frayed emotions, I felt depressed and sorry for myself.

The doorbell rang. A dear friend greeted me. Her face glowed with a brilliant smile. She held a bouquet of yellow daisies. She extended the flowers then stepped forward and drew me into a hug. "I knew you were having a bad day," she said. "I wanted to let you know I cared."

I felt ashamed of myself and humbled. Despite all the trials of that particular day, life was good. I was blessed. Someone cared. I was not alone. "Thank you," I whispered. Tears brimmed and ran down my cheeks. "Thank you!"

The flowers were a simple gesture. My friend's words were brief and to the point. Yet, magically, the dark clouds of emotion hanging over me dissipated. Everything, even my messy house, looked much brighter. For days to come, I smiled each time I thought of how powerful a simple gesture can be in evoking feelings of joy and in strengthening bonds of friendship.

Someone may not show up at your door today with flowers, but you can show up at theirs. Do you have a friend who's having a tough time? If no one comes to mind, pray to be guided to someone who needs you. Give them genuine love and care.

MAY 21
Nurturing the Blessing of Friendship
The more we nurture friendships, the greater the happiness that comes our way. —Author unknown

A little forethought and organization work wonders in nurturing friendships.

Thank-you notes: Stock up on thank-you notes at the dollar store. One or two heartfelt lines can bring great joy to a friend. Thank you for the lesson you taught last Sunday; you're a wonderful teacher. Thank you for the tomatoes you brought over; you certainly have a green thumb!

Friend book: A small notebook helps keep track of important friend facts. Some entries to consider are a favorites list (favorite food, color, perfume, flower, books and music, etc.), and important dates (birthdays, anniversaries, dates of the loss of a loved one). Buy a selection of birthday, get-well, thinking of you, and sympathy cards, and put them with the book so you don't have to scramble for a card at the last minute. Print off address labels and keep stamps on hand so you can quickly get cards and letters into the mail. The favorites list will be a handy reference when shopping for gifts for birthdays and other special occasions.

The personal touch: If you love to take treats to friends but don't have a lot of time to spend in the kitchen, premade cookie dough and brownie mix are great timesavers. Even better are inexpensive gifts geared to specific interests. For a sewing friend, put colorful threads and a package of needles in a cute gift bag. Include a personal note that explains how you admire your friend's love of and talent for sewing. For a gardening friend, a little plant tied with a bright bow. A terra cotta pot with packages of seeds and small garden tools. For cooking friends, colorful hot pads and useful kitchen tools. You can find a wealth of old potato mashers and vintage flour sifters and cheese graters at thrift stores. Favorite candies or chocolates in a decorative jar or gift bag are always a hit, as is a bouquet of flowers from the local market.

Make traditions: Designate time for regular phone calls to check in on those you don't often see. Together plan ahead to allot time for girls' nights, movies, lunch on birthdays, going to the spa together, or getting a manicure or pedicure.

Simple things: The greatest gifts have no price and take little time to offer. Smiles and hugs are easy to give and quick to be received.

As things come to mind, add to this list of simple gestures and nurture your friendships.

MAY 22
From the Heart
The heart of the giver makes the gift dear and precious. —Martin Luther[87]

I am come that they might have life, and that they might have it more abundantly. —John 10:10

We expend much time reorganizing, rearranging, cleaning, dusting, fixing, packing, moving, insuring, and locking up all we have. Though our things require much effort, they are dear to us.

Having witnessed the dispersal of my grandparents' personal belongings, I came to see the benefits of giving things away while we're still alive. To the best knowledge and ability of surviving family members, possessions were distributed in accordance with what was hoped were my grandparents' wishes. The process was arduous, painful when someone wanted something another had received.

Spencer W. Kimball affirmed that living an abundant life has little to do with the acquisition of material goods. He noted that scriptural reference to an abundant life is the spiritual result of our service to others and of the investment of our talents as we serve God. True happiness and a sense of abundance begins within us and is not dependent on external means.[88]

Giving away something we value is humbling. It renews focus, however, on the more important spiritual elements of our existence and replenishes appreciation for all God freely gives. When given in sincerity without pressure of expectation, such giving alters our outlook and enhances our enjoyment of what we take for granted each day.

This month give something you never thought you'd part with to a friend.

MAY 23
The Worth of Words

Charity suffereth long, and is kind; charity envieth not; charity vaunteth not itself, is not puffed up. —1 Corinthians 13:4

Words of the Wise: Have you heard the saying "look before you leap"? Doing so can prevent trouble and pain. The same goes for thinking before you speak. Choose your words carefully so you don't offend others. Speak in calm tones. Be quick to compliment and emphasize your friends' strengths and talents. Show respect. Extend encouragement.

Forgive and Forget: Don't let differences of opinion and minor disagreements become major stumbling blocks. Talk things through. Let friends know you forgive them, then forget offenses. Don't let hard feelings continue to simmer. Unchecked, they are likely to boil and cause hurt. Be humble.

Ask if You Don't Understand: Even close friends interpret challenges and joys, storms and sunshine, pain and happiness in differing ways. If you don't understand what a friend is experiencing, ask. Accept what they say; you don't have to provide answers. Just listen.

Don't Betray Trust: When a confidence is shared with you, guard it carefully. Don't gossip. Build your friends up, both in their presence and when they're away. Treat others the way you'd like to be treated. Friends don't brag, speak down to friends, or become authoritarians.

Who can you build up today?

MAY 24
The Balance of Friendship
Friendship is like a bank account. You can't continue to draw on it without making deposits. —Author unknown

We carry around with us a lifetime of experiences. Happiness, triumph, and gladness have their expression in our actions and words—verbal and written sonnets of joy. Yet sorrow, disappointment, and regret are often packed away into the recesses of shame and shadow. If we continue to add to them, they become burdens—easier to box up than banish. We can come to view our friends as box keepers. The longer we know our friends the more we may expect of them. When we come to anticipate that they should act according to only our desires, frustration occurs on both sides.

Elder Marvin J. Ashton said that a friend should help us be better, improve our attitude, comfort us, and boost our self respect. He further stated that someone is *not* a friend if they contribute to our trials and struggles.[89]

Likewise, if a friend expects us to carry more than our share of their load, the relationship can strain and break. It's the difference between someone asking us to carry around one box versus ten. While friends are indeed intended to help bear one another's burdens, the process is a delicate balancing act for both parties.

Work for balance in your friendships. See the good in yourself and your friends. Focus your energy on the positive aspects of friendship rather than on burden sharing. Doing so will save resentment and provide long-term contentment.

MAY 25

Courage: Being Part of the Solution

The most I can do for my friend is simply to be his friend. I have no wealth to bestow on him. If he knows that I am happy in loving him, he will want no other reward. Is not friendship divine in this?
—Henry David Thoreau[90]

Knowingly or unknowingly, friends let us down. Disappointment and bitterness surge as we experience feelings of betrayal and rejection. But no matter how much our feelings are hurt, we can choose to be part of the solution. Broken trust requires forgiveness. Miscommunication requires restorative communication—healing words—and humility. With time and age come wisdom and maturity; we must use both to overcome bitterness.

Heavenly Father and Jesus are our constant friends—at all times and in all circumstances. They will help us cope with whatever letdowns or injustice we perceive. Even in times of great despair, we need to remember we are daughters of God.

In her book *A Mother's Influence: Raising Children to Change the World*, Sister Margaret D. Nadauld reminds us that as women of God we can't be like women of the world. She asserts that rather than being tough, coarse, or rude, famous, rich, or greedy, vain or popular, we need to strive to be tender, kind, refined, faithful, good, virtuous, and pure. How can your knowledge that you are a daughter of God help you mend or maintain friendships?

MAY 26

Facing Our Bullies
For still in mutual sufferance lies
The secret of true living;
Love scarce is love that never knows
The sweetness of forgiving.
—John Greenleaf Whittier[91]

In high school, I knew a girl who caused me great distress. I saw her as beautiful, gifted, and smart. I also perceived her as someone who thrived on putting me down. And she wasn't the only one. When I received an invitation to a reunion, I took the opportunity to respond with what had been simmering inside me for years. I detailed how circumstances in my teenage life had been difficult—so difficult that going to school was a major endeavor; the girls who tormented me made me want to succumb to grief and depression.

To my amazement one girl—*the* girl—wrote back. A nice, handwritten card that branded itself on my soul. She admitted her wrongs and apologized—profusely. She told me of struggles her own daughter was having. I knew I needed to thank her. But, still holding a grudge from years past, I stuffed the card away. Days later I felt a surge of guilt. For all the time I'd spent detailing her unkindness, her compassion surely deserved at least a word of gratitude from me. Too late. I'd managed to misplace the envelope with her return address.

In years since I've often thought of that girl, now woman. Many, many times I've hunted for the envelope so I could retrieve her married name and address. One day, I must overcome myself and ask a classmate for her contact information. Any embarrassment I suffer will be a reminder that when I'm prompted to act in a positive way I need to do so.

Begin the work of extending forgiveness or releasing grudges you may still be holding.

MAY 27

Love: Growing and Giving
Good things are not done in a hurry. —German proverb

Plant an indoor herb garden. Buy a selection of pots from your local thrift store. Chives are among the easiest herbs to grow inside. Start them from an already established plant purchased at your local garden center. Break the chives, including the roots, into sections, and plant them in potting soil. Basil, thyme, rosemary, parsley, mint, and lemongrass are also easy to grown indoors. Buy lemongrass stalks at your grocer. Insert sections in containers with three to five inches of water. Roots and shoots will soon appear.

When your herbs have taken firm hold, share them with friends. Include your favorite recipes for using your homegrown herbs.

MAY 28
Sharing Joy: The Birthday Lady
How wonderful it is that nobody need wait a single moment before beginning to improve the world. —Anne Frank[92]

A decade ago in our small town, a ladies club published a calendar which listed birthdays of friends and relatives. Sometime during the early 1990s, an unknown "Birthday Lady" started calling everyone whose name appeared on the calendar to wish them happy birthday.

"Is this Lori?" she queried. Following my reply in the affirmative, she began to sing, "Happy burffdayh . . ." When she finished crooning, she added in a lilting voice, "And I hope you have a very special day." Without identifying herself, she hung up. Days later, my husband and daughter received calls on their birthdays.

The first year, I dismissed the elderly woman with a chuckle, but the following year, precisely at seven a.m., she phoned again. "Is this Lori? Happy burffdayh to yooouuuu . . ."

Year after year, my family and I looked forward to calls from the Birthday Lady. Others in town, however, weren't pleased with her early-morning pleasantries. Recognizing her distinctive voice, a couple of residents complained to the ladies club. I never again received one of her calls. Not long after, she passed away.

Now when I celebrate birthdays, I miss the Birthday Lady. I regret I never asked when her birthday was. I don't sing, but I could've wished her my best. I could've thanked her for the joy she brought with her thoughtfulness. I hope one day I'll be given the chance to tell her what her calls meant.

Today, join me in finding someone with whom to share joy.

MAY 29

Friend Stuff: Create a Summertime Cookbook

Good food is like music you can taste, color you can smell. There is excellence all around you. You need only to be aware to stop and savor it. —Chef Auguste Gusteau, *Ratatouille*[93]

A cookbook brimming with summertime recipes is handy when you need to plan quick meals or provide something for a barbecue or family reunion. Gather your friends, family, or neighbors, and compile your favorite summer recipes. Delegate jobs. Have someone divide the recipes into categories such as appetizers, main dishes, salads, soups, and desserts. Decide how to print the book and how many copies you'll need. Appoint someone to oversee printing. Morris Press (www.morriscookbooks.com) specializes in cookbooks. Other popular options for budding cookbook authors are www.Lulu.com and www.createspace.com, where you can upload your own cover. If you're on a budget, use your local copy center. Talk to others who have already compiled cookbooks for ideas that will work best for your needs.

Odds are you'll have so much fun putting together your cookbook you'll want to do more. Here's a list to get you thinking:

* A cookbook for chocoholics
* A cookies-, dessert-, salad-, or barbecue-only cookbook
* A cookbook filled with favorite family recipes handed down through the generations
* A cookbook for the dads in the family (real food for real men!) or a cookbook by and for kids

Whatever kind of cookbook you choose to produce, make it fun. The process of creating the book will yield as many wonderful memories as making and eating the recipes.

MAY 30
Family and Friends Fun: Dutch Oven Peach Cobbler
*A good meal makes a man feel more charitable toward the whole world
than any sermon.* —Arthur Pendenys[94]

Start a neighborhood cobbler night; here are a few tips to get you started.

Make assignments. If you provide the cobbler, have others bring ice cream, bowls, spoons, and napkins. Assign someone to garbage duty to ensure everything gets picked up when the evening comes to a close.

Set ground rules. Doing so will save misunderstandings later. For example, if you don't want children in a certain part of your yard, express your preferences. We conveyed that throngs of kids needed to walk back to their own homes to use the bathroom rather than having everyone use ours.

Tell everyone to bring their own lawn chairs. That way you won't need to worry about finding seating for everyone or about putting chairs away later. We decided our driveway was the perfect spot for everyone to congregate. We also hand deliver a few bowls of cobbler to those who are homebound or at first reticent to join the cobbler group.

In the patch of gravel near our driveway, my husband lays out several cast-iron griddles. On each griddle, he lights a stack of charcoal briquettes. The number of briquettes he uses depends on the size of the dutch oven we plan to cook in. For best results, use high-quality briquettes. Our rule of thumb (to achieve a temperature of 350 degrees) is to take the size of your dutch oven in inches. Add five briquettes to that number for the top, and subtract three from that number for beneath the oven. For instance, if you use a size twelve oven (this is what we use for a double batch of peach cobbler) put seventeen briquettes on the lid (12 + 5 = 17) and nine briquettes underneath the oven (12 − 3 = 9). If you're new to dutch oven cooking or would just like to brush up, here are two books to get you started: *New Frontiers in Dutch Oven Cooking* by Lynn E. Child and Susan

G. Clendenin and *101 Things to Do with a Dutch Oven* by Vernon Winterton.

Cobbler night can be a lot of work, but it's a lot of fun. We've been able to meet new people and form new relationships as well as catch up on life with old friends. There are many recipes for dutch oven cobblers. Some of my favorites are on the following pages. The directions are for a standard oven, but they can all be adapted to a dutch oven.

May Recipes

Blue Ribbon Apple Cobbler

4 cups apples, cored, peeled, and sliced
⅓ cup brown sugar
2 Tablespoons butter, melted
½ teaspoon cinnamon
12 cups flour

½ cup brown sugar
⅛ teaspoon baking power
½ cup quick oats
½ cup crushed corn flakes
½ cup butter, melted
⅛ teaspoon soda

Mix apples, sugar, 2 Tablespoons butter, and cinnamon, and place in a greased 9x13 pan. Mix together flour, brown sugar, baking powder, oats, corn flakes, ½ cup butter, and soda. Sprinkle oat mixture over apples. Bake at 350 degrees for 45 minutes.

Peach and Blueberry Cobbler

1 package Duncan Hines Wild Blueberry Muffin Mix
½ cup granulated sugar
½ teaspoon cinnamon
¼ cup butter
½ cup chopped pecans

2 (1 lb. 6 oz. each) cans peach pie filling
¼ cup sugar
1 teaspoon cinnamon
1 teaspoon almond extract

Rinse the blueberries from the muffin mix and drain. In a medium bowl, combine the dry muffin mix, ¼ cup sugar, and ½ teaspoon cinnamon. Cut in butter, then add nuts; mix until crumbly. In another bowl, combine the pie filling, ¼ cup sugar, 1 teaspoon cinnamon, almond extract, and blueberries. Pour the blueberry mixture into a well-greased 9x13-inch pan. Spoon the crumb topping over the peach mixture. Bake for 35–40 minute at 350 degrees.

Easy Family Reunion Cherry-Cranberry Cobbler

2 (20 oz.) cans cherry pie filling
½ cup orange juice
1 cup milk
1 teaspoon vanilla extract
1 teaspoon lemon extract
1 (18 oz.) box Fisher Original Fair
    Scone and Shortcake Mix
¾ cup ground pecans
½ cup butter, melted

Preheat oven to 350 degrees. Spread both cans of cherry pie filling evenly over the bottom of a well-buttered 9x13 baking dish. Sprinkle ½ cup of pecans over the top of the cherries. In a medium bowl, combine orange juice, milk, vanilla, and lemon; stir in scone mix just until blended. Spread (or drop by spoonfuls) scone mix over cherries. Sprinkle with remaining pecans. Drizzle with melted butter. Bake at 350 degree for 25–30 minutes or until scone mix is done and lightly browned.

JUNE

Walking in the Light

Forgiving Others and Looking for the Good in the World

CORRIE TEN BOOM AND HER family were instrumental in helping numerous Jews escape the horrors of Nazi concentration camps. The benevolent actions of the Dutch woman and her family were discovered, and they were arrested. Her father died in prison. Corrie and her sister, Betsie, ended up in the infamous women's camp Ravensbruck. They suffered through grueling labor, extreme malnourishment, and subhuman conditions. Despite their plight and imminent peril, they held Bible study groups. Betsie died in the camp. In what has been termed a clerical error, Corrie was released at the end of 1944. Starving and exhausted, she fought to regain her health. Of her time at Ravensbruck, Corrie noted, "God does not have problems. Only plans."

Corrie never lost faith. She realized her life was a gift from God. When she met a former guard from the camp, a man known for his cruelty, she prayed to be able to forgive him. She and Betsie had learned that "there is no pit so deep that He [God] is not deeper still."[95] Corrie elected to embrace true forgiveness. She realized that when hearts are willing, God grants us the measure of love we need to be able to forgive our enemies.

Spring ends in June; summer begins. Forgiveness and seeking the good in the world are vital elements of our journey. Forgiveness allows the living water of the gospel to nourish us; the light of Christ burns brightly in our hearts. Enhanced growth flourishes and yields abundant joy. As always, Heavenly Father guides and sustains us.

Making the Most of June

* June is National Fresh Fruits and Vegetables Month. Use your fondue pot, melt chocolate, and dip strawberries, pears, bananas, grapes, orange sections, apple slices, and pitted cherries. Melt cheese and dip broccoli, cauliflower, carrots, and zucchini.

* Fly the flag with pride on Flag Day.

* Make a Father's Day gift basket for your dad. Do a theme basket based on his favorite sport, movies, or music. Or a basket filled with his favorite foods; a basket with outdoor gear, such as a water bottle, compass, lip balm, mosquito spray, waterproof matches, etc.; a fishing basket with fishing gear. Write a tribute to your father. Tell him how his example impacted your life. Thank him for all he has done.

* Visit flea markets and garage sales, and look for colorful but inexpensive dishware that you won't be afraid to use outside.

* While the kids are playing with neighborhood friends in the yard, gather the moms and have iced lemonade. Try different flavors like lemon-limeade, raspberry lemonade, blueberry lemonade, strawberry lemonade, or lemon-peachade.

* Arrange summer pen pals between your children and their out-of-state cousins. The only rule is that they have to handwrite their letters. Buy inexpensive, fun stationery for them to use.

* Try new walking or running routes that will allow you to take in the sights and add extra miles to your usual routine. Give a sincere, friendly wave to everyone you meet.

* Christmas lights aren't just for Christmas. Add a touch of summer magic with white twinkle lights strung on a tree, fence, or arbor.

* Refine the art of the picnic. Plan the first one of the year. Go all out with a colorful tablecloth and the dishware you found for outside. Plan a full meal, even if it comes from take-out boxes.

* Have a yard sale where everything costs only a dollar. Include some real deals and watch the excitement on the faces of attendees when they find what you're offering.

* Start a summer reading club with your friends or neighbors. Plan a night to meet each week or each month. With your group, compile a Best Books for Children list. Categorize by picture books, middle grade, young adult, etc. Type up the list and give it to the moms in your reading group, ward, or community.

* Dust off the grill and begin barbecue season in earnest by trying the recipes following this section.

JUNE 1

Seeing the Best in Others

For with what judgment ye judge, ye shall be judged; and with what measure ye mete, it shall be measured to you again. —3 Nephi 14:2

One day while I was talking on the phone, my daughter wanted my attention. She had a question. I gave a motherly hang-on-just-a-minute gesture—my forefinger pressed to my lips. She nodded and left a stack of playing cards and a note on my desk. I read my daughter's words: *Do I have a full deck?* I knew she wanted me to count her cards, but I had to laugh. On occasion I'd asked myself the same question! The old saying "a few cards short of a full deck" is a euphemism used to describe someone perceived as different.

There are people like Corrie Ten Boom who have endured the numerous kinds of abuse one human being can inflict upon another. People who suffer mental, emotional, or physical ailments and limitations. People who've never had the opportunity for the same economic benefit or academic privilege as others. Add in the fact that each of us interprets the things that impact our lives in often enormously dissimilar ways. We're *all* different!

Yes, there are those whose life choices divide us on matters of principle. But wouldn't it be wonderful if we could see the good in one another? Glimpse wonders of heavenly nobility inherent in all God's children? By definition, many people—including myself—could, at one time or another, be accused of being a few cards short. However, the fact is that it's what we do with the cards we have that really matters.

JUNE 2

Count to Ten

And now the Lord shew kindness and truth unto you: and I also will requite you this kindness. —2 Samuel 2:6

Often people strike out in anger because they believe they have been mistreated. They project anger or feelings of insufficiency onto others in misguided attempts to relieve or justify their pain. In haste or frustration, they wound our hearts and pride. On occasion, sentiment directed at us may be so caustic that a sharp response could be considered justified. But not giving in to the temptation to reciprocate hurt allows us to instead strive for understanding.

Regardless of outside influences, our reactions need to be tempered with the realization of—and in honor of—the kind of women we are striving to become. My friend Jill once shared how to best respond to those who hurt, offend, or simply annoy: before you react, first ask if your intended response is true, kind, and necessary. The age-old adage of counting to ten can also work wonders, allowing time to reign in raw, unchecked emotion.

Would counting to ten—thinking before you speak—help preserve the level of integrity you desire to maintain? How can considering if your responses are true, kind, and necessary improve your life and relationships?

JUNE 3
Make a Difference
And to godliness brotherly kindness; and to brotherly kindness charity.
—2 Peter 1:7

A while back, I overheard a group of women discussing whether or not their simple acts of kindness made a difference. The majority seemed to think their benevolent words and tokens of friendship had made little or no impact. As evidence they threw out examples that they felt substantiated their point. Almost as an aside, one woman noted she really hadn't been trying all that long. Another lamented it wasn't worth her time.

I pondered their question. Many times I'd desired to evoke a lasting difference in someone's life. I followed intuition and the Spirit, and I sometimes went to great lengths to change circumstances, often with no tangible results. Did that mean I'd failed? I thought back to simple acts of kindness expressed on my behalf. I was surprised how clearly I remembered the warm feelings evoked by each occurrence.

So do simple acts of kindness make a difference? Even if the recipient never expresses any sort of sentiment in return? I believe the answer is yes. If our efforts are sincere, our concern and goodwill real and not manufactured, something of the Spirit emanating from us must surely touch them to some degree. Maybe it will be only a seed they tuck away until years later. But perhaps on a rainy day, that seed will begin to sprout and eventually blossom as they reflect on our actions and feel the benevolence we long ago attempted to plant.

June is a month when flowers are in full bloom. How can you nourish others with your kindness? What seeds of goodwill can you plant this month in anticipation of a bright season of future blossoms?

JUNE 4
Verbal and Emotional Offenses: A Choice
Never does the human soul appear so strong as when it foregoes revenge and dares to forgive an injury. —Edwin Hubble Chapin[96]

In Luke 17:1, Christ teaches that being offended is a certainty: "It is impossible but that offences will come." Verbal or emotional offenses can come from anyone. Those that cause the most heartache are inflicted by friends, family members, neighbors, or Church members. The more we love or care about someone, the more acute our misery and anguish.

Whether or not the offending act was intended to cause us distress is not as important as our state of heart. If we become hardened and retreat into self-pity, we convince ourselves that the depth of our pain justifies whatever we might feel or do—even if it's not in harmony with what Christ teaches. We need to stay close to Father in Heaven and be prepared to keep our priorities at the forefront of our mind when we're faced with painful emotions.

By my front door hangs a picture of Christ. Below it are the words *What would Jesus do?* I try to remember to look at the picture every time I leave home—and when I return. In addition, I keep a 2 X 3-inch print of Christ, painted by artist Liz Lemon Swindle, on my dashboard. When other drivers cut me off or make rude gestures, I'm reminded to stay focused on acting and driving in a manner appropriate for a daughter of God.

Thanks to cell phones and other personal devices, taking your scriptures wherever you go is easier than ever. Carrying scriptures or keeping a small print of a temple or of Christ with you can help keep your eternal focus sharp.

JUNE 5
If We Offend: The Nurturing Power of Repentance
Will ye not now return unto me, and repent of your sins, and be converted, that I may heal you? —3 Nephi 9:13

When we think of nurturing ourselves, we might consider taking better care of our health or spending more time on things that bring us joy. Repentance may be something we least associate with pleasure. Indeed, the process is not to be taken lightly. We must recognize and express sorrow for behaviors that prevent us from enjoying the companionship of the Spirit and from partaking of blessings.

Habit can be a strong force that binds us to past mistakes by urging us to continue to err; we might feel our efforts to change are futile. The opinions we hold about ourselves that disparage our true identity can bind us as well. When we don't feel good about ourselves, it becomes easy for us to criticize others. If we adopt the practice of finding fault, we risk causing offense. Recognizing our urge to pass judgment, relinquishing it, and making necessary recompense—no matter the depth of difficulty—restores the fullness of eternal promise and hope.

Repentance is a means to finding joy, a vital element in nurturing our spirit. When we repent in full, Father in Heaven forgives us fully. He does not hang our old habits over our heads or wait for another misstep. We are not expected to continue to shoulder blame, retreat into a dark cave of guilt, or berate ourselves emotionally.

JUNE 6
Bliss and Abundance: A Better Life
All things whatsoever ye would that men should do to you, do ye even so to them. —The Golden Rule

Courtesy is doing unto others what we would like them to do unto us; so is kindness, compassion, trust, and respect. This week, review the qualities of friendship from May 18. The same qualities that apply to friendship apply to the way we should treat everyone. How would you prefer others treat you? Start a trend of extending the qualities you most admire in others. Record your impressions in your journal.

JUNE 7
Finding Beauty
The Lord is my strength and song, and he is become my salvation: he is my God. —Exodus 15:2

Emotional abuse can have long-lasting effects on self-esteem. It is characterized by the repeated use of harmful words or actions for the purpose of control. Emotional abusers seek to rule the lives of their victims by implied threats of harm, embarrassment, or abandonment. Verbal abuse is defined by any words that devalue and demean, such as put-downs and disparaging remarks that erode a sense of worth and potential. It includes negative comparisons with others, shaming, blaming, name-calling, yelling, excessive anger, and criticism.

Like emotional and verbal abuse, physical abuse may take many forms. Others endeavor to deliberately frighten, offend, or otherwise harm due to their anger, misguided perceptions, or for their own pleasure. Like delicate glassware, our lives and emotions can seem shattered beyond repair by circumstances out of our control. When we remain in a state of fear and distrust, our spirits suffer as much as our minds and bodies.

Victims of abuse should not bear the burden of guilt for the damaging or hurtful actions of others. If there are situations in your life that cause you to be fearful or confused or that are in any way harmful, pray for direction and get help. Start with a trusted loved one or Church leader. It's never too late. Even the remnants of our lives that become shattered can, with God's help, be transformed into things of beauty.

JUNE 8
The Land Called Forgiveness
And ye shall also forgive one another your trespasses; for verily I say unto you, he that forgiveth not his neighbor's trespasses when he says that he repents, the same hath brought himself under condemnation.
—Mosiah 26:31

Others can injure us emotionally and physically with rude comments, manipulative behavior, and abuse. As we realize that others are responsible for their own happiness and we are responsible for our own, we may—with the Lord's guidance—need to reexamine or leave a relationship. What then? Do we walk through life with our guard up, determined to never be hurt again? If so we're missing out on a lot. We distance ourselves from opportunities to know good and loving people. But how can we avoid falling prey to manipulation or abuse again?

The sure answers come from time spent on our knees in earnest supplication for direction from our Father in Heaven. He can help and guide us through the Spirit and through leaders whose stewardship we are under. Not hardening our hearts comes through extending forgiveness. If we harbor ill feelings, if we extend any measure of energy to carry a grudge, those feelings will grow over time and hostility may settle on us like a dark, impenetrable cloud.

Forgiveness doesn't mean acceptance or a return to mistreatment. There will always be those who refuse to accept responsibility for their actions. The question is, what can we do to assume responsibility for the choice we have to forgive?

JUNE 9
Seeking the Good
For it must needs be, that there is an opposition in all things.
—2 Nephi 2:11

For the past few days, the newest canine member of the family has challenged our rules. When the puppy thinks no one's watching, she bolts upstairs to dog-forbidden zones. She runs in my youngest daughter's bedroom to the birdcage. Her favorite bird is a young, yellow parakeet. The two of them regard each other with curiosity. At first it was cute; now it's annoying. When the dog decides to run out of the kitchen, she totally ignores me and runs too fast for me to catch her. I don't have time to continually police her.

After she darted upstairs yet again this morning, I lost patience. I sentenced her to solitary confinement in her kennel. Almost half an hour later, I heard yells of, "The dog's out!" *Great.* I fully thought I'd find the boisterous puppy making lunch of the parakeet. Instead, I found her lying quietly on her rug by the back door. The latch on the kennel had somehow come undone. My first inclination was to scold her for her escape. Then I realized that no matter the circumstances of her break out, she was nevertheless endeavoring to do the right thing. I laughed it off and pulled her into my lap. She looked up at me with soulful eyes as if to say, "Sorry about this morning. I'm trying to do better."

All of us are in differing stages of learning. Today, look for the good in someone who you usually don't see it in. Even if it's something relatively small, praise them for it.

JUNE 10

Giving: Extending the Benefit of the Doubt
For if ye forgive men their trespasses, your heavenly Father will also forgive you. —Matthew 6:14

Have you ever thought of giving "the benefit of the doubt" as a gift? The term means to consider a person as innocent, to choose to adopt a favorable view of a person or circumstance. Consider someone not returning a smile or a wave. You could convince yourself they intentionally snubbed you, or you could assume something else was going on that had nothing to do with you personally.

Have you ever not returned a smile or wave? Was it perhaps because you didn't see someone's gesture of kindness? Or maybe you were just having a tough day. For others to make a snap judgment and decide you intended offense would have only added to your distress.

Giving the benefit of the doubt is akin to forgiveness, and the results have the same healing properties. God knows what we do not, and He can see what we cannot see in others; only He can judge. If someone doesn't return your gesture of goodwill or somehow fails to meet your expectations, give them the gift of the benefit of the doubt. Endeavor to do so until they feel the light of Christ emanating from you. It just may be that your goodwill and friendliness is an answer to their prayers.

JUNE 11

Know Where You're Going: Repurpose to Find Purpose

The man without a purpose is like a ship without a rudder—a waif, a nothing, a no man. Have a purpose in life, and, having it, throw such strength of mind and muscle into your work as God has given you.
—Thomas Carlyle[97]

It's true others sometimes intentionally hurt and offend us. But if we harbor anger, sorrow, and resentment, we can become so steeped in discord we unwittingly become not only a magnet for, but a source of ill will. The more negative emotions we allow ourselves, the more difficult it becomes to notice the positive. Consider what could happen if we were to repurpose intended offenses. The word repurposing is often used as a term for giving a new function to household items that were originally intended to be used for something else. Deciding to repurpose downbeat emotions into constructive action helps us navigate decisively away from potentially harmful feelings that could become true obstacles in our lives. Easier said than done? Yes! Yet it's definitely a goal worth pursuing.

If you stockpile offenses, resentment will eventually crowd out your ability to see the best in yourself and others. Stores of antipathy will later lend nothing of value. Instead, work past negative emotions. Repurpose hurt feelings by using the energy stirred inside you to accomplish things of value. Write a letter that will make a constructive impact on a person or situation. Write a card of thanks— or apology—that is long overdue. Help someone less fortunate. The possibilities are endless.

Repurposing the negative, deciding to transform it into something productive and meaningful, will guide you to your life's true purpose.

JUNE 12
Being the Better Person
No person was ever honored for what he received. Honor has been the reward for what he gave. —Calvin Coolidge[98]

My youngest asked why she needed to be the better person when someone else was deliberately rude. I gave a mom-patent answer: because it's the right thing to do. She rolled her eyes. I rejoined with the age-old, "We can't change anyone else, but we can change ourselves." She rolled her eyes a second time and stomped away, unconvinced and feeling slighted. World: one. Mom: zero. I had not been an effective teacher.

In the silence that followed, I sat and pondered. Why should any of us strive to be the better person? I found her and told her what I came up with. People who treat us poorly don't, themselves, have self-esteem. And, by returning rudeness, we alienate goodness and joy. Inner peace, I asserted, from being the better person is priceless. She rolled her eyes—again.

I decided not to be discouraged. The time I spent searching my heart and soul for core beliefs conjured up a good reminder lesson for me. Over the course of my lifetime, I have enjoyed opportunities to learn from many people far wiser than myself. At times, however, I let their teachings slip from my mind as I commiserated over what I perceived as day-to-day injustices. I realized I needed to remember that the opportunity to be the better person doesn't just arrive in the course of a week or even a day. It is afforded on a minute-by-minute, sometimes second-by-second, basis.

Like when your child rolls their eyes at you for the umpteenth time and you resist the urge to do the same, having faith your word and example will one day take root.

JUNE 13
The Healing Power of Forgiveness
Forgive us our debts, as we forgive our debtors. —Matthew 6:12

Resentment and anger are burdens that prevent us from living and acting freely. When hurt continues to grow inside us, we subconsciously begin to nurture only our pain. We come to expect it. We look for more to feed a growing a crop of discontent. Brambles of anguish entwine us. Rooted in feelings of injustice, unhappiness is our harvest.

President James E. Faust told us that our self-esteem and well-being will increase if we extend forgiveness.[99] Indeed, forgiveness is a gift we can give to ourselves that will free us from emotional bondage and help us begin the process of healing. Christ admonished us to forgive one another and further stated in no uncertain terms, "I, the Lord, will forgive whom I will forgive, but of you it is required to forgive all men" (D&C 64:10).

The physical benefits of forgiveness are many and include reduced stress, reduced blood pressure, lower risk of debilitating disease, and enhanced quality of sleep. The emotional benefits are improved self-esteem, renewed sense of optimism, and better quality of interpersonal relationships. The spiritual benefits are numerous as well. The Holy Ghost cannot abide with us if we are nurturing ill will; life-saving guidance and direction may well be lost.

Today, pray to be aware of forgiveness you need to extend. With Heavenly Father's help, plan to release hurt and resentment so you can enjoy the blessings of happiness and increased physical, emotional, and spiritual well-being.

JUNE 14
Hope for the Future: Forgive and Move On
Forgiving does not erase the bitter past. A healed memory is not a deleted memory. Instead, forgiving what we cannot forget creates a new way to remember. We change the memory of our past into a hope for our future. —Lewis B. Smedes[100]

Elizabeth Smart was kidnapped at knifepoint from her home when she was fourteen years old. She spent nine months as a captive. Her mother expressed to her that though nine months were taken out of her life, she must not allow her captors to take one minute more.

Jeralee Underwood was an eleven-year-old from Pocatello, Idaho, who was abducted and murdered. After her body was discovered, her parents publicly expressed thanks to searchers. As recounted by President James E. Faust, her mother stated, "I have learned a lot about love this week, and I also know there is a lot of hate. I have looked at the love and want to feel that love, and not the hate. We can forgive."[101]

Forgiveness bears the blessing of once again discovering the hope and peace we might believe we've been robbed of. In the topical guide to the scriptures, reference and study forgiveness.

JUNE 15
Christlike Attributes: Strength in Mind and Heart
Forgiveness is the attribute of the strong. —Mahatma Gandhi[102]

In his October 2005 general conference address, President Gordon B. Hinckley spoke of the abundance of unkindness, abuse, intolerance, and hatred in the world. He stressed the need for repentance and forgiveness. He noted the human tendency toward unwillingness to forgive and forget, and the inclination to dwell on the shortcomings of others and exaggerate their offenses.

The ultimate act of forgiveness, he pointed out, was the Atonement; Christ's suffering and agony were so extreme we can never grasp the depth of his act of love. President Hinckley then called on us to extend more kindness, tolerance, and willingness to forgive.[103]

Today, if it's not already there, add forgiveness to your list of Christlike attributes on your to-live-by list.

JUNE 16
Communication: Listen to the Spirit
How can we exercise the grace of contentment, if all things succeed well; or that of forgiveness, if we have no enemies. —John Tillotson[104]

The pain was mine. The blood too. I was married to the man who'd inflicted both. Though we had been sealed in the temple, he pursued his agency: his choice was to wound me emotionally and physically. I endured years of abuse. I learned to hide the bruises on my body and the scars in my soul. A family member told me it was my duty to stay with him, no matter the consequences. A divorce, she said, would bring scandal and embarrassment.

By day, I worked and held my head high. By night I hid in shame, guilt, and terror. I wanted to honor my covenants. Surely, I believed, I was to blame for everything that happened. If only I could do more, be more, I could make myself worthy of his love. With increasing vigor, the Spirit bore witness that I was not at fault. My situation was one of true and imminent physical danger.

I've now been married to my second husband for over twenty-five years. I'm grateful for promptings I received that testified of my worth and of how to remove myself and my daughter from peril. I know now that while Heavenly Father expects us to fulfill responsibilities and covenants, He does not want us to bear the burden of guilt that is not ours. Nor does He want us to knowingly place ourselves in situations where our bodies and spirits will be harmed.

Attune yourself to the Spirit and listen intently to the promptings you receive.

JUNE 17
Commitment: Peaceful Living

Peace is not something you wish for; it's something you make, something you do, something you are, and something you give away. —Robert Fulghum[105]

Blessed are the peacemakers: for they shall be called the children of God.
—Matthew 5:9

Our words and deeds are tools of either contention or harmony. When others hurt our feelings, wound our pride, or injure us in any way, it becomes easy to convince ourselves that we are justified in engaging in a bit of score-evening. Yet Elder Russell M. Nelson counsels that peace can only triumph when we overcome our human tendency to fight with another and determine to live as God would have us do. He encourages us to be peacemakers, living peacefully with all those around us, and to teach our children to love and serve one another.[106]

In the hymn "Reverently and Meekly Now," Joseph L. Townsend admonishes:

Bid thine heart all strife to cease;
With thy brethren be at peace.
Oh, forgive as thou wouldst be
E'en forgiven now by me.
In the solemn faith of prayer
Cast upon me all thy care,
And my Spirit's grace shall be
Like a fountain unto thee.

Peace begins with you. What can you do to bring peace into your life and the lives of others?

JUNE 18

Learning: Make the World a Better Place

He who dares to teach must never cease to learn. —John Cotton Dana[107]

Children's writer Michael Morpurgo is the author of *War Horse*, a touching story about a horse and the young man, Albert, who loves it. In England at the outset of World War I, the horse is sold and shipped to France. The book and subsequent movie follow the creature's determination to survive extreme tribulation. The horse's journey is nothing less than astonishing, as is that of Albert, who embarks on a desperate search to find his beloved companion. The bond between them is heartwarming. Equally as compelling are the people they both encounter who, despite their own hardships, extend genuine compassion.

President Thomas S. Monson praised those who extend loving care, compassion, and concern through their service to others and assured us that God will know of our efforts.[108]

Despite hardships in your life, what can you do to make the world a better place?

JUNE 19

Forgiving and Believing: Christ

*And there came a voice unto me, saying: Enos, thy sins are forgiven thee,
and thou shalt be blessed. And I, Enos, knew that God could not lie;
wherefore, my guilt was swept away. And I said: Lord, how is it done?
And he said unto me: Because of thy faith in Christ.* —Enos 1:5–8

Within the pages of his book *Believing Christ*, Stephen E. Robinson
tells us, "We have all done things that shame us, and we have felt the
horrid weight of guilt and remorse and self-reproach." The good news,
however, is that "imperfect people can be reconciled to a perfect God
and be allowed to dwell in his presence . . . God assures us that no
son or daughter has ever been loved by a mortal father more than we
are loved by him."

Stating instances from his years as a bishop, counselor, and
teacher in the Church, Brother Robinson tells of those who essentially
claimed to believe in Christ yet had no faith in His ability to exalt
them. "Believing in Jesus' identity as the Christ is only the first half of
it," he says. "The other half is believing in his ability, in his power to
cleanse and to save—to make unworthy sons and daughters worthy . .
. We must not only believe in Christ, we must also believe Christ when
he says he can clean us up and make us celestial."[109]

The same holds true for those in our lives who may have hurt us.
The Atonement is as much for them as it is for us, unworthy sons and
daughters made worthy.

Pray for the strength and courage to forgive.

JUNE 20

Guidance: Overcoming Discouragement with Others

*Shallow understanding from people of good will is more frustrating than
absolute misunderstanding from people of ill will.*
—Martin Luther King Jr.[110]

A friend wants you to go shopping with her. You tell you her you can't.
She perseveres. "No, thank you," you say. "Not this time." She asks,

"What's wrong? Don't you like me anymore?" No matter your reasons, she's not happy. She says you're not a true friend.

Sometimes it seems even our best intentions get us into trouble. We don't want to lose a friendship. We want others to be able to depend on us. We may feel we should give in—just once. Too often, however, just once turns into others taking advantage of our good intentions, intentions we often reserve to maintain our own health and well-being or to fulfill other obligations. Likewise, comments we make in goodwill may be turned against us. Communication and understanding—necessary qualities to good relationships—need to be in sync and can be strengthened by the Spirit. Yet if someone attempts to make us feel bad, blames us, guilts us, or gives us ultimatums, the conversation becomes decidedly one-sided.

If your best efforts to communicate fall short of conveying what you know to be right, remember that the agency of others allows them to choose to become discouraged. Don't let yourself fall into the same trap. The opposite of discourage is courage—which is exactly what friendships often require.

Practice listening intently to the Spirit as you communicate with others. Listen for direction on what you should say. Strive to emulate the Savior.

JUNE 21
Read All about It! Spread Good News
*We believe in being honest, true, chaste, benevolent, virtuous, and
in doing good to all men; indeed, we may say that we follow the
admonition of Paul—We believe all things, we hope all things, we have
endured many things, and hope to be able to endure all things. If there
is anything virtuous, lovely, or of good report or praiseworthy, we seek
after these things.* —Article of Faith 1:13

Gloom and doom permeate the airwaves, print media, and personal conversations. We heed bad news because it plays on our fears. A volcano is going to erupt and spew life-threatening ash. Will we be in its path? A satellite or huge chunk of meteor is going to smash into earth. Are we all going to die? The economy is crashing. Are we in for imminent financial ruin? There is murder and mayhem, drugs and divorce, plagues and famine. What will happen next? While we need to understand world events and prepare for the future, obsessing over the darkness of bad news robs us of vital light and truth.

The good news is that, though often unnoticed and unreported, there is much good. Practice focusing on virtues and wonders that are just as prevalent in the world as the not-so-great stuff. Tell your friends and family about the unexpected note you got from an old friend, about the kind e-mail you received, about the courtesy of other drivers, about the testimony of a member of your ward who has been struggling—how wonderful that they've found happiness. Tell others about the good stories, articles, and books you've read; about miracles, large and small; about news reports that focus on people being kind and honest.

Looking for and celebrating good news is faith in action. Collect good news, things that are praiseworthy and of good report. Distribute it in abundance.

JUNE 22
Loving Others
Let the heavens be glad, and let the earth rejoice: and let men say among the nations, the Lord reigneth. —1 Chronicles 16:31

When people are treated unkindly, especially over a period of time, it's common for them to project their feelings of pain onto others. I think that's what happened to the old man. For as long as I can remember, he drove past our house twice each day: once on his way to check the peacocks he kept and once as he returned home. The dirt road he used to reach his barn was the same road my family used for running, walking, and four-wheeling. When I saw him pass, I smiled and waved. I attempted to approach his old black truck to extend pleasantries.

His expression and manner were always the same: Jaw set in angry determination. Eyes narrowed. He stared me down in defiance.

Sometimes, his gnarled fingers clenched into a fist, which he shook in my direction. I talked to others and learned he once owned a flock of over fifty peacocks. Vandals, however, had killed most of the beautiful birds. People in our neighborhood had nothing to do with the travesty, yet we managed to garner his scorn. Over time, his angst had a boomerang effect—anger was returned to him as people grew weary of his manner, likely leading him to feel even more justified for being angry in the first place.

I love that summer is bursting forth with promise. I also love that the old man has a new blue—almost neon blue—truck. It seems a stark contrast to his old black one. Maybe I just imagined it, but he seemed to sit a little taller in the seat when he drove past the other day. Part of me can't help but hope that maybe something in his outlook has changed.

Maybe, just maybe, this will be the summer he waves back.

Today, look for the best in others and determine to continue to do so.

JUNE 23
In a Word: Worth
A good example is the best sermon. —Benjamin Franklin[111]

Kathy Hadfield's smile let you know you were valued. It was a smile that conveyed her knowledge that she was loved by God and her desire to spread that love to others. Kathy was a woman in a ward I attended when I was a child. To my young mind, the most impressive thing about her was her refusal to speak ill of anyone. No matter the deed, no matter the vein of current gossip, Kathy would not participate. Instead she inserted comments into conversations about the virtue and value of a person. She never had to take something back or be embarrassed by a comment she thought she had made in confidence. To her, all were worthy of praise. As a result, her smile never dimmed and the light of Christ in her indeed shone and blessed many lives.

Though I admit I'm still far from perfect in practicing it, the impact of Kathy's example is one I've never forgotten.

This week, contemplate the infinite value of kind words.

JUNE 24
The Echo
The trouble with talking too fast is you may say something you haven't thought of yet. —Ann Landers[112]

One of our past bishops shared the following story:

> George had not the least idea of an echo. One day he happened to cry out in the fields, "Hello-Hello!" Instantly he heard the same words repeated from a neighboring thicket.
>
> Surprised at the sound he asked, "Who are you?"
>
> The same voice replied, "Who are you?"
>
> George cried out, "You must be very foolish!"
>
> "Very foolish!" repeated the voice.
>
> George began to grow angry. In order that he might avenge himself, he searched through the woods for the boy who he supposed was mocking him. After searching in vain for some time, he ran home and complained to his mother.
>
> "You are complaining about yourself," she said. "Don't you know that you have heard nothing but your own words? Even as you have seen your face reflected in clear water, so you have just heard your own voice in the woods. If you had said something kind, you would have received the same in reply."

It is thus in everyday life; the conduct of others toward us is generally an echo of our own.

In Matthew 12:36–37 Christ teaches: "But I say unto you, That every idle word that men shall speak, they shall give account thereof in the day of judgment. For by thy words thou shalt be justified, and by thy words thou shalt be condemned."

If the words you speak to others were to come back to you, how would they make you feel?

JUNE 25

Love: God Helps Us to Forgive

But as oft as they repented and sought forgiveness, with real intent, they were forgiven. —Moroni 6:8

Satan uses tools of despair and discouragement against us all. Often the most challenging trials come as the result of the actions of others. The world is always ready to tell us how inferior we are because, in the world's eyes, we're never enough. Those we love most or those we want to love us can inflict pain and heartache and perhaps cause us to question ourselves and what we believe in. We may come to fear failure, fear getting hurt, and fear being judged to such an extent that the light of Christ within us becomes obscured. Sometimes we can even forget it's there.

Negative emotions usually come from an inherently negative source, just as positive comes from a positive source. We can learn from others what we don't want to become. We can find peace in extending forgiveness, knowing that forgiveness is not acceptance. Knowing we are loved by our Father in Heaven despite our sins and shortcomings helps us love others.

JUNE 26

Receiving His Image in Your Countenance

Every man according as he purposeth in his heart, so let him give; not grudgingly, or of necessity: for God loveth a cheerful giver.
—2 Corinthians 9:7

Even when facing difficult challenges and difficult people, we can choose to be part of the solution. It is within our power to have Christ's image engraven in our countenance as we refine characteristics and behaviors that lead us to become more like Him.

Let the Lord comfort and guide you through both joy and despair. Feel the sweetness of each moment. Serve Him. Love Him. Rejoice in the gospel, and pray with full purpose of heart that you might understand the importance of your discipleship and receive His image engraven in your countenance. President Dieter F. Uchtdorf joyfully tells us that the path to discipleship begins right where we are and that taking the first step requires no prequalification.[113] What step can you take today that will lead you to Christ?

JUNE 27
Steps of Forgiveness

For if ye forgive men their trespasses, your heavenly Father will also forgive you: But if ye forgive not men their trespasses, neither will your Father forgive your trespasses. —Matthew 6:14–15

* Recognize the source of grudges, judgments, resentment, anger, bitterness, and the urge to get revenge.

* Take the matter to the Lord so He can help you sort out how you feel and look for solutions. The Savior and His Atonement are the source of all healing. Turn to Him to recover; allow Him to comfort you and remove sorrow and pain. Seek a priesthood blessing.

* Seek for understanding, not only of what has happened to you, but of how you may be contributing to your own pain. Is your chief source of suffering coming from within? Your current thoughts can cause more anguish than what happened five minutes or five years ago. Understand how not forgiving will impact your physical, emotional, and spiritual health. Forgiveness doesn't necessarily imply reconciliation or condoning. Ask yourself what you can learn that will help you to avoid similar circumstances in the future.

* Turn away from the incident. Don't keep replaying it over and over in your mind. Doing so only prolongs the healing process. Heavenly Father doesn't want you to continue to wade through unhappiness, sorrow, and despair. Forgiveness will allow you to return to happiness, joy, and sense of purpose. When you change your thoughts, you can change your life. Invest your energy in positive things. Celebrate your choice to forgive. Choose to see the good in others.

✴ If you are in danger, frightened, or have thoughts of harming yourself, get help. Tell someone. Sometimes all you need is someone to listen with an open heart. Some situations, however, require expert advice. Abuse can destroy both body and spirit and trigger mental anguish and illness. You can benefit from direction on how to process abuse and heal. Shame and guilt are not yours to bear.

JUNE 28
Navigation: The Road of Life
Among the things that require careful contemplation are rough roads and perceived offenses; misunderstanding can either impede or stall progress.

The main character in my novel *My Gift to You* is carrying a burden she doesn't know how to deal with. Trish is haunted by her past, memories of a day she doesn't understand. The emotional baggage she's been carrying around for years causes her to unintentionally drive away her husband and daughter. With their loss, she faces a challenge. She must find the courage necessary to transcend the shadows of her past.

Though she is keenly aware of the maxim, "Be kind, for everyone you meet is fighting a hard battle," she struggles with forgiving herself and the person who forever altered the course of her life. That person, her mother, committed suicide. Trish doesn't know where to begin to make sense of why. Forgiveness comes as both a difficult choice and a precious gift.

Forgiveness must be coupled with understanding. Understanding, however, is often hard won. Others do things that seem to make no sense. For various reasons, we can't always communicate with them to find out why.

Today, pray to understand a person whose actions you've had trouble comprehending. Extend to them the gift of love.

JUNE 29
Letting Go
Know all, and you will pardon all. —Thomas à Kempis[114]

Is there someone in your life who needs forgiveness? A friend, family member, neighbor, or ward member who has done something unkind or hurtful? Elder Jeffrey R. Holland has taught that we should not question whether the victim should need to forgive the perpetrator of an offense; or if it shouldn't be that the laws of justice demand the opposite. Rather, we should heed the words of Christ as recorded in 3 Nephi 12:44: "Love your enemies, bless them that curse you, do good to them that hate you, and pray for them which despitefully use you, and persecute you."[115]

Resolve today to begin processing and discarding negative feelings and resentment:

* Clear up misunderstandings. Make amends. Cry if you need to.
* Write a forgiveness statement declaring your freedom from self-limiting pain and your intention to forgive. For example: I forgive Jane Doe for ruining my flowers with the lawn mower. I can always buy new roses, but I can't replace our friendship.
* Write a letter to the person (deceased or living) explaining your feelings and how you have overcome the negative influences of hurt or injustice. Tell them you have forgiven them. Release them from blame. If necessary, say good-bye. Decide whether you should mail the letter, tear it up, send it off to sea in a bottle, or burn it in the fireplace.
* Note examples of those who have overcome great adversity, forgiven, and moved on. Notice how they used their circumstances to make the world better for others.
* Journal your impressions, and explore the process of forgiveness through personal writing. No one else has to ever see what you've written.

JUNE 30
Becoming: The Process of Getting Wings
Never underestimate your power to change yourself. —H. Jackson Brown, Jr.[116]

Does a butterfly feel pain? In its transformation from crawling being to tightly cocooned metamorphosis to waiting for delicate wings to dry and strengthen, what does it think? Surely, on some level it realizes its life will never be the same. Does it fear the change that melds legs into wings? Through its progression, does it long to return to its former self when the only cares were searching for leaves to munch or the underside of twigs for lengthy, shaded naps? When change gifts wings for flight, does the butterfly gape in wonder at new opportunity or cower at the prospect of previously unattainable heights?

Similar to the process of a butterfly gaining its wings, mortal life comes with the potential of attaining greatness. Learning and growing—transforming—can be painful. Overcoming fear, forgiving, and adapting are part of the territory. Even as we are pressed on all sides with adversity, we must trust. Heavenly Father is always mindful of us. He knows and loves us completely. Everything we experience, when navigated with faith, brings us closer to becoming more like Him.

The gospel teaches us to return home. Doing so successfully is our responsibility. Keeping in mind why we're here is half the battle. With summer in full swing, give thanks for your ability to learn and grow and your choice to forgive during the process of becoming. What the caterpillar calls the end, the butterfly calls the beginning!

June Recipes

Tropical Grilled Shrimp and Fruit with Pineapple-Orange Marinade

Fresh-caught precooked shrimp   Fresh, ripe mango sections
Fresh, ripe pineapple sections   Sweetened shredded coconut

On wooden skewers, alternate shrimp, pineapple, and mango. Place skewers in a shallow baking dish. Pour pineapple-orange marinade over top, cover tightly with foil, and refrigerate overnight.

Grill skewers over medium-low heat, basting with marinade. Sprinkle with shredded coconut before serving.

Pineapple-Orange Marinade

½ cup water   ½ cup orange marmalade
½ cup granulated sugar   ¼ cup pineapple juice

Combine all ingredients in a saucepan. Bring to low boil; boil 5 minutes, stirring constantly until sugar is dissolved. Reduce and simmer over low heat; remove from heat, and cool.

Glazed Apricot Pork

1 (18 oz.) jar apricot jam or preserves

1 (8 oz.) bottle Russian dressing

1 can Sprite or lemon-lime soda

1 (2 oz.) package dry Lipton Onion Soup mix

Pork loin pieces

In a large, sealable bowl, stir together jam, dressing, Sprite, and soup mix. Add pork loin pieces. Marinate overnight. Grill over medium heat, basting with glaze, until cooked through.

Summer Smokies and Apple Bake

1 (14 oz.) package Turkey or Applewood Smoked Chicken Lit'l Smokies

4–5 golden delicious apples, cored, skins on, cut into bite-sized pieces

10–12 baby bella mushrooms, washed and sliced

8–10 brussels sprouts, parboiled and quartered

½–1 cup shredded gorgonzola or Monterey Jack cheese

Preheat oven to 350 degrees. Cut Smokies into thirds. In well-buttered 8x8 baking dish, toss together Smokies, apple pieces, mushroom slices, and quartered brussels sprouts. Add apple marinade, and toss to coat well. Bake at 350 for 15–20 minutes or until apple pieces are fork-tender. Stir once halfway through cooking. Sprinkle with cheese, and serve warm.

Apple Marinade

½ cup apple jam or preserves

2 Tablespoons butter

1 Tablespoon barbeque sauce

In a small saucepan, combine all ingredients until blended.

JULY

Letting Your Own Light Shine
Serving and Giving Joy

IN THE MONTH OF JULY, amid vacation and camps and yard work, we remember and celebrate abiding examples of pioneer conviction and sacrifice. Steel-hardened faith, a lasting legacy etched in our hearts. When the pioneers crossed the plains, they not only endured peril and extreme hardship, but they served those with whom they traveled. From sharing food and provisions to lending their voices in song and their hearts in prayer to rendering aid for physical maladies and spiritual wounds of doubt, they bore one another's burdens and lifted the hands that hung down. They toiled, wept, and moved forward together.

Moving forward on our journey, we are always accompanied by traveling companions. Some abide with us for only a short time, some for a lifetime. All have needs. Working with our hearts as well as our hands, we can effect miracles in their lives and ours. This month discover the blessings of Christlike love.

Making the Most of July

* LDS.org has a wealth of information on ways to serve, including information about Latter-day Saint charities, humanitarian projects, how to serve in your community, and the Mormon Helping Hands program, which provides community service and disaster relief to those in need. Vineyard.lds.org provides participants from around the world the opportunity to complete service activities online.

* Start looking for end-of-season sales for good deals on clothes.

* The book *Great American Documents for Latter-day Saint Families* by Thomas Valletta discusses fundamental documents of American freedom and liberty. Rich with historical background and heritage important to our history, it's a good way to start a discussion with your family about religious freedom and heritage on the Fourth of July. Plan a way to commemorate the blessings of both. Dine al fresco while you watch the fireworks.

* Bring the colors of red, white, and blue into your cooking. Strawberries, raspberries, and cherries. Creamy yogurt, sour cream, vanilla frosting. Blueberries, blue punch, blue Jell-O.

* Plan a road trip; list things you want to see and do along the way.

* Go to an outdoor concert.

* Rediscover popcorn—not the microwave kind but the kind you pop on the stove. Make bowlfuls to take outside and eat on the lawn.

* Have a candlelight dinner in the backyard. Save up salsa jars and make candleholders. Dot the jars with bright paints, and wrap lengths of wire around the mouths of the jars, leaving enough for handles. Insert tea lights, and hang in the yard.

* Watch the movie *17 Miracles*, which tells of the Willie Handcart Company.

* Give summer scripture reading a boost by gathering everyone to read scriptures in a tent in the yard or living room. Have treats ready.

* Visit a farm. Buy fresh eggs. Make your favorite omelet.

* On July 24, 1847, Brigham Young and the first company of Mormon pioneers arrived in the Salt Lake Valley. Celebrate the 24th by remembering your ancestors and serving foods from the countries where they originated. Or have friends and family over for potluck pie or dessert night.

* Leave husbands in charge at home and hold summer reading club at a restaurant to give you the night off.

* Try new kinds of summer sandwiches or salads like those following this section.

JULY 1
Serving: Followers of Christ
I am among you as he that serveth. —Luke 22:27

As followers of Christ, we commit to serving others. Service means helping those who need some form of assistance. We lend help through social, emotional, physical, economic, and spiritual means. We serve when we take meals to needy persons as well as when we give fast offerings. We serve by doing yard work for someone who is unable to do it as well as by visiting that person and lending a listening ear, a shoulder to cry on, or the comfort and strength of shared testimony. We serve by caring for the ill as well as by being a friend to someone who is lonely. We serve by means of sacrificing large amounts of time as well as a few seconds spent giving a warm hello, smile, handshake, or hug.

We may not have pioneer ancestors. We may be converts, the only Church member of our circle of family and friends. But we are never alone. Heavenly Father guides and protects us, ministering to our needs as we press forward with trust. In turn, ministering to the needs of others is an integral part of our journey.

As summer brims with limitless prospect and promise, so do our lives. Service brings with it the opportunity for spiritual development and rich blessings as God works through us to fulfill His work. There are no prequalifying requirements for service. Whoever we are, whatever we have, whatever the season of our lives, we can give of ourselves. When our hearts are attuned to Christ, love and concern for our fellow beings is the natural product. If at times we find our fears and self-doubts stand in the way of our good intentions, we can be assured that our personal best is all that's required.

JULY 2
Your Best Means Best, not More
I see something that has to be done and I organize it.
—Elinor Guggenheimer[117]

Best means most satisfactory, suitable, or useful. As in, the best solution to a problem. Depending on the time, place, and your energy level, the best solution to what needs to be done will differ—helping with a Relief Society dinner, quieting the kids before bedtime, or deciding what to eat for dinner. Doing your best doesn't mean doing more. It means giving the best you have to offer at the time to whatever you're doing, no matter the size of the task.

Whether you're making elegant centerpieces or simply putting a jar with a single flower at the center of each table for a Relief Society activity, you can do your part with care and a smile. Even if you reheat leftovers for dinner—for the second or third time in a row—you can serve the meal on the good plates and use placemats or a tablecloth. Or use pretty, colored paper plates. Offer a blessing of gratitude for the food and for those with whom you share it.

King Benjamin tells us, "And see that all these things are done in wisdom and order; for it is not requisite that a man should run faster than he has strength" (Mosiah 4:27).

It is not requisite that a man should run faster than he has strength. Nor should a woman!

In whatever you do, practicing giving your best—not by exhausting yourself to do more and more but by giving the best of what you can reasonably offer at the time.

JULY 3
Celebrate Acts of Service

To the end that my glory may sing praise to thee, and not be silent. O Lord my God, I will give thanks unto thee for ever. —Psalm 30:12

Your daughter did the dishes without you asking, reminding, or begging her to. Your husband watered the flowers in the front planter, ensuring they didn't wilt under the heat of the summer sun. Your son drew a picture for you and told you he loved you. One, maybe two loads of laundry got washed and dried by someone else; you didn't think anyone even remembered how to turn on the washer or dryer. A loaf of bread or plate of cookies was delivered anonymously.

Recognize an act of service, no matter how small, that has been performed for you. Express thanks. If the act was performed anonymously, give thanks for the effort in your prayers. If you feel you weren't the recipient of service today, express thanks to your Father in Heaven for the many blessings He has bestowed upon you.

JULY 4

A Heritage of Freedom

And it came to pass that thousands did flock unto his standard, and did take up their swords in the defence of their freedom, that they might not come into bondage. —Alma 62:5

Red, white, and blue. The colors of the United States of America. Parades and pride, picnics and patriotism, celebrations of heritage and privilege dot the landscape. Freedom in America was fought for and attained by those who believed in God and who wanted the right to worship as they saw fit. Now, freedom of religion is in peril, even in the country that gave birth to it.

The eleventh Article of Faith states, "We claim the privilege of worshiping Almighty God according to the dictates of our own conscience, and allow all men the same privilege, let them worship how, where, or what they may."

This month, communicate gratitude for your choice to worship as you choose. Think of ways you can practice, protect, and preserve the freedoms you enjoy.

JULY 5

The Selflessness of Service

And when he had called the people unto him with his disciples also, he said unto them, Whosoever will come after me, let him deny himself, and take up his cross, and follow me. For whosoever will save his life shall lose it; but whosoever shall lose his life for my sake and the gospel's, the same shall save it. For what shall it profit a man, if he shall gain the whole world, and lose his own soul? Or what shall a man give in exchange for his soul? —Mark 8:34–37

In our stakes and wards, service projects might entail striving to meet the goals of those in need on a grand scale. In our families or in the acts of service we render alone, the service we give may impact fewer lives. Yet the underlying principle and importance of providing service with the right state of heart is the same. Gratitude for our opportunities to serve and our role in God's plan is key. If service is performed because we desire acknowledgments, it becomes a disappointment and a burden.

Throughout July, contemplate your state of heart when it comes to giving service and how gratitude for your opportunities to serve impacts the quality of your service. Commit to giving unselfishly and without regard for recognition.

JULY 6

Simple Things Transform

Love comes on velvety butterfly wings, softly alighting in our hearts to delight us with its magic.

The air around me seems thick, the room warm. My heart races. I scan the crowd for a familiar face, finding only a sea of unfamiliarity. It takes every ounce of conviction I have to propel me into a pew near the front of the chapel—the only open spot. As I force myself to sit down, it feels as though every eye is upon me. Is my hair okay? Should I have worn something different?

I've experienced just these feelings when attending a new ward for the first time. Have you? Even though our heart tells us we're among friends in the gospel, walking into sacrament meeting for the first time in a new ward is hard. In Sunday School and Relief Society—though the crowd is smaller—first and even second and third times can be equally difficult. Feeling at ease begins with the very first person who introduces themselves. A handshake. A smile. A welcome. The act of someone sitting next to us and asking our name. Simple things transform.

We all need to feel accepted. We all need to feel valued. The heart of service starts with sincere compassion and love. This week, be on the lookout for someone new at church. Introduce yourself. Ask their name. As Christ's emissary, let His love flow through you as you make them feel genuinely welcome.

JULY 7
God's Work: Why We Serve
When ye are in the service of your fellow beings ye are only in the service of your God . . . and if I, whom ye call your king, do labor to serve you, then ought not ye to labor to serve one another? —Mosiah 2:17–18

When we serve others, we are in the service of God, whom we are commanded to love with all our heart, might, mind, and strength. When we love our Father and Elder Brother without reservation, we are able to extend the same kind of heartfelt love to friends and neighbors. We show our love the way the Savior would: through word and deed.

God's work is done through each of us. To some degree, we are dependent on each other to survive the journey of life and make it safely back to Him. Service is love in action. When we are young, our parents or other adults serve us through their loving care and attention to our physical and emotional needs. Teachers serve us through teaching us academically and spiritually. Friends serve us through their kindness and willingness to stand by us in both joy and sorrow. Spouses and other family members serve us through sharing in daily household tasks and comforting us when we are downtrodden and ill.

In the topical guide in your scriptures, look up *serve* and *service*, and read a few of the verses listed. Some to start with are Galatians 5:13, Hebrews 12:28, Alma 42:4, D&C 42:29, Ether 2:9, Moses 1:15, 2 Nephi 2:3, Mosiah 2:17, and D&C 24:7.

JULY 8
Examples: Remember Those Who Give
For inasmuch as ye do it unto the least of these, ye do it unto me.
—D&C 42:38

Numerous people have shaped my life with their selfless service. When I was a child, it was Sister Minnie Jackson. She loved the Primary children in her charge. She overlooked our boisterous behavior and excited chatter that often interrupted her lessons. We knew we were always welcome in her home. She invited us to visit; she waited with open arms.

In my years of seminary attendance, Brothers John Valberg, Richard Ellis, and Winston Benson all took an interest in me and my life trials. I was buoyed by the respect they accorded me. Their examples of unconditional love of others and their devotion to the gospel left a lasting impression. After I left home, Bishops Wes Whiting and Reed Beck both impacted my life in dramatic ways. I am indebted to them for their service and care.

In later years, Sisters Rhea Kidman and LeeAnn Packer demonstrated to me, through their acts of charitable service to others, what elect women of God are really made of. Sisters Phyllis Valentine and Marvel Young showed me how creative abilities can bless lives. Phyllis's handmade rugs, green tomato relish, potato salad, and gift of conversation brought brightness and joy to all as did Marvel's knowledge of gospel doctrines and the special homemade fudge (see February recipes) she delivered to friends, dispensing it from a basket as she walked through the neighborhood.

Remember those who've changed your life. When time permits, write a note of thanks. If they've passed on, share your memories of them with one of their family members.

JULY 9
Listening: Follow Promptings
For whosoever will save his life shall lose it: but whosoever will lose his life for my sake, the same shall save it. —Luke 9:24

In his November 2009 talk, "What Have I Done for Someone Today?" President Thomas S. Monson asked how many times our hearts have been touched as we have witnessed need, and how often we have had the intention to help. He then asked us to consider how frequently we have let other matters interfere, leaving the circumstance to someone else to deal with.

As President Monson noted, we often become caught up in the busyness of life, in the thick of thin things. We expend much time attending to that which does not matter as we neglect important causes such as serving. Attending to spiritual necessities of prayer and scripture reading and keeping our covenants will help attune us to promptings. We will be directed by the Spirit to minister to needs that the Lord knows we are uniquely qualified to meet.

Listen for and heed spiritual promptings that advise you of the needs of others.

JULY 10
Maintaining the Spirit of Service

*And now, for the sake of these things which I have spoken unto you—
that is, for the sake of retaining a remission of your sins from day to day,
that ye may walk guiltless before God—I would that ye should impart
of your substance to the poor, every man according to that which he hath,
such as feeding the hungry, clothing the naked, visiting the sick and
administering to their relief, both spiritually and temporally, according
to their wants.* —Mosiah 4:26

King Benjamin taught we should succor those who are in need of succor, administer our substance to those who are in need, and not "suffer that the beggar putteth up his petition to you in vain, and turn him out to perish" (Mosiah 4:16).

Once in a while, serving according to the wants of others can put us into a position where they may seek to take advantage of us. While we should follow King Benjamin's admonition not to judge based on mortal perceptions, it is a delicate balancing act wherein we must communicate with the Lord through prayer. Heavenly Father does not expect us to allow our common sense to be compromised. When others demand things of us that exhaust or deplete our physical, emotional, or spiritual strength, we need to reexamine the situation and earnestly seek guidance of the Spirit.

Moroni 7:16 teaches, "For behold, the Spirit of Christ is given to every man, that he may know good from evil; wherefore, I show unto you the way to judge; for every thing which inviteth to do good, and to persuade to believe in Christ, is sent forth by the power and gift of Christ; wherefore ye may know with a perfect knowledge it is of God."

JULY 11
Hearts and Hands: The Language of Love

Beginning today, treat everyone you meet as if they were going to be dead by midnight. Extend to them all the care, kindness and understanding you can muster, and do it with no thought of any reward. Your life will never be the same again. —Og Mandino[118]

The conditions I lived in during my first marriage were humble, often desperate. When the Relief Society president asked me to take another sister to a prenatal visit, I was hesitant. Time and money were short; I was struggling. When I met the sister, however, I felt a surge of compassion. She was from the Hmong tribe, a group of refugees— boat people—from Laos. Her diminutive body was stick thin, brown skin stretched tightly over birdlike bones. Straight black hair framed her childlike face. In her eyes I saw joy.

Though there was a huge language barrier, we communicated with smiles and hand signs. She was required to undergo an ultrasound. Fear filled her eyes. I felt panic—I had no idea how to comfort her. The Spirit whispered all that was necessary was love. The sister's eyes locked on mine. I didn't break from her gaze. I smiled for all I was worth, trying to express with every fiber of my being that things were going to be okay.

In the end, it was her sweet spirit that gave the most comfort—to me. She seemed to relax in my presence. She returned my smiles with confidence. Through my simple service of being with her, I learned I had value. Something I held onto when I again returned to the despair of my own life. Like the boat that had at some point carried the dear Hmong sister to safety, hope likewise carried me.

Never underestimate the power of the language of love.

JULY 12

You: Time for Nurturing

The really efficient laborer will be found not to crowd his day with work, but will saunter to his task surrounded by a wide halo of ease and leisure. There will be a wide margin for relaxation to his day.
—Henry David Thoreau[119]

He enjoys true leisure who has time to improve his soul's estate.
—Henry David Thoreau[120]

On the first day of February, we talked about making a fortune jar that contained slips of paper, each with an idea of how we could nurture ourselves. Summertime generally means vacation time. Yet balancing day-to-day home, family, work, and Church responsibilities with summer obligations—like trying to keep up with the yard work— sometimes feels less like leisure and more like stress.

If you still have your fortune jar, get it out. If you don't have it, make a new list of activities that appeal to your senses and your need for the replenishing qualities of peace, serenity, and comfort. Throughout the month, set aside time to nurture yourself and enjoy it.

JULY 13

Worth: Ways to Serve

But be ye doers of the word, and not hearers only. —James 1:22

Lyricist and composer Will Lamartine Thompson wrote the text and music of the well-known hymn "Have I Done Any Good?" While the first verse is most frequently referred to, the second verse bears valuable insight as well:

There are chances for work all around just now,
Opportunities right in our way.
Do not let them pass by, saying, "Sometime I'll try,"
But go and do something today.
'Tis noble of man to work and to give;
Love's labor has merit alone.

Only he who does something helps others to live.
To God each good work will be known.

What are the ways service is given? The following are simple acts that will not only help another but let them know they have worth as a child of God:

* Hold the door for someone and smile.
* At the grocery store, return a shopping cart for a busy mother.
* Help someone achieve a goal, or patiently teach a skill.
* Faithfully do your visiting teaching.
* Fulfill your callings with optimism; teach someone the gospel.
* Communicate effectively and with respect.
* Share your talents.
* Invite someone to share a meal with you and your friends or family.
* Offer your seat to someone.
* Share your gratitude for life.
* Be a true friend; build others up; encourage them.
* Give someone a Book of Mormon; bear your testimony.
* Give a ride to someone; attend a medical or dental appointment with them.
* Comfort someone who is grieving.

How else can you serve others and build their worth?

JULY 14

The Blessings of Service: Giving Our Honest Best

For I was an hungred, and ye gave me meat: I was thirsty, and ye gave me drink: I was a stranger, and ye took me in: Naked, and ye clothed me: I was sick, and ye visited me: I was in prison, and ye came unto me. Then shall the righteous answer him, saying, Lord, when saw we thee an hungred, and fed thee? or thirsty, and gave thee drink? When saw we thee a stranger, and took thee in? or naked, and clothed thee? Or when saw we thee sick, or in prison, and came unto thee? And the King shall answer and say unto them, Verily I say unto you, Inasmuch as ye have

done it unto one of the least of these my brethren, ye have done it unto
me. —Matthew 25:35–40

President Spencer W. Kimball noted that it is in service to others that we find ourselves.[121]

Service enhances our ability to love others. It grounds us in the present. We come to appreciate life's blessings; our focus shifts from ourselves to more complex issues faced by those around us. We become more compassionate. Despair is made easier when we give of ourselves to those who have lost more than we can comprehend. Loneliness is made bearable. Strength, confidence, and connectedness brim.

If you thirst for a deeper sense of self and purpose, don't simply skim the surface of service. Dive into it with your whole heart. Expect nothing but the satisfaction of knowing you have given your honest best.

JULY 15
The Value of Serving Family
And ye will not suffer your children that they go hungry, or naked;
neither will ye suffer that they transgress the laws of God, and fight and
quarrel one with another, and serve the devil, who is the master of sin,
or who is the evil spirit which hath been spoken of by our fathers, he
being an enemy to all righteousness. But ye will teach them to walk in
the ways of truth and soberness; ye will teach them to love one another,
and to serve one another. —Mosiah 4:14–15

Each day, parents make sacrifices for their children. Mothers forego personal objectives to raise their offspring. Fathers too give up opportunities as they devote their time and attention to their families. Yet, righteous parents are ultimately blessed beyond measure as they agree to partner with God in His work. Families are a great training ground where individuals learn the arts of compromise, forgiveness, patience, unconditional love, and selflessness. Parents grow and are strengthened; wisdom, humility, and life-sustaining Christlike attributes are attained.

The service you give your family may go unnoticed, but it is service nonetheless—love in action, your efforts to do your best and be your best. Daily nurture and care should never be undervalued. Today, praise yourself for serving your family through daily tasks, such as making a meal, ironing a shirt or skirt, giving someone a ride, or scrubbing a spill off the kitchen floor.

JULY 16

Willingness to Serve

The time when you need to do something is when people are saying it can't be done. —Mary Frances Berry[122]

The word *nursery* crackled across the phone line. A division in our ward boundaries left the Primary president without a nursery leader. She was looking for volunteers. My mind said no even as my mouth said yes. My heart sank. My last experiences in the nursery were frenzied. An only child, I had never grown accustomed to large groups of small children.

On Sunday, I hadn't yet put down my purse when a mother delivered a crying, hysterical child—my worst fears already bearing fruit. I would be no more than captain of chaos. From out of nowhere came a couple I didn't know. Observing the crying child, the husband knelt down beside her. Then his wife scooped the toddler up to rock and quiet her. Both husband and wife, I discovered, came from large families. They were adept at dealing with young children in multiples. As it turned out, not another child came to nursery that day. The sweet woman who cradled the screaming girl did so until the child feel asleep. I was treated to getting to know the couple and the extraordinary people they truly are.

We never know, when we answer a call to serve, what the outcome may be. Temporary service as well as formal callings are as much for our benefit as they are for those whom we may serve.

JULY 17

Life: What Brings Enjoyment

Wherever you go, no matter what the weather, always bring your own sunshine. —Anthony J. D'Angelo[123]

While it's true that the most important things in life aren't things, there are things in life that lend beauty, comfort, wonder, fulfillment of purpose, and sheer enjoyment:

Thunderstorms

The fresh, clean smell that follows a rainstorm

The sound of loved ones' voices

Meaningful conversation

Candlelight

Starlight

The warmth of the sun

Rainbows

The ability to smile

Working with your hands

Quiet times

The smell of a new baby

Crisp, clean sheets

Holding hands

The chirp of a cricket on a summer night

Music

Written words

The feel of your favorite shirt or jeans

Hugs

Meeting an old friend again

What are some of the other dear and sweet benefits of life? Write about them in your journal; then share them with someone else.

JULY 18

The Miracles of Service

A favor does not consist in the service done, but in the spirit of the man who confers it. —Author unknown

In the aftermath of Hurricane Katrina, I helped assemble personal hygiene kits, clothing, shoes, and toys for children in Louisiana. My heart was touched by a letter we received from Sister Marbely Barahona of the New Orleans 2nd Ward (Spanish speaking):

When we left our house with our three children, the Saturday before Hurricane Katrina, my little eleven-month-old did not walk yet, so I did not bring any shoes for him. We did not know we were going to stay out of our homes for more than a month . . . My son made his first birthday while we were in the church shelter, and he started to walk. We received donations from very generous people, and I kept on the lookout for shoes for Jared until we received your box from Utah. I found these beautiful black boots that were exactly his size, perfect to go to church.

I know that material things are not important, but at that moment, I felt like my Heavenly Father was going to take care of all our needs, not only the temporal things but also our spiritual needs. Jared's little boots were like a symbol that our Heavenly Father took care of us, even through the very small things and that He used His very special children (like you all) to deliver His mercy. I can tell you that we were really blessed during all that time, our testimonies got better, stronger, and once again, we confirm that we are in the true Church—the Church of Jesus Christ.

We may never meet the people we serve. Yet, when we give what we can, miracles happen.

JULY 19
Gaining a Testimony: A Beautiful, Sacred Journey
That which the Spirit testifies unto you even so I would that ye should do.
—D&C 46:7

When we bear our testimony, it does not need to be lengthy, teaches Elder David A. Bednar. Nor do our words need to be eloquent. Our testimony of what we know in our hearts can be borne anytime, anywhere—not just on fast Sunday. Yet our words should be heartfelt and sincere, and our every action should uphold the words which we speak.[124]

As you endeavor to build or strengthen your testimony, be patient with yourself. Like delicate brushstrokes laying down layers of paint on canvas, a sure testimony of the gospel comes with time and effort spent in dedicated pursuit.

President Henry B. Eyring lovingly reminds us that casual scripture study can lead to casual prayers—prayers which lack the level of genuine, well-thought communication we should strive for with our Father in Heaven.[125] The scriptures—like letters from home—can assist us in knowing God and His love a little better each day. As we draw closer to Him, our testimonies will be nurtured and grow.

Enjoy the beautiful, sacred journey of gaining or strengthening your testimony.

JULY 20

Knowing: Sharing Testimony
Therefore, declare the things which ye have heard, and verily believe, and know to be true. —D&C 80:4

A testimony is what we know in our hearts and minds to be true, as witnessed to us by the Holy Ghost. A testimony that Heavenly Father and Jesus live is a rare treasure, as is a testimony of gospel truths. Such testimony is a sure foundation for our faith that dramatically improves our outlook and life. Sharing our knowledge of the gospel with others is enhanced by bearing witness of how Heavenly Father has worked in our lives. Bearing our testimony brings to mind our many blessings. Every time we share our testimony, our faith and the faith of others is reinforced. Sharing our testimony with spouses, loved ones, and friends strengthens them and fortifies relationships.

This week, verbally or in writing, share your testimony with someone you have never before shared it with before. If your testimony is still new and growing, pray for help in strengthening it so that one day you may share it with others.

JULY 21
Enjoy Life's Blessings
When you focus on being a blessing, God makes sure that you are always blessed in abundance. —Joel Osteen[126]

An Irish Blessing

May you always have work for your hands to do.
May your pockets hold always a coin or two.
May the sun shine bright on your windowpane.
May the rainbow be certain to follow each rain.
May the hand of a friend always be near you.
And may God fill your heart with gladness to cheer you.

Today, think of ways you can enjoy your blessings even more by sharing them with others.

JULY 22
The Art of Letter Writing
The art of art, the glory of expression and the sunshine of the light of letters, is simplicity. —Walt Whitman[127]

My paternal grandmother lived over two hundred miles away, yet her determination to be part of my life was great. I often received handwritten cards and letters from her. As I grew older, the letters never ceased. Assuring me of her confidence in my integrity and her belief in my abilities—and always signed, "Love, Gram"—her words of love, wisdom, and encouragement were my most cherished possessions.

When I married and had children, the letters came with less frequency. Grandma's once flawless handwriting became jagged as her gnarled hands shook with age. Knowing how difficult the process had become for her, I loved her more dearly with each letter. They became a priceless line of communication from her heart to mine and also to the hearts of my children.

I look forward to passing on the art of letter writing. In the future, my granddaughters and I will surely use e-mail to communicate.

However, I am already giving priority to creating time to sit at my desk and record things I want to share with them. I want to teach them what I have learned and relate all that I have yet to learn, hopes and dreams as well as things both sacred and miraculous. In doing so I pray they will be proud to come to know who I really am and what I stand for. I believe that one day they will recognize my efforts as an act of love and know how much I value them through the letters I will sign, "Love, Gram."

JULY 23
Blessing Lives with Our Words

And upon these I write the things of my soul, and many of the scriptures which are engraven upon the plates of brass. For my soul delighteth in the scriptures, and my heart pondereth them, and writeth them for the learning and the profit of my children. —2 Nephi 4:15

You don't have to be a grandmother to utilize written communication to strengthen the relationships in your life. Nephi tells us that when he recorded many of the scriptures engraven upon the plates of brass, he also wrote the things of his soul—loving memorandums, no doubt, of what he held most dear.

The scriptures themselves bear to our willing hearts and minds the clear message of God's love for us, the assurance of who we are, and how much we are valued by Him. Who in your life could benefit from your handwritten, heartfelt words? Set aside a corner of the kitchen or dining room table or another place where you can sit and ponder the things you'd like to write. Beforehand, gather note cards or stationery, envelopes, and a dependable pen or pencil. How long has it been since you penned a love letter to your husband? Tell him with gentle expression all the reasons you fell in love with him and why you love and treasure him still. How about the teenage child with whom verbal communication has become all but nonexistent? Do you admire the kindness they showed to someone in recent days? Did you appreciate their help during a family event or crisis? Put your thoughts and emotions into writing, and tell your loved ones how you feel.

JULY 24

Honoring the Pioneers

And each man stands with his face in the light of his own drawn sword, ready to do what a hero can. —Elizabeth Barrett Browning[128]

In Utah, today is celebrated as Pioneer Day, a statewide holiday. A commemoration of the arrival of the Mormon pioneers on July 24, 1847, in the Salt Lake Valley. Parades, rodeos, fun, food. Games and entertainment. Reverent gatherings. Voices lifted in song and praise. Reminiscings and reenactments and tributes. Festivities are ongoing in most larger communities as well as in many smaller towns.

Pioneers have lived in every era. Today pioneers, Elder Dallin H. Oaks says, include anyone who forges on ahead in order to show others the way. He further affirms that we need to do more than just learn about the pioneers. We need to recognize the eternal principles they applied to their lives and then apply them to our own.[129]

Reflect on the examples of your ancestors. How can you show others the way?

JULY 25

Different Is . . . Loved of God

Let us love one another: for love is of God; and every one that loveth is born of God, and knoweth God. —1 John 4:7

I once lived in a neighborhood with a family that was different. On warm summer evenings, when others were out walking or biking or talking as neighbors do, they were never seen. Only a summer or two passed, and the talk began. Why did they not want to associate with others? Did they think they were better than everyone else? Sundays found them in church, smiling, laughing, teaching, and fulfilling their callings. But after church, they pulled into their driveway, and the garage door was shut tight. The blinds were drawn. They were only seen again during their brief forays into the yard to mow or weed flowerbeds or when the husband left for work or the children for school.

Over half a decade passed. Five or so years of them declining invitations and passing most of their time at home in the house—even on those warm, pleasant summer evenings. Five years of speculation over what was "wrong" with them. Finally, the wife confided that a member of the family had a medical condition. A condition that, if not treated with care, could have life-threatening implications. Thus out of necessity, their lifestyle was different.

For many, life is complex—more complex than we can see with our mortal eyes or comprehend with our often limited understanding. Practice extending compassion to those who you might view as different or unusual. Don't miss opportunities to give the gift of your unconditional love.

JULY 26

Charity: The Pure Love of Christ
Wherefore, my beloved brethren, pray unto the Father with all the energy of heart, that ye may be filled with this love. —Moroni 7:48

In Moroni 7:47, the prophet Mormon explained: "Charity is the pure love of Christ, and it endureth forever; and whoso is found possessed of it at the last day, it shall be well with him."

Charity is a state of heart and mind that prompts us to love one another. It is in our offerings of service that charity is made manifest. The Relief Society motto, "Charity Never Faileth," is a wonderful promise. Charity refines our state of heart. In the topical guide in your scriptures, look up charity. Select and read verses of scripture that communicate more about the virtue. A few you can start with are 1 Corinthians 13:4, Moroni 7:46, 1 Corinthians 13:13, and Ether 12:34.

JULY 27

Cultivating the Virtue of Charity
Charity never faileth. —1 Corinthians 13:8

In her book *If Life Were Easy It Wouldn't Be Hard*, Sister Sheri L. Dew writes of times when we don't handle situations well. Occasions when we gossip or judge others—despite not having all the facts. Of jealousy over the successes of others. Of envy and division. Of trying to justify our actions as we assuage our wounded pride. Yet, as she aptly notes, God never intended for us to seek revenge of any kind—under any circumstance.

Charity is the answer.

By definition, charity is benevolent goodwill toward or love of humanity as well as generosity and helpfulness given to those in need; it is lenient—or better yet, withholding judgment—of other's mistakes. One of the many wondrous blessings that accompanies unselfish charity is that we ultimately find more of it to extend to ourselves.

What are ways you can cultivate the virtue of charity in your own heart and mind?

JULY 28
Teaching by Example
Eternal life, which gift is the greatest of all the gifts of God.
—D&C 14:7

The bowl slipped from my hands.

I didn't pay attention to its tinfoil cover, slick from buttered noodles, when I tried to put it back into the refrigerator. The foil slipped against the glass, betraying my fingers. I stared in disbelief, a moment's hesitation, as the precious milk-white container toppled downward. My hands flew toward it. Too late. It fell and shattered on the floor.

Not long ago I would have cried, knelt beside the broken shards of the antique glassware, and lamented the loss as evidence of my own foolhardiness. I would have berated myself and battered my own emotions for the rest of the day.

Not this time.

Instead . . . I smiled.

My daughter and I worked, side by side, placing the pieces into the waste can, sweeping bits too tiny to grasp, vacuuming, then scrubbing the buttery noodle residue from the floor.

"Things happen." We laughed.

Then we stood up and moved on.

Earthly possessions can never compare to the wonders of eternity that stretch before us.

JULY 29
Light the Way Home
Darkness cannot drive out darkness; only light can do that.
—Martin Luther King Jr.[130]

In summertime, I love to make outdoor candles. All year long, I save old spaghetti sauce and salsa jars. After they are washed and dried, I cut a three-foot length of heavy florist's wire. I tightly wrap the wire around the mouths of the jars, leaving half the length as a loop for hanging. I take the end of the loop and tuck it under the already wrapped wire. The end is drawn back up and twisted around itself to secure the loop in place. I settle inexpensive tea lights into the bottoms of the jars and hang the creations in trees or on fences, outdoor furniture, and arbors. At night, the lights become bright, welcoming spots of cheer in the darkness. They serve to light the way home through our backyard from the swing set and tree house.

Changing lives comes one at a time—one smile, one hug, one loaf of bread, one jar of jam, one song, one sonnet. In the service of Christ, we are privileged to have the power to reach out and lift and bless those in need.

In times of sorrow or loss, what have others done to express love and care for you? What helped most to heal your heart? In times of trial and struggle, what words touched and blessed you? In times of illness, what service was of most benefit? In times of loneliness or despair, what uplifted you? Think of ways service has benefited you in the various times and seasons of your life. List ways to serve others as they endure similar circumstances. Like the glow of a candle on a dark night, you can light the way with your love and warmth.

JULY 30

Believe in Yourself: Heavenly Father Does

We cannot tell what may happen to us in the strange medley of life. But we can decide what happens in us . . . how we can take it, what we can do with it . . . and that is what really counts in the end.

—Joseph Newton[131]

Several years ago while working on a book about the plan of salvation, I experienced great opposition. There were serious challenges to work through to complete the book plus severe trials among my family and friends.

Walking upstairs to my office, my mind pleaded with Heavenly Father: what should I do?

In the early hours of morning, I observed a burst of light in the usually darkened stairwell. On a shelf was a never-used, battery-operated candle. I hadn't turned the candle on—no one in my family ever touched it—but it was on. The candle's bulb shone like a beacon, illuminating a sign I'd made at Enrichment Night: "Did you think to pray?"

I dropped to my knees and prayed with all the energy of my soul.

The trials in my life did not lessen, but continued prayer reassured me Father in Heaven was on my side. Miracles accompanied the mayhem. Distinct heavenly help uplifted me mentally and emotionally as well as spiritually and physically. I was able to finish the book.

No matter the twists and turns of life, don't ever stop believing in your capabilities. Heavenly Father believes in you and loves you more than you can comprehend. Whether the determined glow of a candle illuminating a homemade sign or the gentle whisperings of the still, small voice, know for a surety that despite all opposition He is always with you.

JULY 31

Seasons of Service

Everyone thinks of changing the world, but no one thinks of changing himself. —Leo Nikolaevich Tolstoy[132]

Depending on your age and personal circumstances, in some seasons of your life you'll be able to offer more of yourself, your time, or your substance; in other seasons less. Remember, your best is what's required. In all your seasons of service, simple and genuine acts offered with Christlike love bring the richest blessings and joy.

Serve up calmness and serenity; both are priceless gifts. Music bestows inner peace and harmony as it soothes and comforts. Share uplifting songs of praise. Share your gifts and talents, whatever they may be. Have passion and enthusiasm for what you do. Show others they are worthy of respect and understanding. Heal others with your words and deeds. If you offer unconditional love, you're more likely to get it in return. Nourish others with your care. Buried under hurt and disappointment is someone who needs you.

Service brings refinement to our mortal state as well as to our spiritual state; serving others and serving with others can restore your faith in yourself and in humanity. When you serve, tell others they are important and valued. Help them see that they are children of God. Share laughter and tears. Service helps satisfy the spiritual need for emotional connection. What we're searching for often comes within the hours of service we give to others. You can serve all God's creatures, even pets and other animals. Sharing miracles of life and nature nurtures the senses.

Remember your inherent value; the gift of you is unique and special.

July Recipes

Orange Fluff 'n Stuff

3 cups cold water
1 (3 oz.) package cook-and-serve
    tapioca pudding
1 (3 oz.) package cook-and-serve
    vanilla pudding

1 (3 oz.) package orange Jell-O
1 (8 oz.) carton Cool Whip
1 (15 oz.) can mandarin orange
    slices, well drained

Put water in a medium saucepan. Stir in tapioca pudding, vanilla pudding, and Jell-O. Bring mixture to a boil, stirring constantly. Remove from heat. Allow to cool slightly, then fold in Cool Whip and oranges. Chill until set. Variations: use raspberry Jell-O and 15 ounces of raspberries, or blueberry Jell-O and 15 ounces of blueberries.

Turkey Spinach Salad with Peach Poppy Seed Vinaigrette

From *Peachy: A Harvest of Fruity Goodness*

7 cups fresh baby spinach
½ cup toasted sliced almonds
¾ cup cooked turkey (or chicken),
    cut into thin strips

2 cups fresh, ripe peaches, cut
    into bite-sized pieces

Toss spinach and almonds. Place on plates and top with turkey strips and peaches. Drizzle with Peach Poppy Seed Vinaigrette.

Peach Poppy Seed Vinaigrette

⅓ cup peach jam
⅓ cup white wine vinegar
¼ cup olive oil

1 Tablespoon honey, warmed
1 teaspoon poppy seeds

Combine all ingredients in a jar. Chill, shake well, serve.

Raspberry Fruit Salad

1 (6 oz.) package raspberry Jell-O
1 ½ cups boiling water
1 (3 oz.) package cream cheese, cut into cubes and softened
1 cup fresh raspberries, washed

1 banana, sliced
1 cup crushed pineapple
1 cup mandarin orange slices
½ cup pecans
1 cup whipped cream

Dissolve raspberry Jell-O in boiling water. Gradually add the cream cheese and blend until smooth. Chill until slightly thickened. Fold in raspberries, bananas, pineapple, orange slices, and pecans. Beat whipped cream until stiff, then add to Jell-O mixture. Chill until well set.

AUGUST
Flowers along the Path
The Miracle of Motherhood

ADOPTIVE MOTHER. SINGLE MOTHER. MOTHER wanting to be. Mother soon to be. Divorced mother. Mother who has lost a child. Stepmother. Mother of one. Mother of ten. New mother. Mother waiting to be. No matter our circumstances or season in life, developing a mother heart readies us to fulfill the divine, eternal role of motherhood.

Whether motherhood comes in this life or the next, developing a mother heart is an integral part of our journey.

Children need our righteous examples of love, kindness, and goodness. The flowers that brighten life's path, children provide us the opportunity to work in direct partnership with God. This month, enjoy the journey through August as you discover and put into practice the qualities of a mother heart.

Making the Most of August

* The Primary was organized August 11, 1878. Send your children's Primary teachers a note of thanks for their efforts. If you are a Primary teacher, write thank-you notes to the children in your class, highlighting their positive attributes and contributions.

* The first Sunday in August is Sister's Day. Do something special for your sister or a friend.

* Hold a luau. Have fun decorating the backyard, and make grass skirts for everyone. You can use green crepe paper.

* Lie on the lawn, and watch for falling stars. Or have movie night on the lawn. Bring out a projector or television set, and watch your favorite movie under the stars.

* Set up a revolving-sitter schedule with your friends. Have each mom take a turn sitting so the others can get away for a few hours.

* Enter something you've created in your state or county fair.

* Write a poem based on one of your favorite summer memories.

* Take advantage of summer's bounty. Harvest time means lots of fresh, delicious fruits and vegetables. Apples, cherries, peaches, raspberries, pears, and watermelon; tomatoes, peppers, pumpkin, squash, and lettuces. Visit a farmer's market, fruit stand, or produce farm where you can pick your own. Take a class on pie or jam making.

* Give cooking lessons to your kids and their friends. Help them compile a cookbook.

* Make a dinnertime tradition of going around the table and having everyone tell one item of good news from the day, what they are thankful for, or kind words of support to other family members.

* Talk to your children about reverence. The book *Monday I Was a Monkey—A Tail of Reverence* by Jennie McClain helps kids learn how to act on the Sabbath day.

* The Tabernacle Choir was founded in August 1847, one month after the pioneers arrived in Salt Lake. Attend one of their performances or listen to their recordings. Learn more about the choir at MormonTabernacleChoir.org.

* August is National Eye Exam Month. If you haven't already done so this year, make appointments for you and your family members to get their eyes checked.

* Make an ice cream treat with one of the recipes following this section.

AUGUST 1

Savoring Motherhood
Who ran to help me when I fell,
And would some pretty story tell,
Or kiss the place to make it well?
My mother. —Ann Taylor[133]

The pitter patter of tiny feet. Children of our spirits: adopted; children of our bodies: birthed. They dance into our lives and hearts. Cherub-faced infants with tender, rosebud toes. Baby smell of just-born freshness. Somewhere between the time they're first placed in our arms to their first serious illness, we begin to perceive a bond that defies logic and is defined by love.

Starry-eyed motherhood dims a little when they reject (at any age) our best attempts to soothe and sustain; exhaust our reserves of energy and patience with their personal preferences; try our stamina when household workload soars. Yet . . . we are mothers. Co-creators with God in the marvel and miracle of life.

If you're already a mother, this month you may find wet swimming suits and towels plopped in the unlikeliest of places. Sand and mud, melted Popsicles, and spilled pop on floors you think will never again be clean for more than a few minutes. Out loud you proclaim that, on many levels, you can't wait for school to start. In recesses of the heart—where images of sweet, cherubic infanthood are stored, layed up against reality of demanding toddler, cranky adolescent, and individualistic teen—you feel a twinge: time and childhood passing.

Whether your children are of your spirit: adopted; of your body: birthed; or of your heart: blessed to you by blended family—all too soon the floor will be clean for days and weeks on end. The washer and dryer will groan in boredom. The fingerprints that crept higher on the walls and refrigerator will vanish.

Motherhood. Savor it a little longer . . .

AUGUST 2

A Mothering Mission Statement

A mother's love is . . . patient and forgiving when all others are forsaking,
it never fails or falters, even though the heart is breaking.
—Helen Steiner Rice[134]

No matter the mix of family members, children look to the adults in
their lives for examples of how life is to be lived. When love is found
in abundance, it is likely to be emulated. A mother can teach that
regardless of the circumstances of how a family comes to be, they are
tied together with heart strings.

In April, you wrote a mission statement: twenty-five words
defining who you are, how you intend to live, and the goals you
aspire to attain. Reread that statement, then write a mothering
mission statement in twenty-five words or less. Here's mine: Through
my words and example, I will teach my children truth and love that
they might find their way back to God.

Once your mothering mission statement is complete, place it
next to your personal mission statement. Read both often.

AUGUST 3

The Gifts That Children Bring

Only those who look with the eyes of children can lose themselves in the
object of their wonder. —Eberhard Arnold[135]

The gift of patience does not show up on the front porch wrapped in
colorful paper and festooned with ribbons and bows. For us to know
and appreciate its true value, patience must be learned firsthand.

President Dieter F. Uchtdorf notes that patience is not
submissively resigning ourselves or simply not acting because we are
afraid. Patience requires faithful resilience no matter the circumstances
or challenges we face. It is pressing forward with a firm brightness of
hope—thriving instead of merely surviving.[136]

When we do not passively resign ourselves to the tantrums and
arguments of our children or allow our mood to become one of anger

or despair, patience is being learned. We teach through example what proper behavior is. Our confidence is bolstered as we learn we have the power to retain the Spirit and remain calm. That confidence transfers to situations outside the home. If we can maintain composure and self-assurance while dealing with a cranky or demanding child, we find that problems with others can likewise be handled. Look closely for the precious gifts you can learn from your children.

AUGUST 4
Regifting: Optimism
The heart remembers with fondness the feeling of being cherished.

There are no trivial moments for children. Everything is vital and interesting, surprises waiting to be discovered. The world is a place of adventure and wonder. In the delight of children, we learn much about optimism—the gift of looking on the bright side. Mud becomes mud pies. A bad hair day brings giggles. Finger paint creates masterpieces.

As children grow older, frustration and trials often dim optimism. We can't always alter the pressures of the world, but we can teach our children to continue to see the bright side. Our mood, words, and deeds convey optimism. They mold our children's beliefs about success and failure.

Here are a few ways to bless your children's lives by regifting the gift of optimism:

* Encourage your children to take notice of and celebrate good things in life. Every situation has a negative and a positive side. Help them practice looking for the silver lining of every cloud.
* Teach your children that they are inherently good even if their decisions are sometimes not so great. They need to know that bad things pass—that they are not to blame for situations over which they have no control—and that changing their way of thinking can impact negative situations for the better.
* Children need to know that not trying something because they're too afraid can lead to a self-fulfilling prophecy of defeat. Henry

Ford said, "If you think you can do a thing or think you can't do a thing, you're right."[137] If something doesn't work for them, laud it as a valuable learning experience. Point out that they'll be better prepared for the next time.

AUGUST 5
Joyfully Living in the Moment
Children have neither past nor future; they enjoy the present, which very few of us do. —Jean de la Bruyere[138]

Mommies are just big little girls. —Author unknown

The term "child's play" is an idiom, a phrase that denotes something as easy to do. The gift of joyfully living in the moment can be as simple as child's play. Yet as adults we make it harder than it has to be. Joyful living is not merely surviving the moment, and it's more than savoring what is provided by the senses. It is finding gratitude for the blessing of now. Instantaneous enjoyment of life is taught by those who are experts in it: children. When they play, they devote themselves wholeheartedly. We admire their fun but worry that engaging in it will make us look, well, childlike.

Plato tells us, "You can discover more about a person in an hour of play than in a year of conversation." How many times have you tried to question a child about their day only to have them ignore you? If you get down on the floor, help build a castle with blocks, find missing pieces to a puzzle, catch the vision for an invisible road that leads from kitchen to dining room, you'll learn. Perhaps slowly at first, but observing and listening between the lines shows you what's going on in a young child's world. The same holds true for older kids. Their toys are bigger and more complex, but consistently try in sincerity to play right along with them, and you'll begin to understand their minds and hearts.

Take time to play with your children. While you're learning about them, you'll also be learning the value of joyfully living in the moment.

AUGUST 6
Learn: Teach Me
The doctors told me I would never walk, but my mother told me I would—so I listened to my mother.
—Wilma Rudolph, US Olympic gold medal winner[139]

Two words can help bring out the best in your relationship with your child: teach me. Teach me what you learned in school today. Teach me how you fixed the problem with your bike. Teach me how you feel about what happened. Teach me about the colors you used in your painting. When you sincerely ask a child to teach you something, and they sense your interest, they immediately feel valued and important.

Asking them to tell you is a command. But teaching is important; they know that's usually your job. When you give them equal standing, they generally rise to the occasion. Plato's philosophy was, "Do not train a child to learn by force or harshness; but direct them to it by what amuses their minds, so that you may be better able to discover with accuracy the peculiar bent of the genius of each."

Ask your children to teach you because it's a wonderful experience to learn from a child's point of view. And because knowing how they think and learning about the remarkable people they truly are will build your appreciation of them. Respect fosters respect. Then when you're the one doing the teaching, the quality of the time, attention, and esteem that you have bestowed on your children will be the caliber of what you receive in return.

AUGUST 7
Motherhood Circuitry: Take Five
I'd like to be the ideal mother, but I'm too busy raising my kids.
—Author unknown

In the early days of telephones, switchboard operators connected calls by plugging a set of wires into jacks on a switchboard. Each pair of wires comprised a circuit: a means of getting a message from one person to another. The term getting your wires crossed stems from old telephone circuitry, manual switchboards, when someone was inadvertently connected to the wrong place.

As mothers we have good intentions, but sometimes we simply try to do too much at once. Mommy multitasking, trying to be everywhere doing everything for everyone, quickly becomes exhausting. When we're tired or stressed, the message we try to convey in love and concern comes across to our child as something less than loving.

In other words, we get our wires crossed.

If what you're trying to do or say isn't coming across the way you intend, stop, look, and listen to what you need. Rewire your motherhood circuitry by taking five. Five minutes to yourself so you can figure out how to connect the way you'd like to—both with your children and with yourself as God's daughter. For five minutes, focus only on you, on positives that will revitalize you. Take five to pray or read the scriptures. To breathe, rethink things, or talk to your husband or a friend. Take five behind a closed door. Take five to eat some chocolate, laugh, or go for a walk. Whatever you need to do to uncross wires and gain fresh perspective.

Tell your kids in advance that Mommy is going to have some take fives during the day. Outline what you expect of them while you do. Set guidelines, and stick to them.

AUGUST 8
Quality in the Quantity
The quality of a person's life is in direct proportion to their commitment to excellence, regardless of their chosen field of endeavor.
—Vince Lombardi[140]

The emotional support that comes from quality time with our children builds healthy parent-child relationships and influences relationships they develop outside the home. Some days, forging quality time is difficult. One-on-one opportunities get crowded out by the quantity of time we give to other responsibilities. Author Beppie Harrison asserts quantity time can have quality. "We can help our children learn that love requires time as much as it requires attention. The child listening to his mother arrange for dinners to be taken to a mother with a new baby or set up appointments for visiting teaching is learning something about compassionate service."

She also notes that within quantity time there is room for both mother and child to learn and grow as individuals. "In the quantity of time we have together, there are hours to spend jointly and hours to spend separately . . . They [children] need us to read the scriptures to them, but they also need to see that we as adults read the scriptures for ourselves, not simply to be good examples but to gain spiritual food . . . Quantity time is really the child's glimpse into the life of his parent as a person, the person who existed before the child himself was born, and who will continue to grow and develop after the child has moved into independence."[141]

Elder M. Russell Ballard stresses that no singular, perfect way exists to be a good mother. What is most important is that a mother freely extends love to her offspring and treasures them above all else.[142]

Quality and quantity. Both can be precious.

AUGUST 9
One Brush Stroke at a Time
Little by little one walks far. —Peruvian Proverb

American artist Minerva Teichert produced around 1,000 paintings in her lifetime, including over 400 murals. Her work captured enduring and endearing emotion in familiar scenes. In addition to her well-known religious subjects, she captured struggle and serenity, gratitude and grace, heritage and home, in portraits, still lifes, and western scenes. Both East Coast art student and rural West rancher's wife, she has been described as having lived her life on the border of rustic and refined. To canvases she tacked to the wall of her living room, she added strokes of color at every opportunity. Minerva was as adept as she was innovative at mothering and painting, chores and chickens, living the gospel and standing up for what she believed in.

Your future is a work in progress. One brush stroke at time, you paint it with your own unique blend of devotion to family and passion for living. Every day, a rainbow palette of options awaits your touch of creation. Your kind words can paint a masterpiece of love for your children. Your caring and compassion can create the artwork of miracles in their lives.

With the gifts and talents you have been blessed with, what will you paint today?

AUGUST 10
Wishes and Love and Thanks
Write it on your heart that every day is the best day of the year. —Ralph Waldo Emerson[143]

Cotton candy at the fair. A horseback ride. A new home. A better life. The chance to express your love to someone who has passed away. Saying I love you to Heavenly Father and Jesus. A new puppy. Pizza for dinner. Gratitude for the blessing of a new baby sister. Thanks for a new bicycle.

Together with your child, talk about your wishes and what you're both thankful for. On small slips of paper, write down what you come up with. Use lengths of ribbons to tie the papers to helium balloons. Hold hands while you watch the balloons float skyward. Or spread a blanket on the lawn and lie under the stars. For each star you see, make a wish or express something you're grateful for.

Happy wishing!

AUGUST 11
Nobility: Raising Heavenly Father's Children
The bravest battle that ever was fought;
Shall I tell you where and when?
On the maps of the world you will find it not;
'Twas fought by the mothers of men. —Joaquin Miller[144]

At birth, my second daughter had only a thirty percent chance of living. After an emergency C-section, I was in critical condition. Fragile time hung in the balance. What could I give to a baby who might not live? Especially when I was so ill?

I closed my eyes and prayed, begging for courage. Agonizing hours later, when my condition had been upgraded, I was taken by wheelchair to the NICU to see my three-pound, three-ounce daughter. "I'm your mommy," I began, endeavoring to keep my emotions under control. "And I love you!"

For the next week, I kept a vigil by her isolette. Though my daughter would require months of specialized care, she did live. At eight days old, her ventilator tube was removed, and I held my baby for the very first time. As I cradled her featherweight body in my arms, our eyes met, burning into my heart the knowledge that her life had special purpose. Unexpectedly, there came the understanding that my life and my role of mother would be enhanced; raising this special-needs child would require great devotion and sacrifice. That Heavenly Father had entrusted me with her felt both humbling and ennobling.[145]

Even if none of your children possess what in recent years has become termed as "special needs" because of an illness or disability, all children are special in that they possess a noble birthright. As such they need to be raised and nurtured in the ways God directs. Honor each of your children by seeking to help them reach their divine potential.

AUGUST 12
Trials: Motherhood Refined
It must needs be, that there is an opposition in all things.
—2 Nephi 2:11

Motherhood brings the unexpected. Children suffer illness and disease; bear burdens of disability; experience emotional or social obstacles; endure debilitating doubt about themselves, their family members, or the principles they were raised with. Such challenges are borne equally in the hearts of loving mothers. The trials of motherhood refine the process. They require us to search long and hard for answers we never imagined there would be questions to.

Elder Jeffrey R. Holland assures us that when we as mothers have humbled ourselves unto the Lord and done all we can on behalf of our children, we will receive His help. Elder Holland urges us to claim the promises of the Savior; with steadfast resolve he affirms that we can have faith that all things will be made right. [146]

Erin Herrin, the mother of conjoined and then separated twins and author of *When Hearts Conjoin*, confirms, "Life as a mother is busy and exhausting, but, as any mother knows, rewarding . . . We thank our Father in Heaven every day for the privilege . . . Happiness and joy can be found in the most heart-wrenching circumstances when it brings us closer to God, family, and friends, This love, combined with faith, helps us endure any trials that come our way."[147]

In your journal, record unexpected trials you've encountered as a mother. Then list the refining properties of each experience.

AUGUST 13
Are You Proud of Your Children?
Children are the hands by which we take hold of heaven.
—Henry Ward Beecher[148]

No matter their current demeanor, all kids have done something compassionate or thoughtful at some point. Remember the dandelion given to you in innocent love? The handmade birthday card? Breakfast in bed? It doesn't matter the kitchen was a mess. Kitchen floors and counters and dirty dishes will pass. Love lives on forever. Their rendering of pancakes was a genuine offering of true love—Christlike charity. We need to hold such moments firmly in our mind through days of turmoil or strife.

Are you proud of your children? Heavenly Father is. Was the C on their report card their best work? Maybe so. Maybe not. But the fact they were in class long enough to receive a C and not an F may be commendable. He recognizes their efforts to attend church, just sitting in the foyer, as progress. He knows that their apology to a crying sibling—even if they started the fight in the first place—needs to be complimented. He looks for the best in them. So can you.

We are naturally disappointed when a child makes a choice that is clearly incorrect or not in harmony with Christ's teachings.

Yet we should strive always to feel pride and express it for points of light—shining moments when a child's divine nature and character is evident. The fact that they are here on earth means that in the preexistence they made a righteous choice to follow God's plan. They accomplished much and were magnificent beings. How grateful and proud we ought be! When we enter eternity, we will know for a surety of their greatness once again.

Why not regard them accordingly now?

AUGUST 14

Teaching: The Rainbow of Motherhood

Take joy and pride in your role as mother and nurturer of God's children.

When you take time to sit down with your spouse and talk over a problem with regard and respect for one another's opinions, your child learns positive communication.

When, despite obstacles, you patiently finish a task, your child learns perseverance.

When you apologize, your child learns humility.

When you talk compassionately to pets and make certain their needs are met, your child learns kindness.

When you accept an apology, your child learns forgiveness.

When you care for your body and mind, your child learns self-respect.

When you return to the check stand with an item you weren't charged for, your child learns honesty.

When you pray, your child learns you value God.

A mother's example creates rainbows in the stormy skies of life. What will you teach your children today?

AUGUST 15

Sacred Things: Your Testimony

And now, after the many testimonies which have been given of him, this is the testimony, last of all, which we give of him: That he lives!

—D&C 76:22

Tell your children the stories of Jesus, Elder Neil L. Anderson exhorts, stories of His birth, life, and crucifixion. Our children have significant responsibilities and great spiritual aptitude. Preparing them for life is not a task to be taken lightly. You can testify of the Savior in all aspects of daily life. You can speak of your feelings toward Him and your debt of gratitude. You can bear verbal testimony of your knowledge that He is the Christ. The Spirit will carry your conviction into the hearts of your children.[149] In addition to bearing testimony verbally, write it down. Give a copy to your children to keep in their scriptures or in another safe place. Let them know your feelings about things sacred: the gospel, the prophet, the Book of Mormon, and all you hold dear. Talk with them about how they can have a testimony of their own.

AUGUST 16

Respect Is a Two-Way Street

The bond that links your true family is not one of blood, but of respect and joy in each other's life. —Richard Bach[150]

Sister Marjorie Pay Hinckley observed that children rise higher when they are treated with respect. In her book *Small and Simple Things,* she admonishes, "Use courteous and respectful language when you talk with your children and others. You don't teach a child not to yell by yelling. We cannot expect to be respected if we treat others in demeaning ways."[151]

Children who are treated with respect are most likely to become happy, healthy adults even in the face of dire circumstances and challenges. They will be more able to withstand pressure from friends who might encourage them to use dangerous substances and engage in spiritually disabling activities. They will be more optimistic as well as more confident in making correct decisions when the world beckons. They will also be more willing to treat others with love and respect.

Use respect and kind words abundantly in your conversations with your children.

AUGUST 17

Breaking the Cycle of Emotional Abuse

Be ye therefore merciful, as your Father also is merciful. —Luke 6:36

The forms of emotional abuse include

Belittling: Verbal abuse that erodes a child's sense of worth and potential—telling a child they should never have been born, that they are a mistake, or that they are bad or stupid; negative comparisons with others; guilting or blaming; any word or act that devalues or demeans a child.

Harassment: Threats or intentional infliction of stress-inducing situations, such as doing something to frighten a child; using extremes in punishment; or deliberately playing on a child's fears, such as being alone. Repeated episodes severely diminish a child's capacity to cope with day-to-day life and cause debilitating anxiety.

Coldness: Depriving a child of emotional security, stability, and love. Coldness and its more severe form, cruelty, are acts of mistreatment that destroy confidence and hinder intellectual progress as well as the ability to form healthy relationships and make positive social interactions.

Inconsistency: Intentional change of rules, consequences, or responses; malicious unpredictability damages trust in self and others.

Ignoring: Disregard for a child's thoughts, opinions, and feelings. Rejection or withholding love and affection. Neglecting a child's physical or emotional needs stunts vital social and intellectual development and compromises emotional stability.

If you were a victim of emotional abuse when you were a child, take steps to ensure you don't continue the cycle. Adults should take care to avoid using words and derogatory comments that have been used against them as weapons against others—especially children. Positive affirmations can literally change the course of a child's life.

AUGUST 18

Words Heal: Twelve Things Your Children Need to Hear You Say

Train up a child in the way he should go: and when he is old, he will not depart from it. —Proverbs 22:6

* I love you. Nothing will change the way I feel.
* I value who you are. You are special and unique, and I want to know about you as a person. Whatever you have to tell me, I'll listen.
* I forgive you. Everyone makes mistakes; when I make mistakes, I hope you will forgive me. It's important to forgive yourself. Life isn't about doing everything perfectly but about trying to do our best in an imperfect world.
* Crying is okay. Even adults cry. It's a healthy way to deal with sadness, fear, and frustration.
* I am proud of you. It's okay to be proud of yourself and to feel good about your accomplishments.
* I believe in you. You've got what it takes to succeed. You can do whatever you set your mind to. I support your dreams and goals.
* I have confidence in you. I know you will make good choices. Choosing what's right isn't always easy; it takes courage. Truth can be hard, even lonely, but integrity is priceless.
* I will always be here when you need me. When you need help just ask, and I'll be ready.
* I admire your kindness. Compassion not only builds others up but helps us to feel good about ourselves and gives us a sense of who we are destined to become.
* I'm sorry. I was wrong. Please. Thank you. Excuse me. I respect you and will show you that I do by my words and actions.
* I want your opinion. How you feel is important to me. I want to understand your viewpoint.
* I'm glad I'm your mother. You bring great joy to my life—thank you for being you.

AUGUST 19
Building Your Child's Inner Strength
Your children will become what you are; so be what you want them to be. —David Bly[152]

Would it surprise you to know that your children will grow into what you think they are? If you consider them an annoyance, they may not understand exactly why, but they'll live up to your expectations. If you see them in positive light and extol their positive attributes often, they'll see themselves as being of worth and will strive to live up to your expectations.

Provide verbal and emotional support for your children by recognizing deeds and attributes that demonstrate the kind of characteristics you wish to reinforce. Celebrate your child's unique abilities: comforting a sibling, showing concern for others, unselfish behavior, expressions of love, gestures of compassion, a positive attitude when under stress, making correct choices when faced with peer pressure, choosing to pray and read scriptures. Compliment them by naming the specific character traits they exhibit: compassion, kindness, selflessness, generosity, honesty. Take it a step further and help them realize the personal impact of their deeds. For example, "When you were nice to your brother, it made him feel better about himself. It's nice to see how happy he is now." Consistently notice good behaviors as they occur, and children are likely to model them often.

Make a list of your child's positive attributes and tuck it into your journal. Based on the list, contemplate ways you can express your approval and belief in them. Think of things you wish your parents would have expressed to you.

AUGUST 20
You Are Wonderful: Let Me Count the Ways
Care for your family like you would a precious garden, carefully tending them with time, effort, and love to ensure they flourish and grow.

If we only tell our children what they're doing wrong, they won't discover all that is good about themselves and the greatness they are capable of. As you become more aware of your child's abilities, make a list of things you admire about them. The list could include some of the following:

* I love how you make me smile.
* Your laughter reminds me of all that is good in the world.
* I feel the Spirit when I hear you pray.
* In your eyes, I see light and hope that uplifts and encourages me.

* I treasure the time we spend together.
* I am grateful for your help washing the dishes.
* You have the gift of a kind and listening heart.

Add to the list. When you have assembled at least twenty positives, handwrite them on a decorative piece of paper. Or type and print them using a special font. Give the list to your child as a birthday gift or when they are having a hard day. A variation would be to list each positive on a separate piece of paper and give them to your child when you feel it is appropriate. Leave the messages under their pillow, taped to their mirror, or send the messages through the mail as personalized greetings. Make lists for children who are still at home and for those who are away from home.

AUGUST 21
Always a Child of God
*Self-worth cannot be verified by others. You are worthy because you say
it is so. If you depend on others for your value it is other worth.*
—Wayne Dyer[153]

Respect your bodies. No matter the shape or size. Love them.
—Stephanie Nielson[154]

Author and self-worth analyst Karen Eddington shares self-worth education and outreach through her community work, mentoring programs, media appearances, motivational speaking, and books. She has mentored over 10,000 women and teens in developing self-acceptance and confidence and has conducted multiple research projects. She tells us, "Self-worth is explainable. Confidence is not a magic thing that just happens to a lucky few people. There is a principle of choice, action, and accountability to developing confidence. Feeling self-worth is a result of choice and accountability. Every day, we create ourselves . . . If kids base their worth as a person on how they look, they will limit themselves."

She explains how we as mothers can help: "Teach kids about beauty; beauty is more than skin deep. The more skin you feel you have to show, the more you are saying to the world: My value is only physical. I have no brains, no heart, no talent or gifts, or depth of emotion."[155]

Talk with your children about self-worth. Tell them who they are—their true natures and divine birthright—versus who the world tells them that they should be. Being "imperfect" in the eyes of the world does not mean they are imperfect to their Father in Heaven. Teach them that they are first, foremost, and always children of God.

AUGUST 22
Crafts and Hobbies for Children

Feelings of worth can flourish only in an atmosphere where individual differences are appreciated, mistakes are tolerated, communication is open, and rules are flexible—the kind of atmosphere that is found in a nurturing family. —Virginia Satir[156]

Learning a new skill and finishing the task is fun and rewarding. The act of engaging in creative endeavors provides psychological and emotional benefits that teach children to experience and respond to life in new ways. As television and the Internet threaten to consume more of our children's time, crafts and hobbies can be introduced as alternatives to provide balance.

Two's Company: When introducing a child to crafting, plan for at least one parent to participate. Leaving a child alone, especially those who are younger, will seldom enhance their desire to create. Nor will it build your relationship, a desired outcome of at-home activities. Working with a child can provide a vital means to promoting positive communication and foster a sense of family unity.

De-Stress: As adults, we take pleasure in crafts and hobbies that provide relief from stress—not create it! The same holds true for children. Allow children ample input, and remember desire to learn a skill is paramount. When a craft/hobby is decided upon, encourage the child to make their own decisions on choosing colors and (if applicable) placing objects. They'll learn about planning and organizing. Expressing confidence in them instead of doing it for them will help them discover their own unique abilities.

Encourage Enjoyment, Discourage Perfectionistic Tendencies: Crafts and hobbies can provide a teaching opportunity for parents to foster the attitude that mistakes are a part of learning—not a sign of failure. Praise is vital. Parents should be optimistic and positive and not compare siblings.

Even with careful advance planning, it's normal for children to experience frustration as they go through trial and error to find what works. If your children dwell on perceived mistakes, help them discover the joy in their creations. For example, the broken wall of a popsicle-stick butterfly house can become a patio for butterfly dances!

AUGUST 23
Time for Fun: Camp Mom
You don't really understand human nature unless you know why a child on a merry-go-round will wave at his parents every time around—and why his parents will always wave back. —William D. Tammeus[157]

The end of summer is drawing to a close. Everyone's getting a little restless. There are mixed emotions all around. Soon school will start. If only in subtle ways, schedules and lives will change. Lighten the mood and celebrate the season with a backyard end-of-summer camp.

Older kids can help prepare stations with outdoor games like hopscotch or croquet. Make stations for bird watching, mini-golf, water balloon volleyball, hula hooping, and jewelry making. Roast hot dogs for lunch. Make homemade root beer. If you invite neighbors and friends, have the other mothers bring potluck side dishes and desserts. Have an afternoon story time. Use finger puppets to entertain younger children. While you're reading, the older kids can make personalized pillowcases: buy inexpensive pillowcases, and use fabric paint to write names or messages. Have everyone who attends add their handprints.

Bring the day to a close with an evening bonfire. Make s'mores and sing songs. Give plenty of hugs. Have fun!

AUGUST 24

The Power of Example

I think it must somewhere be written that the virtues of mothers shall, occasionally, be visited upon their children. —Charles Dickens

Example is potent stuff. We can tell our children they should love others, but if they constantly see the negative way we talk to or regard the checker at the grocery store, the waiter at the restaurant, or the beggar on the corner, what lesson will they really learn? Do we talk down to others? Do we only use courtesy and polite expressions and speech for those who have a high social status?

If we relate our belief that we should treat all others with respect, our children will listen—if our example bears up our words. When we underscore our examples of goodness, kindness, and love with gentle words that explain to our children why it is important to act as Christ would, they learn much about the value of Christlike attributes.

Today, when you are kind and compassionate to another human being, tell your child why you felt it was important for you to be so and how it feels to act on Christ's behalf.

AUGUST 25

Focus: How Our Children View Our Example

My father didn't tell me how to live, he lived, and let me watch him do it. —Clarence Budinton Kelland[158]

Elder David A. Bednar assures us that all we are—all we think and do—and who we are becoming is known to the Lord.[159]

As the perceptive sons and daughters of God that they are, our children know as well!

Our children keenly observe how we dress, if we pay tithing, if we reverently partake of the sacrament, and if we attend the temple regularly or are at least working to do so. They notice what we read, watch, and listen to. What we love and spend our time on. The friends we choose and the actions of those friends—including how we allow our friends to treat us and how we treat them. Our children also watch how we treat our parents, siblings, and spouse.

Take notice of the example your actions portray. Are your inner thoughts and convictions evident in your words and deeds?

AUGUST 26
The Remarkable Individuals Called Children
We worry about what a child will become tomorrow, yet we forget that he is someone today. —Stacia Tauscher[160]

Young mothers often tell me how lucky I am that three of my children are grown. "Now you don't have to stress about them anymore," they say. No more keeping track of their whereabouts. No more fretting over what they eat. No more worrying about their decisions. Those well-intentioned women are surprised when I tell them that now my worries are actually bigger. Mothers don't stop being mothers just because their children grow up. Adult choices bring bigger consequences—a verity that becomes all too apparent!

Often we get discouraged, believing all we've done for our children is in vain. They don't seem to listen, let alone care. It helps to know that, ultimately, generations past and future are bound together by hope. In memories of past joys lie promises of hope for the future. Life bears a simple truth: families are made up of independent souls struggling to find their places in the world. What holds everything together is no more, no less, than simple, heartfelt love. Our children are forever our children. No matter how painful, we never stop caring.

The care and concern a mother extends to her children takes many forms. Stress and worry are part of the package. Am I lucky that three of my children are grown? Yes. But not because my work is finished or lessened. It is because three remarkable individuals have taught me more about myself than I would have ever imagined I could learn.

AUGUST 27
Parenting: Dictator or Disciple of Christ?
Some mothers are kissing mothers and some are scolding mothers, but it is love just the same, and most mothers kiss and scold together.
—Pearl S. Buck[161]

In times of stress, we can fall into the trap of wanting a fast fix, of demanding that problems be solved right away. We raise our voice, thinking our tone will drive home our point and thus expedite the process of problem solving. But parenthood isn't about forcing a quick fix. Not thinking before we speak to our children usually causes more harm than good. As does labeling. Negative labels are excuses we formulate that communicate we think a child isn't capable of anything better, that that child is defective.

Certainly, we love our children. Certainly, they must have discipline. Yet there is a difference between constructive scolding and outright criticism. Harshness and blatant criticism does not communicate concern and affection. Encouragement and love are what make children feel comfortable enough to make the kind of choices we'd like them to make—even if it takes them a while—and allows them to feel able to navigate their own journeys with confidence.

If we act and speak in harmony with the Lord's will—as if He were right in the room—more will be accomplished in a few minutes than in hours spent in contention and arguing. We can choose to remain calm and still be assertive and in control of our emotions.

This week, consider how your attitude toward your children can either serve to help or hinder your relationship with them as well as how it impacts their perception of themselves. Think of how compassion and encouragement can serve to help them accomplish what they need to do at home, at school, and in the world, and how it can mold the kind of people they will become.

AUGUST 28
Getting to Know You: A Favorites List
It's not only children who grow. Parents do too. And as much as we watch to see what our children do with their lives, they are watching us to see what we do with ours. I can't tell my children to reach for the sun. All I can do is reach for it, myself. —Joyce Maynard[162]

What's your favorite hymn or scripture? What's your favorite food or color? Do you have a favorite song or favorite kind of candy? How about a favorite season or holiday, book, author, poet, or composer. Write down a list of your favorites, and share it with your children. With very young children, draw or paint a picture for them and explain its meaning. Encourage them to follow suit.

Urge your children to share their favorites with you. Doing so brings up lots to talk about and can be especially helpful for blended families. Share your favorite traditions or recipes, and ask your children to teach you theirs. If your children are grown, send them a postcard every few weeks, giving them the news of home and expressing your love.

AUGUST 29

Loving: The Importance of Being Together

Children are entitled to their otherness, as anyone is; and when we reach them, as we sometimes do, it is generally on a point of sheer delight, to us so astonishing, but to them so natural. —Alastair Reid[163]

My husband and I were late for a concert. Our four-year-old granddaughter, Abbie, assumed she was going too. As we left the restaurant where our family had dined that evening, it became apparent to her she'd not accompany us. "I want my grandma!" she screamed. She threw her little body into my arms. I toppled backward. Sprawled on the pavement, I laughed. I didn't care I was lying prone on the side of a busy street amid dozens of gawking passersby with a crying child on top of me. As Abbie clutched me tightly, all that mattered was the knowledge that she loved and needed me, a moment only a mother or grandmother can understand.

Childhood passes much too quickly. To savor it we must create opportunities for togetherness. Daily routines and customs paint vibrant memories. Mealtimes together where stories of the day are shared. Bedtime rituals that calm, comfort, and relax while strengthening the bond of love and trust between parent and child. If you're not already doing so, kneel with your child at their bedside and say nightly prayers together. Read or tell them a bedtime story or read the scriptures. Sing a lullaby. Exchange good-night hugs and kisses.

Daily rituals include notes, quotes, jokes, or cartoons you place in their lunchboxes. Milk and cookies after school. Walks together. Playing games. Making dinner together or making and eating unhurried breakfasts on the weekend.

AUGUST 30

Through the Generations: Daughter, Wife, Mother
Mothers most of all . . . carry the key of our souls in their bosoms.
—Oliver Wendell Holmes[164]

The poem "Three White Dresses" by Linda Gay Perry Nelson tells of the three white dresses in a girl's life: a blessing dress, baptism dress, and temple dress. This week, write a letter to your daughters and granddaughters telling them what the concept of three white dresses means to you and the importance of each. Express what being a mother and grandmother means to you as well as the values you hope to pass down through the generations.

AUGUST 31

Motherhood: Finding Humor
The heart of a mother is a deep abyss at the bottom of which you will always find forgiveness. —Honore de Balzac[165]

When I had three children under the age of six, I felt inadequate. I vented my frustration with impatience. As they grew, chaos and contention reigned. All too often I was edgy and intolerant. Why not, I one day decided, search for the humor in mothering? In situations that made me a little crazy, look for the silver lining?

Sometimes all I needed was a little chuckle to get me by. Sometimes I needed a minute or two of all-out, uncontrollable giggling. Several times my laughter was accompanied by a steady flow of tears. I decided to begin each day by arming myself with a smile. When my young son colored his hair with Elmer's glue and purple food coloring, I told myself (finding the silver lining) that at least it would wash out. Eventually, it did. When he woke his sleeping sister with an air horn, I told myself the discourse between them would help foster their communication skills. When my youngest painted art projects—and the entire kitchen counter beneath them—I chose to see her as a budding Rembrandt. I then reminded her that putting down paper towels will save her the cleanup. I smiled and embraced the fact that she was still learning about tidiness.

Looking at the foibles of childhood and teen years as learning experiences provides a good starting point for finding humor. In your journal, make a habit of recording the wonder of the humorous moments you share with your children. Even if only one sentence or word, a photo or drawing, commit to doing so at least once a week.

Smile!

August Recipes

Blueberry Ice Cream

3 cups mashed fresh blueberries
¾ cup sugar
5 cups milk
2 cups whipping cream

1 can (14 oz.) sweetened condensed milk
1 can (12 oz.) evaporated milk
1 cup sugar
3 Tablespoons vanilla extract

Combine blueberries and ¾ cup sugar in a large bowl. Stir to combine. Add remaining ingredients. Stir well. Pour mixture in 5-quart freezer container. Pack freezer with ice and salt. Freeze according to ice cream freezer manufacturer's instructions. Pack with additional ice and salt. Let stand 1 hour before serving. Yields 1 gallon.

Peanut Butter Crumble Ice Cream Balls with Caramel Sauce

Vanilla bean ice cream
4 cups graham crackers, coarsely crumbed
¼ teaspoon cinnamon

Optional: ½ cup crushed cornflakes
¼ cup honey
¼ cup butter, melted
¾ cup peanut butter

Scoop 24 2-inch diameter balls of vanilla bean ice cream and refreeze until solid. Combine graham cracker crumbs and cinnamon. If desired, add in optional cornflakes. In a small saucepan, combine honey, butter, and peanut butter; stir over low heat until well blended. Pour peanut butter mixture into crumbs, and work to a coarse, crumbly consistency. Spread mixture onto a platter, and cool to room temperature. One by one, quickly roll and coat ice cream balls in the peanut butter/crumb mixture. For a thicker graham cracker coating, press and mold additional crumbs into each ball. Freeze until solid. When ready to serve, drizzle with caramel sauce.

Caramel Sauce

½ cup evaporated milk   ½ cup brown sugar
½ cup butter   1 teaspoon vanilla

Combine all ingredients in a small saucepan, and stir over medium heat until sugar is dissolved. Stirring constantly, bring to a low boil; boil until thickened. Remove from heat, and drizzle warm sauce over ice cream balls.

SEPTEMBER

Harvesting Blessings

Finding and Bringing Bliss into Your Home, Marriage, and Family

SEPTEMBER BRINGS WITH IT THE season of harvest. Seeds planted in faith months ago, nourished by rain and sun, strengthened by hail and heat, finally bear fruit. In growing a garden we learn many life lessons. Often inexplicably, some plants (like my potato vine) thrive under less-than-favorable conditions, while others, in what might seem to be the best growing environment, droop and wither. In raising a family, conditions may be either fertile or rocky. There are no guarantees a happy family will produce successful, well-rounded children. Likewise, there are no assurances that a troubled family will yield children doomed to fail.

The only certainty is that we can choose to thrive. It can be disheartening when what seems so obvious to us isn't discerned by those we love. How can it be that what the Spirit witnesses—verities and principles—aren't plain to them? We must persist in faith so we can nurture, love, and support our family members no matter their choices.

A favorite quote of mine by an unknown author states, "If you feel like giving up, remember why you held on for so long in the first place." Remember that as you become increasingly aware of your own pace and progress in contrast with the journeys of those you love. Hold on and continue on in faith. Whatever the harvest, bless it with your love. Never cease praying for the promises of heaven.

Making the Most of September

* Have family photos taken while the kids' school clothes still look new.

* With school back in session, schedule an afternoon cookie-and-milk, or fruit-and-juice, time together with your children. Use the occasion to talk over their day at school.

* On Labor Day weekend, find a last summer concert or farmer's market to attend.

* Borrow a telescope, and look at the stars. Identify constellations. Celebrate the autumn equinox.

* Designate a section of wall or place in your home where you can display your children's artwork. At dinnertime, let them tell you about their new pieces and why the works were created.

* Have a family leaf-raking day. Don't forget to jump and play in the piles of leaves! Gather some large leaves, and make a family tree collage.

* Trace the hands of family members on construction paper. Cut out the images, and join them together in a wreath or garland.

* Reassess your food storage needs. Practice cooking with food storage items.

* Sort through the closets. Launder summer things, beach towels, summer clothes, swim suits, camping and hiking gear, etc. Place in storage containers for winter. Donate outgrown and surplus clothing for needy kids.

* Come up with a family award system. Nominate family members, and give weekly awards for the person who demonstrates the most kindness, honesty, integrity, helpfulness, etc.

* Pick apples. Make a fresh apple crisp or apple pie.

* Reexamine scripture reading. Are you being spiritually fed? Is your intake enough to nurture you?

* Plan to write or add to your family history.

* For each act of service or good deed done by a family member, have them write a brief description on a paper heart. Tape or string the hearts together. Work at making the chain of hearts as long as possible. Set a goal: a length that will reach around the kitchen, down the hall, or around the house.

* Make or learn to make homemade bread, and enjoy it with the recipes following this section.

SEPTEMBER 1
Common Threads: Love, Joy, and Satisfaction
Joy is a net of love by which you can catch souls. —Mother Teresa[166]

As M. Russell Ballard stated so eloquently in his April 2008 conference address, "Daughters of God," motherhood can be difficult. Between moments of joy and fulfillment come times wrought with feelings of inadequacy, monotony, and frustration.

The same is true of our families as a whole; putting family first can be difficult. In both immediate and extended families, there are hard and frustrating times and shining moments. Moments of wonder and joy, satisfaction, and incredible fulfillment. In slightly less eloquent terms than Elder Ballard, George Bernard Shaw recognized, "When our relatives are at home, we have to think of all their good points or it would be impossible to endure them."[167] Mother and humorist Erma Bombeck observed, "The family. We were a strange little band of characters trudging through life sharing diseases and toothpaste, coveting one another's desserts, hiding shampoo, borrowing money, locking each other out of our rooms, inflicting pain and kissing to heal it in the same instant, loving, laughing, defending, and trying to figure out the common thread that bound us all together."[168]

This month, seek the common thread of love in your family relationships. Journal your thoughts with joy moments, notations of specific instances that highlight the inherent joy of being part of a family.

SEPTEMBER 2
Building a Firm Foundation
The family is the building block of society. It is a nursery, a school, a hospital, a leisure center, a place of refuge and a place of rest. It encompasses the whole of the society. It fashions our beliefs; it is the preparation for the rest of our life. —Margaret Thatcher[169]

A house is built by hands, a home by hearts. A house provides shelter from the elements; a home affords physical comfort as well as spiritual and emotional refuge. A house must be built on a firm foundation; a home requires one as well.

President Thomas S. Monson teaches that parents are responsible for the home they construct; that building must be done in wisdom.[170] Using the tools of patience, unconditional love, persistence, loyalty, forgiveness—and a great sense of humor—mothers need to have a plan for what they want their families to become.

In his First Presidency Message, President Monson lists the hallmarks of a happy home: a pattern of prayer, a library of learning, a legacy of love, and a treasury of testimony. Read President Monson's "Hallmarks of a Happy Home" talk online at LDS.org. Prayerfully ponder how to implement his instruction.

SEPTEMBER 3
Praying Together, Staying Together
America cannot continue to lead the family of nations around the world if we suffer the collapse of the family here at home. —Mitt Romney[171]

In 2001, President Gordon B. Hinckley admonished parents to safeguard their families by praying together. He further asserted that there is no replacement for a family kneeling together in a regular pattern of prayer. He testified that sincere efforts to hold regular family prayer may not yield results that are immediately evident, yet changes, no matter how slight, would be brought to pass, as God rewards those who diligently seek him (Hebrews 11:6).[172]

Our minds are made clearer, our purpose more defined, our efforts more unified, when we pray together. We wouldn't knowingly send our children into extremes of inclement weather without protection. Why would we send them into the world without the protection of prayer?

Follow the counsel of the prophets, and implement or improve the practice of family prayer in your home.

SEPTEMBER 4
Gratitude Defined
Saying thank you is more than good manners. It is good spirituality.
—Alfred Painter[173]

"Gratitude," says Vaughn E. Worthen, PhD, is garnering "significant attention in the emerging field of positive psychology." In his work as a licensed psychologist, he has extensively researched the use of gratitude in promoting well-being. "Gratitude can have a profound effect on perspective, completely determining or altering the way we look at an experience. Gratitude can be defined as a coping response to challenging or difficult circumstances . . . [which] at appropriate times is helpful in treating depression, reducing anxiety, and introducing a more positive focus to troubled relationships. Experiencing and expressing gratitude can help all of us—whatever our situation—lead fuller, richer lives."[174]

The best way to teach gratitude to your children is to model it:

* In family prayer, express sincere gratitude and appreciation for other family members. State specifically why you are grateful for them and their contributions.

* Thank the waiter or waitress who serves your meal. Thank your children's teachers, principals, cafeteria workers, and janitors. Thank those who serve in your community, state, and country by writing thank-you letters or letters to the editor of a local newspaper. Thank Heavenly Father for ward and stake leaders, General Authorities, missionaries, and the prophet for their selfless service to others.

* Share what you have with others. Let your family know that doing so—taking part of your meal to another family or giving selflessly of your time and means—is an expression of gratitude to God for the blessings you have.

* Send thank-you notes; teach family members to do the same. When they express verbal or written thanks, praise them. Buy thank-you notes for them to keep on hand.

SEPTEMBER 5
Family Mission Statement: A Blueprint for Unity
The family is central to the Creator's plan for the eternal destiny of His children. —The Family: A Proclamation to the World

This month, plan a family home evening to discuss and draft a family mission statement: a blueprint for what your family wants to accomplish collectively. Together, read "The Family: A Proclamation to the World." Afterward, give everyone a pencil and a sheet of paper. Brainstorm ideas about what is important to your family. How you want to help, serve, and strengthen one another. What kind of example you want to be. In short, what your family wants to proclaim to the world about their beliefs and ideals and about how to best put them into practice.

Blend the suggestions together, and write a family mission statement. The statement can either be a few sentences in length, several paragraphs, or even an entire page; allow family members to decide. Type the declaration, and give a copy to each family member. Whether taped into a notebook or tucked into a pocket, encourage everyone to keep their family mission statement with them at all times. Urge them to memorize the statement and keep it always in their hearts. Make a larger copy to frame and hang in your home. The text could be superimposed over a family photo or displayed next to family photos. As part of the same or next family home evening, send your family mission statement to extended family members with a note explaining why you have chosen to write one. Challenge them to write one as well.

SEPTEMBER 6
Living, Serving, and Growing Together: Rules of the Road
Unity: a condition of harmony. —Merriam-Webster Dictionary

Discuss and establish rules of the road for your family so you can live together in harmony. Post them in plain sight, and review them often.

Stop: Traffic signs, lights, and signals alert us to danger. Danger can await family members as well. Are there habits that need to be broken, such as criticizing or tearing one another down? Is there a family member who needs loving roadside assistance to correct their course of travel?

Look: Out on the open highway, we must observe driving conditions. Does fog or darkness pose a hazard? Unified families look for ways to be helpful and light the way by serving one another. Does a child need help with a project that is overwhelming? Does a mother need assistance with dinner or with a younger child? Do prayers need to be offered specifically on behalf of a family member?

Listen: On the road, other drivers honk to get our attention—they have something they want to alert us to. Unified families seek ways to understand one another through prayer, positive communication, and patient listening. What are family members trying to express that we need to listen to? What is the Spirit trying to tell us that we need to heed?

Observe and obey the speed limit: While driving, if we go too fast or too slow, there can be consequences. If we put too much pressure on a family member or if we don't provide enough support, there can be consequences as well. If we undermine family members by not being loyal, by not putting their needs at the forefront of our priorities as often as we can, or by not keeping confidences, we can quickly lose touch with them.

Yield: On the road, we must respect other drivers—even if we don't agree with the way they're driving! Becoming angry and contentious only fosters more anger and contention. Family unity requires each member to strive to be a peacemaker and to treat others the way they'd like to be treated. Each member needs to know they are loved and valued.

Observe detours: Roads get flooded. Highways get washed out. Mudslides can stall our travel. Sometimes we need to take a detour. At different times in our lives, one family member may be stronger spiritually and be able to take the initiative to lead in righteousness, by reestablishing patterns of family prayer, scripture study, family home evening, church attendance, and so on.

SEPTEMBER 7
Trust: A Vital Ingredient of Life
We're never so vulnerable than when we trust someone—but paradoxically, if we cannot trust, neither can we find love or joy.
—Walter Anderson[175]

Elder Donald L. Staheli says that listening to our children and respecting their views results in trust and aids in communication. The resulting unity that comes from understanding and agreeing on the expectations of each family member is priceless. Enduring relationships and trust are forged by personal time spent together.[176]

"Taken in the very widest sense, trust," says author and Emmy Award–winning composer Peter Buffett in his book *Life Is What You Make It*, "is the belief that the world is a good place. Not a perfect place, as anyone can see, but a good place—and a place worth the trouble of trying to make better. . . . The belief—the faith—that people are basically good is one of the core values that allows us to feel at home in the world. . . . It has to start with a loving family that then extends outward to a caring and secure community."

Speaking of his own upbringing, Peter says, "The things that allowed me to feel safe and trusting as a kid had nothing to do with money or material advantages. It didn't matter how big our house was; it mattered that there was love in it. . . . The kindnesses that allowed me to trust in people and in the basic goodness of the world could not be measured in dollars; they were paid for, rather, in hugs and ice-cream cones and help with homework. They were kindnesses that every parent and every community should be able to shower on their children."[177]

Bless the lives of your family by believing in their inherent goodness and divine possibility. Accentuate and extol the virtues of family life as you work to build trust.

SEPTEMBER 8
Rise Above: Believing

Remember to look up at the stars and not down to your feet. . . . However difficult life may seem, there is always something you can do and succeed at. It matters that you don't just give up.
—Professor Stephen Hawking[178]

Stephen E. Robinson writes, "Often the reason some people can't fully accept the blessings of the gospel is because the weight of the demand for perfection has driven them to despair. . . . We are very good at telling each other and ourselves how perfect we must be to inherit the kingdom."

Have you ever felt pressure from spoken or unspoken expectations? Coupled with feelings of inadequacy, that pressure can cause despair, discouragement, and frustration. Brother Robinson says, "Too often we forget to tell each other how this perfection is to be gained. . . . You can burn yourself out trying to become perfect on your own."

As you work to enhance your ability to teach and lead by the Spirit, let family members know that for the Atonement to work in their lives they do not need to first become perfect through their own efforts. Help them understand the core of the gospel, the good news of the Atonement, and what it truly means to each of us. "The great secret," Brother Robinson asserts, "is this: Jesus Christ will share His perfection, His sinlessness, His righteousness, His merits with us."[179]

This week, prayerfully study the Atonement, and share your knowledge with your family.

SEPTEMBER 9
Long May It Wave: A Family Flag
We do not act rightly because we have virtue or excellence, but we rather have those because we have acted rightly. —Aristotle[180]

A family coat of arms is traditionally a symbol of a family's characteristics and values. The designs were once used to identify those who fought in battle. Each soldier selected symbols and colors to represent his family or clan. The designs were then passed down from generation to generation.

Research your surname and discover if your lineage has a coat of arms or family crest. The symbol can then be used in numerous ways: on t-shirts for family reunions, as a letterhead, or on a family flag. Your family mission statement can be included with the crest using favorite colors and your surname. If you can't discover a crest or coat of arms for your family surname or don't have the time to undertake the research, create your own. Draw from values and family ideals and characteristics that are important and unique to your immediate family. You could incorporate sports equipment, musical instruments, camping or fishing gear, or a silhouette of your house. Or use elements or colors from the flag of one of your ancestor's native countries.

Before the end of the year, make it a goal to create a family coat of arms or to discover if your lineage contains one. Design a family flag to fly for important family events and holidays.

SEPTEMBER 10

Love: The One-Winged Angel

The most important thing in life is to learn how to give out love, and to let it come in. —Morrie Schwartz[181]

The three-and-a-half-foot-tall garden angel was exquisite. Her delicate features portrayed grace and serenity. I loved it, but it was well over what I could afford. I waited the entire summer, hoping the angel would go on clearance. When it did, I purchased it and placed it next to the front door. A few days later, my grown son came to clean the siding on the house with a high-pressure sprayer. Somehow, the hose became tangled. It caught the poor garden angel. She toppled. One of her wings splintered into dozens of pieces.

Red faced, my son apologized. He quickly turned away from me. He didn't want to finish washing the siding—just get away from what had happened. The strain of his teenage years had once cut a deep division in our relationship. I didn't want anything to come between us again. A distinct thought flashed into my mind: my son is much more important than a resin angel. I rushed off the porch after him. I needed to express what was in my heart.

Later that same year, he surprised me with another angel: a beautiful stone piece with a bird alighting on her hand. I keep it near my desk. The one-winged resin angel I continue to proudly display next to the front door. A reminder that love is more important than anything else.

What reminds you that love is more important than anything else? Display it with pride, and let others know your feelings.

SEPTEMBER 11
All We Hold Dear

Time is passing. Yet, for the United States of America, there will be no forgetting September the 11th. We will remember every rescuer who died in honor. We will remember every family that lives in grief.
—President George W. Bush, November 10, 2001[182]

When the names of the victims of September 11, 2001, began to spill into the media, one name, one face stood out to me: Lauren Grandcolas. A passenger aboard United Airlines flight 93, she was near my age. Like me, she was a writer. She'd just attended her grandmother's funeral. Although my maternal grandmother had passed away four years earlier, her death and funeral were still on my mind. Lauren was also three months pregnant with her first child. My youngest was three years old. In the weeks and months which followed 9/11, those seemingly insignificant similarities between us caused my mind to latch onto the memory of a woman I'd never even known.

Because of Lauren, life took on new dimensions. Each new thing I tried, I wondered if she had ever tried. Each time I held my daughter or spoke to one of my children, I paid closer attention to little things I'd taken for granted like the cadence and tone of their words. Words spoken between me and my husband, a fireman, became more precious. I was acutely aware that one day some string of syllables would be our last, like the words last spoken by Lauren to her husband, Jack.

Today, focus on your family, the aspects you hold dear. What you would miss most if they were suddenly taken from you. Record your thoughts and impressions in your journal. The details of what you write can nourish your gratitude and appreciation on days you might have difficulty recognizing the good characteristics of your family members.

SEPTEMBER 12
A Taste of Home: What Defines Home?

Wherever a true woman comes, home is always around her. The stars may be over her head, the glow-worms in the night-cold grass may be the fire at her feet; but home is where she is; and for a noble woman it

stretches far around her, better than houses ceiled with cedar or painted
with vermilion, shedding its quiet light far for those who else are
homeless. —John Ruskin[183]

What does your home taste like? Italian food: pizzas, pasta, crusty
bread? Mexican dishes: tamales, enchiladas, and piquant salsas? Roast
chicken, mashed potatoes, and tender, flaky rolls? Something sweet,
something savory, served in heartfelt love?

What does your home smell like? Sugar and spice? The scent of
vanilla and almond, lavender and lemon? Just-mown grass, well-loved
sports equipment, slightly damp and needs-a-bath dog? Just-baked
cookies, apple pie with cinnamon, fresh flowers, a favorite soap?

What does your home look like? Favorite collectables from
vacations; photos, old and new; a family tree of faces? Shelves lined
with personal touches: books and antiques, odds and ends, curios and
knickknacks? Bulletin boards lined with events and accomplishments?
Spiritual sensibilities emanating from framed prints of Christ and
temples and heavenly scenes of grandeur? Fishing poles and camp
gear? Clutter that celebrates life!

What does your home sound like? Heavenly choirs, dance beats,
sacred hymns, childhood songs of delight? Voices joined in praise,
voices expressing concern and love? Your husband's deep, rolling
laughter; the joyful sound of children playing; bedtime stories; stories
of Jesus? Vacuuming and the clatter of dishes being washed, the play-
ful clamor of beloved pets, the chatter of dear friends, the constant
company of a busy washer and dryer?

Today, spend some time thinking about what the sensory aspects
of your home are and what you desire them to be.

SEPTEMBER 13
Emotional Security
For by thy words thou shalt be justified, and by thy words thou shalt be
condemned. —Matthew 12:37

It's easy to find fault. We wouldn't steal material possessions from
another, but would we rob them of their good name? Just as surely as

the good name and reputation of those outside the family circle can be stolen or compromised, so can those of family members when we fail to keep confidences, criticize, dwell on shortcomings, and form harsh opinions—and share those opinions with others.

Never judge another until you have walked a mile in their shoes, even though those shoes may have tracked mud across your new carpet. Disrespect brings distrust, contempt, and contention. To walk in another family member's shoes, to understand them and their motivations, we must first have compassion and the guidance of the Spirit. When possible, problems are best addressed directly with the person we're irritated with.

Practice honoring and revering your family.

SEPTEMBER 14
Safety: What Does Home Feel Like?

Happiness is the object and design of our existence; and will be the end thereof, if we pursue the path that leads to it; and this path is virtue, uprightness, faithfulness, holiness, and keeping all the commandments of God. —Joseph Smith[184]

Raising a child in love and righteousness means raising them in an emotionally and physically safe environment. Abuse is not only physical. It is any behavior that is destructive to body, mind, and spirit. As part of his message during the general Relief Society meeting in September 1995, President Gordon B. Hinckley read from "The Family: A Proclamation to the World": "We condemn most strongly abusive behavior in any form. We denounce the physical, sexual, verbal, or emotional abuse of one's spouse or children."

John C. Nelson, MD, who served as a spokesperson for the American Medical Association Alliance's SAVE (Stop America's Violence Everywhere) program, said, "Spouse abuse involves inappropriate acts of one spouse over the other. It may involve coercive acts in which an abuser forces a person to do something that he or she normally would not do, with no particular concern for the victim. Abuse may also include the use of threats, name calling, yelling, and intimidation." He continues, "I believe that there are people, women particularly, who are abuse victims but wouldn't describe themselves as such. . . . It may not necessarily involve being beaten up, but it is still abuse and is outside the bounds the Lord has set for marriage."[185]

If you, your children, or family members are at risk of physical, mental, emotional, or spiritual harm, seek help. The Church pamphlet "Preventing and Responding to Spouse Abuse" is one of many helpful resources. Search "abuse" on LDS.org. Post a copy of "The Family: A Proclamation to the World" in a prominent place in your home.

SEPTEMBER 15
The Heart of Home: Love and Acceptance
Our most basic instinct is not for survival but for family. Most of us would give our own life for the survival of a family member, yet we lead our daily life too often as if we take our family for granted.
—Paul Pearshall[186]

Whether in our place of work, our ward, or our stake, feeling accepted and valued is vital. The same holds true for family. Just because family members live in the same house doesn't mean they always feel like part of the family. Involving everyone not only in daily chores but in planning for the welfare of the family can help draw members into a sense of belonging. Sharing in responsibilities, such as meal planning and deciding on family vacation objectives, is a good start. Earnestly seeking the opinions of family members involves them even more. If a lonely widow lives next door, what ideas do they have for cheering her? If a family member is going through a trial, what are their ideas for helping? When a family member is struggling, they have particular need of feeling accepted and included as an integral part of the family unit. Though rules and discipline must be enforced, love should never be withheld because of poor decisions.

Belonging and feeling needed are important facets of family life. Today, think of ways you can best help your family members feel love and acceptance. Consider how doing something with a family member instead of for them impacts family relationships.

SEPTEMBER 16

Ten Suggestions for Mothers

To us, family means putting your arms around each other and being there. —Barbara Bush[187]

With the example of his own mother and his wife, Flora, in mind, President Ezra Taft Benson offered ten suggestions specifically for mothers:

1. Take time to always be at the crossroads in the lives of your children, whether they be six or sixteen.
2. Take time to be a real friend to your children.
3. Take time to read to your children. Remember what the poet Strickland Gillilan wrote:

    > You may have tangible wealth untold;
    > Caskets of jewels and coffers of gold.
    > Richer than I you can never be—
    > I had a mother who read to me.

4. Take time to pray with your children.
5. Take time to have a meaningful weekly home evening. Make this one of your great family traditions.
6. Take time to be together at meals as often as possible.
7. Take time to read the scriptures daily together as a family.
8. Take time to do things together as a family.
9. Take time to teach your children.
10. Take time to truly love your children. A mother's unqualified love approaches Christlike love.[188]

SEPTEMBER 17

Blessings: Family Home Evening

Family home evening is a tradition of love that strengthens and unites family members.

Elder David A. Bednar has noted that the best family home evenings don't necessarily take place as the result of structured lessons but come about as families learn together with the assistance of the Holy

Ghost. Children can be invited to ask questions; if parents don't have the answers, the family can seek and discover them together.[189]

The family home evening section of LDS.org contains helps: lesson topics, activities, and resources, as well as a family home evening planner where you can plan your evening and print an agenda.

Speaking of family home evening, President James E. Faust expressed that commitment to God developed in such a setting can help families and individuals gain stability and strength.[190]

Whether you are married or divorced, engaged or single, a member of a large family or small one, living at home or alone, commit to incorporating family home evening each week in your schedule.

SEPTEMBER 18
The Importance of Your Family Story
Our family is a circle of strength and love. With every birth and every union the circle grows. Every joy shared adds more love. Every crisis faced together makes the circle stronger. —Author unknown

Promote family unity by compiling your family story. Assign a family historian; family members can take turns assuming the job on a rotating, monthly basis. Use a notebook or loose-leaf binder. Sheet protectors can hold certificates, newspaper clippings, and other mementoes from family life. Place your family crest or coat of arms at the front with a copy of your family mission statement. The entries don't need to be lengthy or sophisticated and could even be done in pictures.

Make additions to your story at least once or month—or weekly in family home evening—by adding news and events. Encourage everyone to submit ideas.

SEPTEMBER 19
Intent: The Way to Start the Day
If you don't like something change it; if you can't change it, change the way you think about it. —Mary Engelbreit[191]

What makes a perfect day? Not a cloud in the sky? No rain drops or storms on the horizon? No contention, no trial, no challenge? Or is the perfect day one where we have ample opportunities to learn? It depends on our perspective. If we dread the day ahead, it will become a source of anxiety. If we look for miracles, they will come.

As a boy, George Albert Smith attended the Brigham Young Academy in Provo, Utah. While there, President Smith later related, the principal of the academy, Karl G. Maeser, one day stood up and said, "Not only will you be held accountable for the things that you do, but you will be held responsible for the very thoughts that you think."

A boy at the time, President Smith was concerned over the meaning of the statement. He wondered what he should do to align himself with what God required of him. After much contemplation, he realized Principal Maeser meant that since our actions are driven by our thoughts, our mortal lives will be the product of the very thoughts we hold in our minds.[192]

Share your ideas with your family about maintaining a positive attitude. Start a bulletin board where quotes on positive thinking can be displayed. Explain that what we expect for the day will have great bearing on how we perceive what happens.

SEPTEMBER 20
Your Best and Brightest: Smile!
A smile is the light in the window of your face that tells people you're at home. —Author unknown

At the stake girls' camp I attended last summer, there was a smile. From the Maple Rise Campground on the east slope of the Wellsville Range, we saw it shining through the night. Somewhere down in Cache Valley, five streetlights formed a semicircle. A smile. Two more lights above—eyes—completed the picture: a happy, smiling face. We oohed and aahed and took turns pointing it out to others. Those down in the valley who lived in the proximity likely had no idea the large fixtures created such a happy scene when viewed from above. The smile made us smile!

Sometimes we reserve our best and brightest smiles for those who are not as close to us as our family members. This week practice giving those close to you your best and brightest smile.

SEPTEMBER 21

Knowing: A Testimony of What Joseph Smith Saw
Yea, they shall know of a surety that these things are true, for from heaven will I declare it unto them. —D&C 5:12

In his October 2002 conference address, President Gordon B. Hinckley bore firm testimony that God and Christ appeared to Joseph Smith. He recounted his interview with reporter Mike Wallace and his response in the affirmative to the question of whether or not he believed what Joseph claimed to have happened indeed did.[193]

It was on this day in 1823 that the angel Moroni appeared to Joseph Smith. Why is it so important for you to study and pray for a sure testimony that this event—and the First Vision—actually happened? Marjorie Pay Hinckley said, "Either Joseph Smith had a vision or he didn't. If he did not, then we are all engaged in a tremendous hoax; but if he did, then it behooves each of us to give all the time, money, effort, and energy that we can muster to promote the kingdom of God."[194]

Don't build from clay what you should forge out of steel. Begin to strive toward your own sure testimony of what Joseph Smith saw and heard. Read President Hinckley's talk, "The Marvelous Foundation of Our Faith," from the October 2002 general conference.

SEPTEMBER 22

Loving the Sabbath: A Day of Joy
Remember the sabbath day, to keep it holy. Six days shalt thou labour and do all thy work: But the seventh day is the sabbath of the Lord thy God: in it thou shalt not do any work, thou, nor thy son, nor thy daughter, thy manservant, nor thy maidservant, nor thy cattle, nor thy stranger that is within thy gates: For in six days the Lord made heaven and earth, the sea, and all that in them is, and rested the seventh day: wherefore the Lord blessed the sabbath day, and hallowed it. —Exodus 20:8–11

How we regard the Sabbath, either as boring or fulfilling, impacts our family's view of the day. Contentment comes from focusing on what can be accomplished rather than what is given up on the Sabbath. On Sunday we have the privilege to learn and grow, touch hearts and lives, and build and strengthen relationships. We should reverence the Sabbath, but with many wonderful possibilities, it never has to be boring!

Ralph Waldo Emerson said, "Enthusiasm is one of the most powerful engines of success. When you do a thing, do it with all your might. Put your whole soul into it. Stamp it with your own personality. Be active, be energetic, be enthusiastic and faithful and you will accomplish your object. Nothing great was ever achieved without enthusiasm."[195]

Anything worth doing is worth doing well—with enthusiasm. When you love what you're doing, passion and energy are the natural byproducts. As you ponder all that is possible on the Sabbath—God's holy day—refine your observance of it and treasure it as a day to be anticipated with joy as you look forward to future blessings.

SEPTEMBER 23
Making a Difference
He that cannot forgive others breaks the bridge over which he must pass himself; for every man had need to be forgiven. —Lord Edward Herbert, 1st Baron Herbert of Cherbury[196]

Have your family conduct a kindness experiment. For three days, speak only kind, supportive words to each member of the family. Look for every opportunity to sincerely compliment and praise one another. Tell each other of your genuine love. No matter anyone's demeanor, continue for the full three days.

Have each member observe the reactions of others in the household at the outset of the experiment and again at the end. They should also observe how they feel. Does being kind draw them closer to the Spirit? Does it take less energy to be kind than to engage in contention? How does the media in the home—TV shows and music—help or hinder kindness?

At the end of three days, give everyone the choice of repeating the experiment. Ask what the pros and cons are. Teach family members that when they are working toward a goal, such as demonstrating kindness more consistently, they are entitled to assistance from the Lord. They can pray for help and guidance. Talk about how things that discourage or demean come from the adversary and only things that are encouraging and uplifting come from the Lord.

SEPTEMBER 24
Choosing to Slow Our Pace: Love and Nurturing Can't Be Rushed
There is no fear in love; but perfect love casteth out fear: because fear hath torment. He that feareth is not made perfect in love.
—1 John 4:18

As a child, I loved Cream of Wheat. Before I served it to my children for the first time, I told them of its wonders: soft, sweet texture, the fact you could slurp it up through a straw. I placed steaming bowls in front of them and watched them dig in, spoon in one hand, straw in the other. Much to my surprise, dismay and confusion distorted their faces.

"What's wrong?" I asked.

"Lumps," they mumbled. "They're kind of hard to . . . chew. And it won't come up the straw!"

At the time, my husband was working two jobs. I worked part-time and felt the strain of raising our three offspring largely on my own. My attempts at relating to my children were often, sadly, like my attempts at making Cream of Wheat—hurried and not very palatable. After the deaths of my grandmothers, I navigated a good deal of soul-searching, which led me to realize both women had left behind something of incalculable value. Their tireless efforts had created a legacy of devotion and caring both inside and outside family circles. What legacy would I leave? My life had been one of trying to prove myself; I hadn't always been patient. I came to discover that taking proper care of a family—and making Cream of Wheat correctly—require loving attention and care.[197]

Fear of not measuring up to the expectations of the world can cause us to enter a cycle of hurry and impatience. Choosing to consciously slow our pace so that we can contemplate the individual needs of our family members can have a lasting impact. Love and nurturing can't be rushed.

SEPTEMBER 25
Marriage for an Eternity
Therefore shall a man leave his father and his mother, and shall cleave unto his wife, and they shall be one flesh. —Abraham 5:18

In his book *Eternal Marriage and the Parable of the Silverware*, Elder F. Burton Howard tells the story of how his wife lovingly cared for the silverware they received as newlyweds. He writes, "For years I thought she was just a little eccentric, and then one day I realized that she had known for a long time something that I was just beginning to understand. If you want something to last forever, you treat it differently. It becomes special because you have made it so, and it grows more beautiful and precious as time goes by. Eternal marriage is just like that.

"Repentance, forgiveness, long-suffering, patience, hope, charity, love, and humility. All of these things are involved in anything that is eternal. We must learn and practice them if we intend to claim an eternal marriage."[198]

Search the topic of marriage on LDS.org and read one of the conference talks. If you're not married, list ways you can prepare for eternal marriage. If you are married, list ways you can enhance your marriage.

SEPTEMBER 26
Eternal Love
God, the best maker of all marriages, combine your hearts in one.
—William Shakespeare[199]

President Henry B. Eyring expresses that both our greatest sorrows and our greatest joys are found in family relationships. Putting the needs of others before our own is what true love is. Selfishness results from a lack of love. Men and women are required to make and keep sacred covenants to ensure the wellbeing and happiness of one another. [200]

He tells of a gravestone of a mother and grandmother on which the inscription reads, "Please, no empty chairs." The woman requested the wording because she knew the reality of the eternal family she desired is dependent upon the choices each family member makes. She asked please because she realized neither she nor Heavenly Father could force anyone to comply with righteous living and to make wise choices based on gospel principles. President Eyring exhorted spouses to pray for the love to see the best in one another, and to care for and nurture one another. [201]

Make a list of your husband's positive attributes. Tell him of your love and how much you value him and your marriage. Send it to him. If you're not married, write a letter to your future husband expressing your love for the kinds of characteristics you anticipate he will have.

SEPTEMBER 27

He's Number One: Loving Your Husband

What counts in making a happy marriage is not so much how compatible you are, but how you deal with incompatibility.
—Leo Nikolaevich Tolstoy[202]

Marriage means work. It also means joy. Let your husband know that even if the kids take up much of your time, he's still number one.

* Attend the temple together.
* Have regular date nights.
* Share your interests with one another; start a hobby together.
* Pray for him and with him.
* Look him in the eyes when you talk to him.
* Respect him.
* Tell him things that make him special to you.
* Compliment him on the qualities and characteristics that endear him to you.
* Bolster his confidence; compliment him in front of his friends.

* Tell him what's on your mind instead of expecting him to guess.
* Send him encouraging notes, texts, or e-mails during the day.
* Greet him at the door.
* Seek his advice.
* Make his favorite meal or treat without him asking.
* Take walks together.
* Be loyal; don't tear him down, especially in front of others.
* Frequently tell him you love him.

What are some other ways you can let your husband or husband-to-be know he's valued and important?

SEPTEMBER 28
Preserve and Protect: The Covenant of Marriage
Love spends his all, and still hath store. —Philip James Bailey[203]

Elder Dallin H. Oaks tells us that the safest way to prevent a divorce from a disloyal or abusive spouse is to not marry such a person. In other words, we need to know well the kind of husband we want to have and make certain we don't settle for less. Casual conversations on the Internet are not enough to discern the true personality of a person. Only observing a potential spouse's actions in a diverse range of conditions can help us discern their true character. Yet, Elder Oaks notes, marriage doesn't require that both parties be perfect. Just that a prospective husband and wife are determined to work together toward perfection.

For those already married, he counsels that repentance, rather than divorce, is the cure for most marital problems. Selfishness must be overcome with a resolution to improve. Divorce often only serves to complicate situations and compound heartache.[204]

Pray and ponder ways to protect the covenant of marriage.

SEPTEMBER 29
Choices: A Healthier You, A Healthier Family
Every herb in the season thereof, and every fruit in the season thereof; all these to be used with prudence and thanksgiving. —D&C 89:11

I was six when I spotted a poster in the school cafeteria. Its bold red lettering got right to the point: "You Are What You Eat!" Below the words, cartoon fruits and vegetables were crowded into the figure of a boy. The child had radishes and brussels sprouts in his toes and feet. Carrots filled one leg, celery another, and tomatoes, apples, and oranges were packed into his torso. With bananas in his arms and string beans and peas in his hands and fingers, he was a sight! His countenance beamed as if to say: Eating fruits and vegetables is cool!

Well into adulthood, if someone were to have made a "You Are What You Eat" poster of me, my countenance would have said, "Eating junk food is cool!" Unfortunately, it would have also been a good poster for the saying, "A minute on the lips, a lifetime on the hips." I decided to make changes in my diet that would change life for the better.

Eating right can impact us and our families in many ways. Eating foods with sound nutritional value increases our health, reduces the risk of illness, and helps manage conditions like diabetes; food can also impact our state of mind. Start with small changes. Add something healthy to each meal; substitute it for something that is packed with calories, salt, or sugar. Each week, add another healthy element. You'll soon be on your way to maintaining a healthy diet for yourself and your family.

SEPTEMBER 30
Compile 72-Hour Kits
Organize yourselves; prepare every needful thing. —D&C 109:8

General conference is coming up. It's a great time to reassess your 72-hour kits. When compiling your family's kits, don't forget menu cards, ID cards, and seasonal items.

A menu card, detailing at what intervals food should be consumed, is vital to ensuring supplies are rationed appropriately. In a disaster, following a prewritten guide will be much more effective than attempting to make decisions midcrisis. Likewise, an ID card can aid those too stressed to remember important details. On a 3X5 card, record names, address, phone number, and emergency numbers, Social Security number, immunization dates, blood type, and medical needs. Photo and fingerprints can also be added to the card, which can be either laminated or enclosed in a Ziploc bag.

Since disasters have no regard for season, plan accordingly. Each spring and fall, reassess your family's kits. For winter, add thermal clothing, warm hats, gloves, and socks. In the spring, add bug spray and replace winter clothing with items intended for more moderate temperatures. For year-round use, include sunscreen, lip balm, hand warmers, and bandanas. Hand warmers not only warm extremities in the winter but also provide comfort for aches and pains. Bandanas can serve as coverings for the head, hot pads, signal flags, washrags, and first-aid helps (tourniquet, sling, or bandage).

With a little forethought, items you may have overlooked adding to your 72-hour kits will pay big dividends in a disaster.

September Recipes

Green Chile Stew

3 lbs. lean hamburger
2 medium yellow onions, chopped
12 green chilies, cleaned and diced (or 3 small cans)
4 peeled tomatoes, fresh or canned, quartered
1 ½ teaspoons salt

2 cloves garlic, minced, or ⅔ teaspoon garlic powder
½ teaspoon cumin
¼ teaspoon oregano
Optional: canned or frozen corn
Flour tortillas
Grated pepper jack or Monterey Jack cheese

Cook burger and onions until burger is brown and crumbled. Add all other ingredients, and simmer slowly for about 1 hour. Spices can be doubled to taste. Serve in bowls; top with tortilla chips, grated cheese, and a dollop of sour cream.

To use for casserole, layer flour tortilla halves or coarsely crushed tortilla chips, stew mixture, and grated cheese. Repeat layers. Bake covered at 350 degrees for 30 minutes or until heated through.

Bezas' Garbanzo Peach Soup
From *Peachy: A Harvest of Fruity Goodness*

1 (15 oz.) can garbanzo beans, rinsed and drained
¼–½ cup milk (depending on desired thickness)
3–4 fresh ripe peaches, peeled and diced

¼ teaspoon cinnamon
1 ½ Tablespoons lemon juice
¼ teaspoon ginger
2 Tablespoons sugar

Blend garbanzo beans and milk until pureed. Add peaches and blend well. While blending, add cinnamon, lemon juice, ginger, and sugar. Blend for two minutes. Chill overnight. Serve in a bowl with a mint sprig in the middle.

Hearty Beef Stew

3–4 lbs. beef stew cubes
2 ½ cups celery, chopped
7 cups mini-carrots, whole
2 medium onions, diced
7–8 peeled, cubed red potatoes
1 package dry Lipton Onion Soup mix
1 large can stewed tomatoes

4 Tablespoons tapioca
½ teaspoon pepper
1 Tablespoon Worcestershire sauce
¼ Tablespoon sugar
2 Tablespoons parsley
6 beef bouillon cubes or equivalent granules

Brown stew cubes. Transfer into large, well-greased roasting pan. Add celery, carrots, onions, and potatoes. Toss together. Sprinkle with soup mix, tapioca, and pepper. Pour stewed tomatoes over top. Add Worcestershire sauce, sugar, parsley, and bouillon. Mix well. Bake at 375 degrees for 3–5 hours, stirring 2–3 times an hour. Add a little water if it looks dry.

Carrot Soup

1 onion, thinly sliced
¼ cup butter
5 cups water
¼–½ cup white or brown rice
2 Tablespoons chicken bouillon

2 ½ cups carrots, sliced
2 small cloves garlic, minced
Half and half
Parsley

In butter, sauté onion until translucent. Add sautéed onion and remaining ingredients to large saucepan, and cook until carrots are soft and rice is done. Puree in blender. If mixture seems thick, or if desired, add a little half and half. Sprinkle with parsley and serve hot.

OCTOBER
Holding Your Head High
Defining Who You Are and What You Stand For

Novelist Nathaniel Hawthorne wrote, "There is no season when such pleasant and sunny spots may be lighted on, and produce so pleasant an effect on the feelings, as now in October."[205]

The month glides in on gander wings. Golden sunsets dip the day into star-encrusted indigo evenings. Punctuated by wood smoke and the laughter of children enraptured by final fair-weather play, a sweet, crisp stillness settles. Autumn colors charm our sense of sight; the artist's heart within us feasts on the palette. With crimson, amethyst, and saffron accents, fall foliage paints landscapes that flow creek side to mountainside.

We slow with the year, savoring everything with care. Our hearts turn to hearth and home. Wife and mother, sister and friend, we spread comfort and cheer as we journey. It is our profession and pride. Within quiet moments of reflection, we turn inside ourselves. In our travels, have we trod the deepest valleys of introspect? Attained our best skill in climbing with faith when mountains present themselves? Have we embraced all our heritage enables and ennobles us to accomplish?

This month, rediscover and redefine who you are and what you stand for.

Making the Most of October

* October is Breast Cancer Awareness Month. Make an appointment for a mammogram. Plan a special day, and go to lunch with your girlfriends.

* General conference is this month. Find special new recipes to try for both Saturday and Sunday.

* Participate in Fire Prevention Week activities in your community. Ensure that your family has an escape plan, including a prearranged place to meet in case of fire.

* Get reacquainted with your Crock-pot. The simmering smells of Crock-pot foods lend a savory home-cooked aroma of comfort to your kitchen.

* Get a jump start on holiday cleaning. Have the carpets cleaned. Clean or replace shower curtains. Wash the insides of windows. If you have a fireplace, stock up on firewood. Make sure the chimney is cleaned. Clean and dust light fixtures. Wash mirrors. Flip mattresses.

* Start the new novel you want to read or write.

* October is Domestic Violence Awareness Month. Learn more about the subject so you can help yourself or someone else if necessary.

* Learn about US presidents who visited Utah. The book *When the White House Comes to Zion* by Mike Winder and Ronald L. Fox tells stories behind events that brought American presidents to the Zion of the West.

* Take a drive to see the fall leaves. Collect a few favorite leaves, and tape them in your journal. Write about favorite autumn memories from childhood.

* Sort your socks. Donate those you no longer wear. Make a basket of your favorites so you can quickly pull them on during chilly days. Buy a new pair that are irresistibly cozy.

* Get out the scarves, hats, mittens, and coats. Get them ready to go by arranging them on a decorative coat rack. Learn to knit or crochet, and make yourself a scarf.

* Refine the art of homemaking. Dust off the good dishes. Experiment with decorative and festive table settings. Make a harvest soup or stew. Trial-run holiday recipes.

* The Salt Lake Tabernacle was first used for the October 1867 general conference. Learn more about the building and its impressive history.

* Visit a corn maze or pumpkin patch, and select pumpkins for decorating, crafting, cooking, and baking. Plan an all-pumpkin dinner. For dessert use one of the recipes following this section.

OCTOBER 1

Getting out of Comfort Zones: Living Up to Our Full Potential
Everyone needs to be valued. Everyone has the potential to give something back. —Princess Diana[206]

"The attic," recalled Laura Ingalls Wilder, "was a lovely place to play. Often the wind howled outside with a cold and lonesome sound. But in the attic Laura and Mary played house with the squashes and the pumpkins, and everything was snug and cozy."[207]

Like the warm familiarity of Laura's attic, we all seek to linger in comfort zones. Beyond them we fear winds of uncertainty and insecurity. Why would we want to venture out?

Laura later wrote, "Laura felt a warmth inside her. It was very small, but it was strong. It was steady, like a tiny light in the dark, and it burned very low but no winds would make it flicker because it would not give up."[208]

Spend time thinking about what your comfort zones are and why you choose to remain in them. Be willing to step outside and scan the horizon for opportunities. Try something new. Say hello to someone you've never before spoken to. Make a new friend. Agree to speak, if asked, in sacrament meeting. Determine to share the gospel. Pray for help and guidance, and step forward into the task with faith.

Even if the light within you burns low, let no winds make it flicker, and do not give up. All things, even staying in our comfort zones, pose the risk of pain and disappointment, so we are the better for having tried. In trying we strengthen our resolve and fortify our courage. As Laura Ingalls Wilder said, "There's no great loss without some small gain."

OCTOBER 2

Justification: Removing Road Blocks from Your Path
Creative experiences can be produced regularly, consistently, almost daily in people's lives. —Stephen R. Covey[209]

I used to do a lot of thinking about my treadmill. I thought about which would be the perfect room for it. It was first in a room I used as an office. The view was wonderful, but I didn't get much running or walking done. Every time I looked over at the computer, I felt guilty for not writing or attending to office work. I had my son move the treadmill to the family room, but there I found too many distractions. I had him move it back upstairs to another room—a room with few distractions. Still I didn't use it. There it sat for weeks until I finally acknowledged I was making excuses. If I wanted to be in better shape, if I wanted the feeling of accomplishment, I would have to pay the price of dedicated time on the treadmill; leave excuses behind and get going.

Dale Carnegie said, "We all have possibilities we don't know about. We can do things we don't even dream about."[210]

What excuses might you be making that keep you from accomplishing what you want to do?

OCTOBER 3
Try, Try, Try Again: Live Up to Your Full Potential
Courage is the price that life exacts for granting peace. —Amelia Earhart[211]

How many times in life do we have dreams that we don't see through to fruition because of fear? Fear of failure, fear others will judge us, fear we'll somehow get hurt—so much fear that we choose not to take any action. Or we settle for lesser dreams. Like painting the bathroom a new color instead of doing something really big—life changing. Adopting a child. Creating a nonprofit foundation. Building the yoga or dance studio we dream of. Strengthening our faith, gospel knowledge, and testimony so we can serve as a missionary.

The bigger the dream, the bigger the disappointment if we fail—right?

Yet as we travel through life, yearning trickles then floods our soul. We come to know that by dreaming big we honor our Father in Heaven, those who have gone before us, and those who are yet to come. And ourselves for the gift of life we've been given.

If we cower in fear of what might happen, if we never attempt anything of significance, at the end of our existence, we will have failed. If we don't try, we can't gain the chance of living up to our full potential.

Try, try, try . . . then do it again.

OCTOBER 4

If You Think You Can, You Can

*As long as habit and routine dictate the pattern of living, new
dimensions of the soul will not emerge.* —Henry Van Dyke[212]

Look unto me in every thought; doubt not, fear not. —D&C 6:36

One of the biggest reasons we shy away from our potential and
our dreams or from standing up for what we believe is summed up
in just four letters: f-e-a-r. Though a tiny word, fear can have big
implications if we don't work to overcome it.

Faith and fear cannot coexist; each day we must take action
to nurture our faith in ourselves as God's daughters. Allowing in
negative outlooks from the media or others—or memories of past
failures—holds us back from being all we are destined to become.
Thoughts power behavior and, ultimately, our circumstances.

If you haven't looked at them in a while, dust off your personal
mission statement; life list; and the hopes, goals, and dreams you
wrote about in April. What can you do today to change your thought
patterns from doubt and disbelief to faith?

OCTOBER 5

Setting Fears Aside

*You gain strength, courage, and confidence by every experience in which
you really stop to look fear in the face.* —Eleanor Roosevelt[213]

How many fears do you have that you don't need? Write them down
on a piece of paper. Explain them in detail, or note rationale for worries that have held you hostage for a long time. As you write, imagine
each fear leaving your body, traveling through your pen or pencil, and
taking up residence on the paper. When you've written down every
unproductive fear you can think of, seal the paper in an envelope.

Stand back and take a deep breath. What does it feel like to have
those fears on paper instead of inside yourself? Faith now has room to
flourish, as do peace of mind, clarity, and serenity. What else would
you like to replace your fears with? Make a second list. Write down
the opposites of the old fears. For example,

* The ability to succeed
* Faith to face disappointment
* Self-assurance in dealing with others
* Self-confidence in expressing beliefs
* Calm and poise when under fire
* Trust that your Heavenly Father and Jesus won't ever let you down
* Reliance on the guidance of the Holy Ghost
* Assurance of the promise of blessings
* Conviction

Put the second list on your mirror, dresser, or desk—a place where you'll see it often. Do you want to keep your old fears? Decide what to do with the sealed envelope.

Said author Marianne Williamson, "Love is what we were born with. Fear is what we learned here."[214]

OCTOBER 6
Just Keep Climbing

Moral excellence comes about as a result of habit. We become just by doing just acts, temperate by doing temperate acts, brave by doing brave acts. —Aristotle[215]

For years I wanted to hike the Emerald Pools trail in Zion National Park. Photos of the area captivated my imagination. When traveling back from St. George, Utah, following a business trip with my husband and youngest daughter, we had a few hours to spare. We decided to make the hike.

We worked our way up the trail until we arrived at a section encrusted with ice. Standing upright was nearly impossible. Other hikers turned back. We pressed on. I felt great . . . until the trail became very steep. Suffering from a fear of heights, I mustered up courage that my husband and daughter, both unafraid of heights, couldn't understand.

I led out. On a ribbon of sand, where I knew my footing was sure, I felt confident. When the way turned rocky, my confidence ebbed. Each step had to be carefully considered. At one point, the trail skirted the edge of a cliff face. Although the section was not long, I panicked. I told my family to go on without me. While I sat on a rock and thought about my next move, my husband poked his head back around the side of the cliff. "Come on. You can do it. I'll help." Scared but determined, I took his hand, focused on my goal, and proceeded to finish the last section of trail.

We don't all climb mountains in the same way. Some are less confident; some are more skilled. Sometimes we just need time to figure things out. Some of us need encouragement and a helping hand. No matter how you climb the mountains in your life, the most important thing is to keep moving toward your highest potential.

OCTOBER 7
Get Up, Stand Tall, Push On
All you need is the plan, the road map, and the courage to press on to your destination. —Attributed to Earl Nightingale

We can certainly "climb" ourselves into exhaustion. We must rest and reenergize, nourish and nurture ourselves, stop to give encouragement to others passing by, and take the time to enjoy the view. But when we perceive we've been enjoying the respite and comfort of a plateau—a place that neither challenges nor inspires us—we need to get up and push on.

Said W. Clement Stone, "Like success, failure is many things to many people. With positive mental attitude, failure is a learning experience, a rung on the ladder, a plateau at which to get your thoughts in order and prepare to try again."[216] Asserting that we cannot settle for being merely ordinary, President Gordon B. Hinckley urged us all to stand a little taller by rising above the ways of the world to become better people.[217]

How's the view from where you are? Could you figure out a way around obstructions in your path if you got up and stood tall? Could merely pleasant landscapes turn to grand vistas if you pushed on?

This week, think of ways you can get up, stand tall, and push on from plateaus in life.

OCTOBER 8
Got Faith?

*Faith—is the Pierless Bridge supporting what we see unto the scene that
we do not.* —Emily Dickinson[218]

On a family zip line tour in Washington State, I encountered trouble.
Twenty feet from safety, my down-filled coat billowed, slowing me
to a stop. Soon the pulley that held me suspended thirty feet in the
air started to propel me backward. Terror coursed through my body
when I realized going in reverse would put me farther away from help.
In a split second, I had to make a choice: faint, scream, . . . or listen!

Listen to the inspiration that flowed into me: the impression to
focus on our tour guide, Pat, who stood on a platform in a tree, and
to pay careful attention to what he told me to do. His eyes locked on
mine. He instructed me to reach up and put my leather-gloved hand
behind the pulley to stop myself. No way did I want to move my
hands! Let go of my harness and reach above myself to grab the zip
cable? *Listen.* The impression was firm and strong. I grasped the cable
and held on for dear life. Pat clipped himself to the line and made
his way toward me. Reaching my position, he pulled us both back to
safety.

The experience taught me about faith: doing all we possibly can
and then—when we reach the end of our rope (or the momentum of
our zip line)—continuing to cling to hope with the firm belief that
help will come.

What have you learned about faith this year? Write about an
instance where your faith pulled you through a difficult situation.
Include the story in your personal history or as part of your ethical will.
Share your experience with someone who is learning about faith.

OCTOBER 9
Seven Things: Happiness!

Happiness often sneaks in through a door you didn't know you left open.
—John Barrymore[219]

What makes you happy? Your Lord and Savior? He who is your Comfort and Guide through both joy and despair? Your family? (How much you depend on one another for little day-to-day things so often taken for granted!) Your favorite dessert? Smiles that make every hardship fade away? Being able to express yourself creatively? Using your talents to bless and help others? Finding rainbows after a storm, be the clouds a real storm or a life trial? Friends who are friends because they value you for you?

In your journal, take a few minutes to write down seven things that make you happy. On each day of each week, when you first wake, remember one of your happy things and let it light your day.

OCTOBER 10
Decide to Be a Better You
Be sure to put your feet in the right place, then stand firm.
—Abraham Lincoln[220]

In his book *Way to Be: 9 Ways to Be Happy and Make Something of Your Life*, President Gordon B. Hinckley issued a call for us to be our best, to rise above mediocrity and speak for that which is right and true.

All of us on the earth are sons and daughters of Heavenly Father, yet no one is exempt from feeling loneliness, despair, sadness, and fear. No one is exempt from trials and challenges. We can, however, consciously elect to be architects of solutions rather than contributors to difficulty and crisis. A better world starts in our communities, neighborhoods, and, at its core, in our homes and hearts.

Dr. Martin Luther King Jr. said, "Our lives begin to end the day we become silent about things that matter."[221] What things matter most to you? Using the power of your voice and influence in love and compassion, what issues would you like to address for the betterment of others? Or for the preservation of heritage and values you hold dear? What kind of world do you dream of? What kind of family life? It all starts with you . . .

OCTOBER 11
Choosing
Stand up to your obstacles and do something about them. You will find
that they haven't half the strength you think they have.
—Norman Vincent Peale[222]

Is There Anyone Left?

Is there anyone left who will fight
For what's good and what's right and what's true?
Who, facing derision,
Makes firm the decision
To wage battle 'til all wrongs are through?

Is there anyone left who will stand
Against lies and tyranny and theft?
On the truth lay firm hold,
And remain ever bold,
Lest those weakened grow lost and bereft?

Is there anyone left with courage
To take action, use voice, words, to speak.
To uplift and to help,
Without thought of one's self,
Without promise of fame that most seek?

Is there anyone left who cares enough
To spend their own precious time to find cure
For the cries of the weak
And the fears of the meek
Anyone whose heart, intentions, are pure?

Is there anyone left who esteems
Humankind above power and wealth?
Money may make the man
But that wasn't the plan
It can't ransom our inner-most self.

Is there anyone left who can grasp
It's our selves that we'll win or we'll lose?
We're all God's creation,
Regardless of station,
We are granted our conscience to choose.

OCTOBER 12
Cultivating Moral Courage

Yea, and are willing to mourn with those that mourn; yea, and comfort those that stand in need of comfort, and to stand as witnesses of God at all times and in all things, and in all places. —Mosiah 18:9

While courage is taking voluntary action to confront danger, moral courage is a unique variety of bravery that compels us to do what is right in order to stand up for a principle. It is actively doing the right thing even if we are ridiculed, inconvenienced, or even punished. It is doing the right thing even if no one else is and even if no one approves.

Jesus Christ is a prime example of moral courage. He continued to teach the gospel even at the peril of His life. Countless others through history have died for the cause of truth and righteousness. The moral courage of a parent may be giving up time or opportunities to provide their children with a stable home environment. For a sports team, moral courage means always demonstrating good sportsmanship. For a driver, it means upholding traffic laws even in the middle of the night when no one else is around.

Contemplate ways moral courage is exhibited.

OCTOBER 13
Moral Courage Is . . .

Stand up for what is right even if you stand alone. —Author unknown

Moral courage is
> Conscientiously carrying out a Church calling.
> Not participating in gossip.

Being respectful to others even if you don't agree with them.

Praising someone else's talents.

Showing compassion and forgiveness.

Always living by, and fully up to, your standards.

Taking responsibility for all your actions; being honest, admitting guilt, accepting blame.

Doing the Lord's will and not your own.

Keeping promises.

Never undermining others.

Speaking kindly to others.

Not complaining when you are faced with difficult circumstances.

Seeing others the way God does, with eternal potential and possibilities.

Stating your beliefs firmly, clearly, and gently.

Working to earn what you want and need.

Not keeping things you find that don't belong to you.

Standing as a witness of God at all times and in all things and in all places.

OCTOBER 14

Maintaining the Conviction to Have Moral Courage

Standing for what is right when it is unpopular is a true test of moral character. —Margaret Chase Smith[222]

Conviction is the confidence that what we believe is indeed right and true. Courage is the bravery that bears up that conviction. When we sacrifice personal comfort, security, or status to stand for what we believe in, when we uphold an ideal despite persecution, we are exhibiting moral courage. In a perfect world, moral courage would always have a counterpart: understanding. Understanding about what we choose to do.

For example, if a parent or spouse has abused you, you may elect not to speak of the mistreatment. You might, however, distance yourself from your abuser. Without having all the facts, those who don't understand may judge your actions as harsh. If a neighbor is found to be involved in immoral behavior, you will likely feel that gossiping about the situation would not be appropriate. Yet other neighbors may deem you worthy of ridicule if you choose to break ties with the person.

Standing up for what you know to be right can be a lonely prospect. If you have acted in love and respect for yourself, your family, or for one who has done wrong, the Lord will not abandon you. President Henry B . Eyring promises that as we reach out to our Father in Heaven He will lift us, giving us courage to face whatever happens.[223]

OCTOBER 15
The Lord's Will
Character is doing the right thing when nobody's looking. —J. C. Watts[224]

A few summers ago on a girl's camp hike, I wanted to be among the first to reach the top of the mountain. After stopping to help several girls and leaders, however, I reached the summit almost dead last. I perceived only my failure.

Back at camp, I volunteered to drive to a local market to pick up needed ice for the coolers. As I drove away, discouragement loomed. It wasn't that I'd given service grudgingly; I loved the people who I stopped to offer food, water, and encouragement to. It was that my high expectations of myself convinced me I should have been able to do both God's will and mine.

Thankfully, the Spirit whispered that I had not failed. Tears brimmed in my eyes. With appreciation of the confidence He placed in me to care for others, my tears increased. I pulled into an intersection to cross the main highway. Mere yards ahead of me, a car turned onto the road I was on. My daughter and granddaughters! After long, hot, dusty days at camp, they were a sight for sore eyes. I watched in awe as my middle granddaughter saw me, leaned back over the seat, and waved enthusiastically. Had I not given the service I did, I would not have been in that intersection at that precise moment to enjoy the excited waves of love. Had I pursued my will and made it to the top of the mountain early, I would have missed the much-needed gift of seeing my family.

We may not know where doing the Lord's will might lead us, but we can be assured He is ever mindful of us.

OCTOBER 16
Christlike Communication
Character is much easier kept than recovered. —Thomas Paine[225]

Whether the circumstances are emotional or physical, there will be times when you must choose to take a stand to protect yourself and what you believe in. Times when just a few words will suffice. Times when you must battle for that which is right, both on your own behalf and on behalf of others. Yet to live life to its fullest you can't go around with boxing gloves on. If you did, how could you use your hands to effectively comfort those in need of encouragement and to uphold what is good and right and true in a Christlike manner? Your hands would become atrophied in their ability to effect positive outcomes. Likewise, if you used your voice to frequently condemn others, your sensibilities become dulled to praising, extending love, and expressing gratitude.

Today think about how you communicate with others, specifically how you relate to those around you when you're under fire. Practice maintaining your emotional and spiritual equilibrium as you strive to protect your personal rights and what you believe in.

The Holy Ghost will guide and help you.

OCTOBER 17
The Messages We Send
Every idle word that men shall speak, they shall give account thereof in the day of judgment. —Matthew 12:36

To communicate with others effectively, we need to understand that we all have differing perceptions. There are words that imply or have totally different meanings to some people than they do others. We need to use care and compassion and think before we speak. Communication is a skill we build and hone throughout our lifetime. There are kinds of communication we should avoid. Words that erode relationships or others' self-esteem, such as slander or gossip, as well as telling lies, speaking out in anger, deliberately guilting or blaming others, or doling out demeaning criticisms should have no part in our communications. Positive, Christlike communication is undertaken in love for the purpose of edifying and helping others. Mark Twain said, "The difference between the almost right word and the right word is really a large matter—'tis the difference between the lightning bug and the lightning."[226]

Treat others the way you'd like to be treated by using your words to convey love, devotion, support, encouragement, value, regard, admiration, and dignity.

OCTOBER 18

Spiritual Nutrients: Life-Sustaining Nourishment
Whosoever drinketh of the water that I shall give him shall never thirst;
but the water that I shall give him shall be in him a well of water
springing up into everlasting life. —John 4:14

Nutrients are things we need in order to live and grow. They build and repair tissue and regulate body processes. They are used as energy and promote increased awareness and intuition as well as general well-being. Spiritual nutrients are no less essential to us. President James E. Faust taught that the most crucial spiritual nutrient we need is a sure testimony of God; of His son, Jesus Christ; and of the Holy Ghost. He noted that the scriptures, selfless service, and faith are also spiritual nutrients.[227] Can you think of others? How about honesty, integrity, modesty, charity, sincerity, generosity, unity, and purity?

President Faust asserted that our human spirit needs to know about its eternal journey—where it came from, why it's here, and its ultimate destination. Avoiding anything that would damage spiritual nutrients keeps us spiritually healthy and moving forward toward our eternal goals.[228]

This week bless yourself and your family by avoiding spiritual pollution and increasing your intake of life-sustaining and lifesaving spiritual nutrients.

OCTOBER 19

Pride and Passion: Modesty Counts

The great charm of all power is modesty. —Louisa May Alcott[229]

Modesty is more than what we wear. Modesty is purity in thought and action.

The choice to be modest influences our thoughts, impacts our behavior, and molds our character. We don't have to resort to extremes of fashion; use harsh, abrasive, or crude language; or behave in outlandish ways to draw attention to ourselves. Being modest means we don't have to reveal skin to stake our place in the world. Our demeanor reveals who we are. We have an understated reserve; a calm, classy, celestial conduct; an aura of the divine. Not a weakness in manner but an unpretentious deportment that shows we know who we are. Confidence in our power to effect change in others' hearts and lives through our examples. Being modest means we know we come from an incomparable royal lineage. We know that one day we're going back to our heavenly home to claim our inheritance in the kingdom!

Modesty. Let it be your pride and passion.

OCTOBER 20

The Armor of God: Protection

Wherefore take unto you the whole armour of God, that ye may be able to withstand in the evil day, and having done all, to stand. Stand therefore, having your loins girt about with truth, and having on the breastplate of righteousness; And your feet shod with the preparation of the gospel of peace; Above all, taking the shield of faith, wherewith ye shall be able to quench all the fiery darts of the wicked. And take the helmet of salvation, and the sword of the Spirit, which is the word of God. —Ephesians 6:13–17

Elder Robert D. Hales tells us that the helmet of salvation spoken of in the scriptures serves to protect our reasoning, intellect, and thoughts. The breastplate of righteousness assists us in having the

Spirit with us at all times to guard our heart and soul. With our loins girt about with truth we can possess a sure foundation on which to build faith and develop our testimony. The sword of the Spirit is the word of God which will pierce the darkness so that we perceive light and truth to guide our journey through life. The shield of faith allows us to protect ourselves from the fiery darts of the adversary. Having our feet shod with the preparation of the gospel of peace, by reading and studying the scriptures, we will glean assistance so we can obey the laws, ordinances, commandments, and covenants of God.[230]

Are there unprotected places in your armor? Work to strengthen or recommit yourself to serving God and keeping his commandments. Defend yourself with the shield of faith. Be determined to help make shields of faith for all members of your family.

OCTOBER 21
Force of Habit
We are what we repeatedly do. Excellence then, is not an act, but a habit.
—Aristotle

If any of you lack wisdom, let him ask of God, that giveth to all men liberally, and upbraideth not; and it shall be given him. But let him ask in faith, nothing wavering. For he that wavereth is like a wave of the sea driven with the wind and tossed. —James 1:5–6

When we become accustomed to the ways and opinions of humanity, in-depth study of the gospel can seem awkward or unnecessary. Something only for scholars. But just as you become acquainted with the characters of your favorite television show by continued viewing, the people, places, and lessons in the scriptures will become clearer with continued study.

Prayerfully study Elder David A. Bednar's talk "Learning to Love Learning" on LDS.org. Enter the name of the talk in the search field on the main page of the website. As you make it a habit to immerse yourself in learning about the gospel, you will come to feel more and more at home in the culture of things spiritual.

OCTOBER 22

State of Heart: Good Things

When the heart is enlivened again, it feels like the sun coming out after a week of rainy days. There is hope in the heart that chases the clouds away. Hope is a higher heart frequency and as you begin to reconnect with your heart, hope is waiting to show you new possibilities and arrest the downward spiral of grief and loneliness. It becomes a matter of how soon you want the sun to shine. —Sara Paddison[231]

Back in January, I told you about a whale who seemed to express gratitude to her rescuers. In February, we talked about how a grateful heart continues to seek hope. In July, we discussed healing our hearts from hurt or offense: processing sorrow and anger through writing or talking. We need to be quick to acknowledge and express delight and joy. Letting go of pent-up negative emotions allows us to enjoy an increase in both emotional and physical energy. Seek for and find the peace the Atonement can bring. Express emotions in constructive ways. Serve others, and forgive ourselves and those who have wronged us.

How does October find your state of heart? Are you consistently seeking the good in life? The odds of being victorious may at times seem overwhelming, but as President Thomas S. Monson reminds us, David did triumph over Goliath!

Renew your energy and enthusiasm by re-centering your efforts to become the woman you are destined to be. Find ten things that have helped you grow stronger this year in one way or another. Write them in your journal. Celebrate your victories over your Goliaths, and let the sun shine bright.

OCTOBER 23

What's in a Word: Quotable Quotes

Quotations when engraved upon the memory give you good thoughts. They also make you anxious to read the authors and look for more.
—Winston Churchill[232]

In years past, as a contributing columnist for a local newspaper, I sometimes wrote about my belief that each day has something to teach us and can be our best day if we so choose. Sometimes that raised eyebrows. Some days, a few folks contended, are just plain bad. Life is tough. Difficult. Distressing. Rotten. Granted. But I still maintain we can choose to see the best even in the worst. Those who have borne enormous trials and heartaches have been among my greatest teachers—and those I love to quote most.

Encapsulated sentiments, important life lessons, uplifting viewpoints, testimonies—quotations give us a shimmer of thought that can brighten the mood and lighten the load on so-called bad days. Cute quotes. Humorous quotes. Family quotes. Spiritual quotes. Motivational quotes. Quotes for all reasons and seasons. Quotes that fit our mood or describe our brood. Quotes that inspire us to aspire or perspire. Collecting quotes is both a pleasurable pursuit and an educational endeavor. If you haven't already, begin to compile quotable quotes by people you admire. When you have amassed enough for a booklet, print it out and give it as a gift to those you love.

Quoting Ralph Waldo Emerson: "By necessity, by proclivity, and by delight, we all quote."[233]

OCTOBER 24

P.S. I Love You: Expressing Yourself

Learn to express rather than impress. —Attributed to Jim Rohn

It's easy to get so busy we forget the importance of little things that really are big things. Things like saying I love you. Elder H. Burke Peterson once said that a common, everyday tragedy is the abundance of those around us who are not getting the love they need. Countless thousands, he claimed, would give anything to have such. Your family and friends need you—they need to know they are valued and loved. Seemingly simple things can make a dramatic impact. Expressions of love include:

* Uninterrupted time together

* Expressing gratitude
* A gentle touch or holding hands; rocking a child
* Listening and talking without judgment; speaking softly
* Apologizing
* Looking someone in the eyes when they talk to you
* Praying together
* Showing respect
* Giving your time
* Being on time; simply being there for someone
* Sharing a fond memory
* Showing interest in something that's important to another
* Being kind and patient
* Teaching a concept
* Comforting a fear

In whatever you do, don't forget to add an abundance of love.

OCTOBER 25
A Heart-to-Heart Book: Finery and Fine Points
Share the gift of you.

The word *finery* is commonly used to denote our best clothing or jewelry. In my mind it can also apply to life: our best of anything. The fine points of life are the details, particulars we can't afford to overlook or let slip by. For instance, we might spend the entire day planning and preparing a meal. We might put an hour into shopping and as much into cooking. After it's done, tasting what we've made is a fine point we should savor. Likewise, we can buy our children lots of stuff, but we miss the fine points of our gift of time with them if we don't get to know them—or let them get to know us.

Compile some of your life finery: the best of you that you'd like to pass down. Tips, secrets to having a happy home or keeping the windows clean, special memories, recipes, photos, quotes, awards or recognitions you've received, stories you love, stories about you, stories and poems you've written, etc. Make a scrapbook about you:

a heart-to-heart book. Among the memorabilia, add your impressions and memories of life's fine points. Details that make life worth living. Details that enhance happiness and joy. Details that shouldn't be missed by life travelers. Details that thrill the senses and provide uplift, inspiration, and encouragement.

Share your heart-to-heart book with your children or grandchildren.

OCTOBER 26
Badge or Burden: Triumph over Trials
Pray for powers equal to your tasks! Then the doing of your work shall be no miracle. But you shall be a miracle. Every day you shall wonder at yourself, at the richness of life which has come to you by the grace of God. —Phillips Brooks[234]

On August 16, 2008, Stephanie Nielson was burned on over 80 percent of her body in an airplane crash. For three months she lay in a medically induced coma. When she awoke, she worried what her children would think of her. She realized they could perceive her mother heart. Though her exterior appearance wasn't the same, the love she possessed had grown.

We may suffer exterior scarring—disfigurement due to burns or other accidents or other changes in our appearance because of illness, disease, and age. We may suffer interior injury—hurts others cannot see. No matter the cause and effect, we can choose to wear our trials as either badge or burden. By the virtue of our determination to survive and thrive, we can bless, uplift, inspire, and motivate as friend, mentor, teacher, conqueror, and champion of life's inherent sweetness.

Our spiritual beauty never has to become marred by physical or emotional circumstances. As Stephanie noted following her accident, our true beauty—our spirit—is a gift from God which can never be taken from us. Determine to triumph over trials. Embrace and celebrate your spiritual beauty. Find ways to lead out as an example and light to other women who are navigating the rocky slopes you have already traversed.

OCTOBER 27
Knowing: Preparation and Priorities
The most important things in life aren't things.
—Anthony J. D'Angelo[235]

On Friday, August 15, 2008, the day before Stephanie Nielson's plane crash, my family survived perilous circumstances. A wrong turn took us from the safety of well-traveled road into dangerous terrain where there was no turning back. The event compelled me to take a closer look at who I was and where I was going. Wrong turns, I learned firsthand, could present life-altering implications. There had been signs that trouble was around the corner, places we could have turned back had we been paying closer attention. In the aftermath, I wondered what signs there were in my life that hinted of other possible wrong turns. Were my priorities in order? What did I need to do to make certain I was on the right path, accomplishing what was truly necessary to fulfill my earthly mission?

Speaking of the sudden, unexpected death of his wife Dantzel, Russell M. Nelson advised there is an important lesson for us all: now is the time to prepare to meet God.[236] Are you prepared to do so? Are there hints in your life that you may be headed in the wrong direction? Are there priorities you to need to realign? Begin to make any necessary changes.

OCTOBER 28
Living and Dying Well
Ordinary people seem not to realize that those who really apply themselves in the right way to philosophy are directly and of their own accord preparing themselves for dying and death. —Socrates[238]

Planning for your death can seem morbid unless you've witnessed the confusion and heartache that can occur when someone passes away without having left instructions or clues as to their last wishes.

New York Times health columnist Jane Brody says, "There is no cure for mortality. The better and the further in advance you plan for that end, the less traumatic it's likely to be, not just for you but for those you leave behind."[237]

Following are five basic tips that can help you create a plan:

* Ensure that your will and trust are up-to-date. Draft a letter of last instructions or an advance directive to spell out your desires.

* Make sure beneficiary designations are current for life insurance, annuities, pensions, retirement plans, Social Security, etc. Who has power of attorney? Who is the executor of your estate?

* Prepare a list of assets, and note where legal documents can be located, such as deeds, titles, and insurance policies. Designate where you will leave the key to your safety deposit box.

* Plan funeral arrangements. You can make advanced arrangements for a memorial service, such as prayers, music, and poems. Decide on the mortuary and provide specific instructions. Which cemetery do you wish to be buried in? Do you already have a plot? Do you have the temple clothes you want to be buried in? Do you want anything specific to be buried with you?

* Write letters to loved ones expressing your love and appreciation for them and your time together.

OCTOBER 29
The Miracle of Genealogy
Other things may change us, but we start and end with the family.
—Anthony Brandt[239]

Troutdale, Oregon. The name of the city was stamped on every letter my grandmother received from her sister, Veda. Decades later, when I saw the city sign outside Portland, a flicker long burning in my heart turned to flame. There was something in Troutdale for me to find, the Spirit confirmed. Not just yet, however; traveling west, we were due out on the coast.

After a week, we got ready to return home. I looked down at my feet. On the grass was a dime. I picked it up and put it into my pocket.

Hours later, again approaching Troutdale, my heart pounded. At a gas station, I looked in the phone book at a pay-phone booth. I located a number, but my cell phone was in our truck. I glanced across the parking lot to where my family eyed me with impatience. Going back for the cell would mean a chorus of complaints. As I inserted the coins to make a call, the operator told me I needed additional funds—ten cents. I inserted the dime from my pocket! No one answered, so I left a message giving my cell number and hung up. Not five minutes later, a call came. An excited woman told me she was who I was looking for—a cousin I never knew I had.

As we visited with her that evening, she brought out a list of names from an old family Bible. Tears in her eyes, she told me she knew one day someone would come for them.

When you enlist yourself in the work of researching your family history, miracles will unfold.

OCTOBER 30

Life Lessons: Compassion, Empathy, and Gratitude
A house needs a grandma in it. —Louisa May Alcott[240]

My Grandma Minnie passed away when my children were little. My Grandma Esther lived over two hundred miles away. But our next-door angel-in-disguise was named Phyllis Valentine. In the fifteen years we were privileged to know her, Phyllis taught my children about selfless service, compassion, empathy, gratitude, and unconditional love—priceless life lessons my children continue to practice. We've been blessed with other angels as well: Agnes, Hazel, June, Marvel, Leila, Erma, Etta, and our beloved Delone—all strong, valiant women who enriched our lives immeasurably with their insight, wit, and wisdom.

Some families are blessed to have grandparents living nearby. The benefits of time spent one-on-one with them are priceless. For those who don't, nothing beats an adopted grandma. A ward sister or neighbor with a lawn to mow, leaves to rake, and walks to shovel. Someone to make cards for and to hear stories from. A good old-fashioned, new-fangled, or young-at-heart woman for your family to love and be loved by.

Is there a grandma waiting to be adopted near you?

OCTOBER 31
Standing Up for What You Believe
Better keep yourself clean and bright; you are the window through which you must see the world. —George Bernard Shaw[241]

Know who you are; hone your confidence as a daughter of God.

Believe in yourself. Believe you can make a difference.

Know what you believe so you can express it.

Live by your to-live-by list.

Finish what you start; know your priorities.

Respect yourself and others.

Be an example of what you believe in. Be the change you want to see.

Make courageous decisions.

Never compromise your values.

Overcome procrastination.

Pray for wisdom and guidance.

Choose the right.

Avoid making excuses.

Be honest.

Value a clear conscience.

State your views clearly but gently.

Keep commitments.

Embrace opportunity. Love learning.

October Recipes

Harvest Pumpkin Spice Cake with Orange Cream Cheese Frosting

1 yellow cake mix	1 cup skim milk
1 teaspoon cinnamon	4 egg whites
½ teaspoon nutmeg	1 ¼ cups solid pack canned
½ teaspoon ginger	pumpkin
⅛ teaspoon cloves	1 teaspoon vanilla extract
⅛ teaspoon cardamom	1 teaspoon lemon extract
¼ teaspoon soda	

Lightly coat a Bundt pan with cooking spray. Set aside. Preheat oven to 350 degrees. Whisk the dry cake mix, spices, and soda in a large bowl until well combined. In a smaller bowl, whisk milk, egg whites, pumpkin, and vanilla. Add liquid to dry ingredients, and beat with a mixer on medium for 3–4 minutes.

Pour batter into pan, and smooth on top. Bake at 350 degrees for 30–35 minutes or until done. Remove and cool for 15 minutes. Invert on rack. Top with cream cheese frosting.

Orange Cream Cheese Frosting

1 (16 oz.) package confectioners' sugar
1 small (4 oz.) package low-fat cream cheese, softened
2 Tablespoons fat-free sour cream or Greek yogurt
1–2 Tablespoons orange juice
½ teaspoon orange extract
½ teaspoon vanilla extract
Orange food coloring, to desired hue

Mix all ingredients until well blended. Add 1–2 Tablespoons additional orange juice for drizzle frosting.

Lee's Southern Pumpkin Pie

4 ½ cups (2 lbs.) firmly packed dark brown sugar
1 teaspoon cinnamon
1 teaspoon allspice
1 teaspoon nutmeg
½ teaspoon salt
3 Tablespoons all-purpose flour
1 (29 oz.) large can solid pack pumpkin
1 teaspoon vanilla
6 eggs
2 cups granulated sugar
1 cup dark corn syrup
½ cup butter, melted
1 (12 oz.) can evaporated milk

Mix together brown sugar, cinnamon, allspice, nutmeg, salt, and flour. In a separate bowl, mix pumpkin, vanilla, eggs, sugar, corn syrup, butter, and evaporated milk. Blend the dry ingredients in the pumpkin mixture until smooth. Fills four 9-inch pie shells. Bake at 350 degrees for 1–1 ¼ hours or until centers are set and knife comes out clean.

Virginia Parker's Pumpkin Cake Roll

¾ cup flour
1 teaspoon baking powder
2 teaspoons cinnamon
1 teaspoon ginger
½ teaspoon nutmeg
1 teaspoon salt
3 eggs
1 cup white sugar
⅔ cup solid pack pumpkin
1 teaspoon lemon juice

Combine the dry ingredients and set aside. Beat eggs for five minutes, gradually adding sugar. Stir in the pumpkin and lemon juice. Fold dry mixture into the pumpkin mixture. Spread into lightly greased and floured cookie sheet (15x10x1). Bake at 375 degrees for 15 minutes. Turn onto a towel sprinkled with powdered sugar. Start at the narrow end of the towel, and roll the towel and cake together. Cool before carefully unrolling.

Filling

1 cup powdered sugar	4 Tablespoons butter
2 (3 oz.) packages cream cheese	½ teaspoon vanilla extract

Combine ingredients and beat until smooth. Spread on the cake roll. Roll up the pumpkin roll, and chill in aluminum foil.

NOVEMBER
Gratitude for the Joys of the Journey
Giving Back, Giving Thanks

BAKING AND COOKING. CARING AND sharing. This time of year with the holidays on their way, we return to hearty meals and ample togetherness. Simple joys often taken for granted are treasured and cherished. Time weaves itself into memories that will later evoke fond remembrances and smiles. With evening comes the quiet or din of home. Some family members settle down for study or rest. Others are just coming in the door. After dinner, we warm our hands in suds-filled sinks. Doing dishes is time for chatter and enjoyment. The expectations of the world are left at the threshold of our home. We kick off our shoes and don comfort clothes. Laughing and loving, we take pleasure in the gifts of family and friends.

November is a time for counting blessings. There are so many aspects of our journey deserving the expression of thankfulness. This month, celebrate and live in gratitude.

Making the Most of November

* Shop thrift stores to find new-to-you decor. Hunt for attractive serving dishes and glassware for Thanksgiving. Find dishware for yourself as well as for others; you can give baking dishes filled with flavor-packed casseroles or large bowls brimming with savory soups or stews to someone to keep and not have to worry about getting them back.

* Clean your pantry. Involve the kids, and make donations to your community food bank.

* Volunteer to serve Thanksgiving dinner at a homeless shelter or rescue mission.

* Make wreaths now. Start your Christmas cards early, a few at a time.

* Make pinecone turkeys.

* Go ice skating.

* Donate blood.

* Deep clean for the holidays. Clean and organize one or two rooms each week.

* Clean out the refrigerator. Keep disposable containers on hand for stashing leftovers or sending food home with relatives or friends.

* Clean the oven. Sharpen your kitchen knives.

* Compile a list of things to do, including household chores, for when the kids need an activity to occupy them. Make use of friends and family members who may be staying with you. Have them teach knitting, embroidery, crafts, and other skills to younger children and teens.

* Have the kids make a game of finding acronyms for the word *home*: Helping Others Make Effort, Hand Over Mouth Exercise, Heaven-Oriented Meaningful Education, Hands Of Mercy Everywhere, Hope Opportunities Memories Excellence, etc.

✳ Create a profile on Mormon.org. Tell how your faith impacts your life. To register, you'll need your membership record number, which can be obtained through your ward clerk.

✳ Search for ways to go the extra mile; teach those things to your children. Consider helping a military family for the holidays.

✳ Set a goal for reading the Book of Mormon in a set amount of time.

✳ Take a walk and listen for the crunch of your boots in the snow or in the remnants of dried fall leaves.

✳ Sip hot chocolate. Let the creamy goodness fill and warm you.

✳ Try out new appetizers for the holidays.

NOVEMBER 1

The Lord's Tender Mercies

Withhold not thou thy tender mercies from me, O Lord: let thy lovingkindness and thy truth continually preserve me. —Psalm 40:11

Elder David A. Bednar instructs that faithfulness and obedience enable us to receive the Lord's tender mercies, important gifts which His timing helps us to recognize.[242] Each day this month, write down a favorite joy you've experienced this year or a tender mercy you've received. Draw from your Mindful of Me Journal or from sacred and otherwise special events imprinted in your memory. At the end of the month, fold the list and tie it with a bow to give to yourself at the close of the year. Here are some suggestions to get you started:

The joy of small, simple moments. Laughter, hugs, smiles.

A prompting that resulted in spiritual, emotional, or physical safety.

An unexpected call from a long-lost friend or relative.

Finding your purpose in life; being able to realize a lifelong dream.

Financial stability.

Progress made on genealogy.

Guidance in solving a particular problem; strength when you thought you had none.

Gaining the knowledge that happiness is a choice. Consciously choosing it.

Praying and receiving God's counsel and guidance; forging a relationship with Him.

Finding harmony and balance; learning to enjoy peace and serenity.

NOVEMBER 2

A Basketful of Blessings

For each new morning with its light,
For rest and shelter of the night,
For health and food, for love and friends,
For everything Thy goodness sends.
—Ralph Waldo Emerson[243]

In April 2007, Sister Bonnie D. Parkin noted that gratitude is a Spirit-filled principle. Gratitude indeed illuminates the fact that we are surrounded by God's miracles. Living in gratitude, we develop a keen sense of the extraordinary in the ordinary. Sister Parkin also pointed out that consciously being appreciative raises our sensitivity to divine direction as we relate to others and to the Lord, expressing our faith through gratitude.

To illustrate her point, Sister Parkin told of a family experiencing a difficult time. They turned to Father in Heaven and realized that goodness was abundant. They expressed daily thanks to one another and to the Lord. A friend noted their "blessing basket" overflowed. Expressing gratitude became habit, and soon, before nightly family prayers, the family shared in the regular custom of discussing all the blessings that had been added to their "basket."[244]

Wonders, miracles, and acts of kindness can be found in each moment of our lives. Recognize your blessing basket. Acknowledge blessings to yourself, to Heavenly Father, and to your family. Throughout the month, you may want to ask friends and family members to write down their blessings on slips of paper which can be added to a real basket. Read the blessings aloud on Thanksgiving, or compile them in your family's history or scrapbook.

NOVEMBER 3

Putting God First: Who We Serve Determines How We Live
Thou shalt thank the Lord thy God in all things. —D&C 59:7

In Exodus 20:3, we're instructed, "Thou shalt have no other gods before me." Do "all things with an eye single to the glory of God," states Doctrine and Covenants 82:19. When we put God first before all else, loving and serving Him with all our heart, might, mind, and strength, everything in our lives falls into place. Our sincere devotion to Him dictates that all we do and say is undertaken to the best of our ability according to His will, in His holy name, and to His honor. Choosing between our Father in Heaven and others is sometimes difficult. We want to please friends and family; it's only natural to want to fit in and feel we are of value in the mortal world. Yet true and lasting peace and happiness come only through faithful discipleship.

If we consistently put God first in our lives, when others disappoint or hurt us we will be able to follow the Lord's perfect example of love.

Give thanks for being a daughter of God. Write a few lines in your journal about what you have learned about Him this year and how your love of Him has impacted your life.

NOVEMBER 4
His Hand in All Things
Gratitude is a quality similar to electricity: it must be produced and discharged and used up in order to exist at all. —William Faulkner[245]

President Henry B. Eyring promises us that we can experience the gift of the Holy Ghost each day.[246] We can pray with thanks; count our blessings and listen for the Spirit. When we implement faith, the Holy Ghost will help us to see how abundantly we have been blessed. In giving humble thanks for our many blessings, remembrance and gratitude will fill us.

As we express gratitude for blessings we enjoy, blessings of home and family, health and happiness, trials that build character and strength, possessions, and circumstances that enhance our existence, we need to remember to give thanks to Heavenly Father for His presence in our lives. We need to acknowledge His hand in all things. Give thanks for the gift of His Son. For the Holy Ghost. For the gospel and the Church. For devoted and caring leaders that watch over us. For scriptures that help us learn truths. For commandments to guide us. Thanks too for His belief in our abilities, our chance to serve others and fulfill our callings.

What else can you thank Heavenly Father for?

NOVEMBER 5
Examples of Gratitude: Stories
Gratitude is the fairest blossom which springs from the soul.
—Henry Ward Beecher[247]

There are verbal expressions of thanks. Written expressions in cards, notes, and letters. What other examples of gratitude have touched your life? Did your parents or grandparents always give thanks for each meal? Did your grandmothers, like mine, wait patiently for your grandfathers to come to the table before anyone ate as an act of grateful respect? What have you learned from how friends and relatives have conducted themselves? Their reactions to others. Their reaction to sorrow, trial, or calamity that showed gratitude? Courtesy, kindness, dignity. Reverence for things sacred. Appreciation and regard for others. Compassion. Concern. Selfless giving. Care of themselves, their home, their families.

Write a short essay about the example of gratitude and how it impacts those who witness it. Include the essay in your ethical will. The example can come from the life of a loved one or from your own life. If you still have living grandparents, ask them to write a story from their lives about gratitude. Include the narratives in your family history, or with the grandparents' permission, provide copies of it for other family members.

NOVEMBER 6
The Best Gift You Have to Offer: You
Give what you have. To someone, it may be better than you dare think.
—Henry Wadsworth Longfellow[248]

Heavenly Father and our Savior Jesus Christ refer to us with love as theirs. Daughters and sisters, we belong to their divine family. As part of that family, we can learn in the scriptures how vital our roles are. In the Doctrine and Covenants, we learn that prior to their westward journey the Saints at Winter Quarters were admonished to keep pledges with one another, cease to contend one with another, cease to speak evil of one another, and let their words edify one another. The same holds true for us. We are also to

Pray for one another.

Bear one another's burdens.

Love one another.

Encourage one another.
Forgive one another.
Serve one another.
Teach one another.
Fellowship one another.

Whether we are feeding our family, doing the laundry, mediating a quarrel, visiting teaching, taking a meal to someone, giving up our space on a packed elevator to someone else, yielding without anger to a careless driver, offering words of encouragement or a smile, we are entrusted with the love and care of God's precious children. We were made to last for an eternity. Our associations with others will last that long as well. What marvelous gifts of time and genuine concern we have at our disposal to offer. Whether in brief minutes or long hours, give thanks this day and all days for the best gift: you.

NOVEMBER 7

Gratitude for the Gift of Spiritual Strength in Every Season

The Lord shall open unto thee his good treasure, the heaven to give the rain unto thy land in his season, and to bless all the work of thine hand.
—Deuteronomy 28:12

In the moving epilogue of her book *Lighten Up!*, Sister Cheiko Okazaki tells the story of the death of her husband, Ed. She describes the time, which was coupled with other family tragedies, as a season of sorrow. Yet she expresses abundant gratitude for the love and care she received from Heavenly Father. She could have spent her time mourning the loss of her husband. She chose instead to experience the strength of the love of Christ by serving, showing gratitude, and loving God.

Sister Okazaki writes that there are thirty-two times the scriptures refer to seasons. It was her conviction that Heavenly Father knows the seasons of our lives.

Spiritual strength is gained by faith and determination and is honed by prayer, study, fasting, church and temple attendance, service, and abundant expressions of gratitude. As the holidays approach, reflect on the current season of your life. Whether yours is currently a season of sorrow or of service, of learning or of reflection, recommit to fulfilling your responsibilities and take action that will continue to allow you to progress toward your divine potential.

NOVEMBER 8
The Gift of Choice
It is your own conviction that compels you; that is, choice compels choice.
—Epictetus[249]

Prior to our youngest daughter turning twelve, she looked forward to doing baptisms for the dead. She was prepared. As soon as she had her birthday, she seized the opportunity to visit with our bishop. He granted her a recommend and commended her for her enthusiasm and desire to attend the temple.

A day was planned. We arrived at the Logan temple ready to see our sweet child participate for the first time in behalf of another in the vital ordinance of baptism. Her enthusiasm was contagious. We arrived at the baptistry early—only for my husband and me to be turned away. We had neglected to renew our recommends. They had expired just two days before!

Fortunately, our middle daughter was also with us and accompanied her younger sister. With ample time to ponder, my husband and I waited outside. We wanted to be inside with our daughters, but we couldn't be. Our oversight had cost us being where we wanted to be.

Today, celebrate the gift of choice by choosing wisely the things you do that will impact your future.

NOVEMBER 9
Trial and Error
Follow me, and do the things which ye have seen me do. —2 Nephi 31:12

Author and designer Rachel Ashwell, originator of the shabby-to-chic movement, started a furniture company with flea-market finds. Though she didn't have a formal education in design, she worked with items others had cast off and became successful because she tried.

Despite an underprivileged upbringing and a humble demeanor, Scottish mezzo-soprano Susan Boyle became an icon for dreamers worldwide by pursuing her zeal for singing. She tried.

Both women attained excellence though starting out as average. Imperfect circumstances improved because they tried.

From day-to-day dilemmas that need solving to hobbies or interests we want to undertake, it's okay to be average—imperfect. We shouldn't let the knowledge that we are imperfect stop us from trying. Learning to ride a bike, gaining a testimony, playing a musical instrument, or even cooking palatable meals is done by trying. Trying, as in trial and error, enables us to learn from mistakes and imperfections.

Try to be like Jesus, the Primary song tells us. It doesn't say we must be exactly like Him right now; it only urges the effort of trying. Continue to try, and express gratitude for your ability to do so.

NOVEMBER 10
Rewarding Yourself for a Job Well Done
Be kind to yourself. The change you effect by revering and paying tribute to your authentic self will change your life for the better, and in turn the lives of others.

You found time to exercise this week. You lost a pound. You aced a test. You finished a craft project. It's your birthday. You survived another visit from your mother-in-law. The kids are all in bed—early. You worked on family history. You closed an important business deal. You cooked dinner every night of the week. You kept your cool during an argument. You ran your first 5K. You cleaned the whole house.

Each of life's victories are sweet. It's fun to celebrate. It's great to reward ourselves for reaching a goal or milestone. But how? Often we turn to food or shopping, reasoning that celebrating gives us an excuse to indulge, but we need consider whether the rewards we offer ourselves for reaching short-term goals are in line with our long-term goals. There are numerous ways to reward ourselves besides indulging in food or spending too much money:

* Enjoy a favorite or long-anticipated book.
* Attend a theatrical production or concert.
* Start a collection of favorite items.
* Redecorate a room with thrift-store finds.
* Put a certain dollar amount into your savings account.
* Give yourself permission to have a night off.
* Share the news of your success with a friend or loved one.

A goal reached, a job well done brings the intrinsic reward of feelings of satisfaction and accomplishment. Be sure to acknowledge to yourself that you are pleased with your efforts.

NOVEMBER 11

Heroes: Gratitude for Those Who Serve
As we express our gratitude, we must never forget that the highest appreciation is not to utter words, but to live by them.
—John Fitzgerald Kennedy[250]

A few years ago, there was a terrible car accident. As a volunteer fireman, my husband, Brian, responded. A teenager on his way to visit his grandmother lost control of his car. The vehicle careened into a field at nearly 90 miles per hour. The boy was ejected, his body lacerated in several places by a barbed wire fence. His femoral artery had been torn. He was bleeding to death. My husband put pressure on the teen's leg and talked to him to help prevent shock. As Life Flight prepared to land, he shielded the boy's body from flying debris with his own body. The teen mentioned he liked my husband's sunglasses. The two of them made a deal: if the boy would fight to live, Brian would give him the sunglasses.

My husband couldn't stop thinking about the teen, wondering if he'd lived. We found him in a hospital in another town. He faced a year of rehabilitation, but he was alive and his leg had been saved. Brian handed over the sunglasses.

My husband's efforts were nothing out of the ordinary for an emergency worker. Every day throughout the world, countless thousands of acts of service are given by emergency personnel who put their lives on the line to help others. Police officers, firefighters, ambulance personnel, servicemen and women. Heroes without number. Today, thank someone who protects and saves lives even at the risk of losing their own by performing an act of service for them.

NOVEMBER 12
Smiles to Share
Peace begins with a smile. —Mother Teresa[251]

Smile acronyms worth smiling about:
Spiritually Minded Is Life Eternal.
Service Makes Individual Lives Exciting.
Students Mastering Important Life-skills Enthusiastically.
Self-Motivation Is Lasting Energy.
So Much Improvement Is Exciting.
Significant Milestones In Loving Everyone.

The worth of a smile is infinite. Smiles boost our physical, emotional, and spiritual health. They connect us to others and ground us in what's most important; smiles speak the language of love. Sister Julie B. Beck tells us that because we have a Savior, we are able to awaken each day with hope smiling brightly. Worry need not overtake us because we can be assured Christ has us in His care. All we need do is press on in faithful discipleship.[252] Smiles celebrate gratitude. Who can you share a smile with today? Remember to be happy; you never know who might be falling in love with your smile!

NOVEMBER 13
Find the Good in All Things
All things bright and beautiful,
All creatures great and small,
All things wise and wonderful,
The Lord God made them all.
—Cecil Francis Alexander[253]

There's a new baby in the house. The furry kind—with four paws and a tail. Oakleigh is a six-week-old German shepherd puppy who has a lot to learn. So do I. When we brought her home, I had visions of her being as well behaved as her canine mother. I started trying to teach her to sit, wait, and lay down. She ignored me. She nipped and bit and chewed rugs, chairs, hands, fingers, and toes. "No, no, no!" The loud words made her misbehave more. She seemed frantic; she ran everywhere. We gave chase. She didn't want to be held by anyone. I put her in her crate and retreated to the computer to read about puppy behavior. What I learned was what I'd forgotten in twenty years: Oakleigh was acting out because she was overstimulated and overwhelmed by my expectations.

I tried a different approach. Assertive but calm. No power struggle. By noon, she was a changed puppy. When it was time for her nap, she came to where I sat with a notebook and pen. She laid her head on my leg and fell asleep. Gratitude for her sweet spirit filled me. I appreciated her simple act of trust. Peace settled on the house once more.

In our striving to gain control of situations, we sometimes lose patience. Who or what might you be expecting more of than is reasonable? Practice being grateful for the good that already exists.

NOVEMBER 14
You Are Awesome!
The thing that is really hard, and really amazing, is giving up on being perfect and beginning the work of becoming yourself.
—Anna Quindlen[254]

On February 27, did you write a love letter to yourself? Did you tell yourself how pleased you are just to be you? Did you write about your triumphs and achievements? Tell yourself of your best qualities, your laugh, your sense of humor, your patience, your compassion, your determination? I hope you keep your letter handy and that you read it often!

Today, spend a minute writing to yourself again. Convey gratitude to yourself. Write a thank-you note to you, or make a special entry in your journal. Write about how thankful you are for both your strengths and your weaknesses. Give thanks for all you have learned because you put forth the effort. Express appreciation to yourself for the body you have and all it enables you to do. For your mind; for your energy and enthusiasm to set and reach temporal and spiritual goals. For qualities you've decided to cultivate and practice; for those you're still working on. Thank yourself for your wisdom. Your willingness to study the gospel so you can know who you are. Credit yourself for paying heed to the Spirit. Thank yourself for your determination to overcome struggles. For your strength in battles you're still waging.

Why? Because even if you forget once in a while, you are awesome!

NOVEMBER 15
Sunday Thank-You Notes
Courtesies of a small and trivial character are the ones which strike deepest in the grateful and appreciating heart. —Henry Clay[255]

During the holiday season, we frequently focus on those less fortunate, as we should. Yet there are others who deserve our thoughts. When was the last time you thanked your mayor, bishop, or a city worker? Your children's principal, teacher, or librarian? What other people provide life-enhancing or life-sustaining services that rarely receive a thank you?

Sundays can be wonderful days to contemplate who you're thankful for. Let them know by sending cards or letters. Making out thank-you notes is a perfect Sabbath activity for families to initiate in November—when thoughts turn to gratitude—and a wonderful tradition to maintain all year long.

NOVEMBER 16
Gratitude for Memories
God gave us memories that we might have roses in December.
—J. M. Barrie[256]

I recently found myself craving a milkshake from a quaint burger joint that occupies a permanent place in my heart. When I was a child, Grandma Minnie and I would take our regular seats at the counter; I loved to spin circles on the old silver stools. Grandma ordered the same thing every time: one burger with fries for us to split. If I was very good, I got a root beer all to myself. It didn't matter that the fries were greasy or the burger buns a bit stale. Listening to the oldies blare from the jukebox, watching Grandma smile, and spinning on my stool, I felt I was the luckiest kid alive.

Years later I frequented the place with friends. Everyone knew that a visit to the old drive-in wasn't complete without a visit to my grandparents' home a few houses away. After parking and ordering, we'd all pile out of the car and head down the street. Grandma Minnie and Grandpa Frank would welcome us with open arms. All my friends loved them.

Good memories.

I did go for the milkshake. I hadn't visited the place in a long time. Sitting at the drive-in with my daughter, we savored creamy mint-chocolate goodness. I told my daughter—again—about her great-grandparents and the wonderful times we shared together.

Lighten your day by sharing your treasured memories with someone you love. Tell them of your gratitude for time passed, for memories made and lessons learned, and for memories yet to be created.

NOVEMBER 17
Gratitude: The Best Yet
When our perils are past, shall our gratitude sleep? —George Canning[257]

After my friend Stacey died in 2007, the seventeenth of each month became my Stacey Day. A day to celebrate life instead of mourning her death. Then came a month that was harder to enjoy. Stacey was about to become a grandmother. On January 17 there was a baby shower. I arrived way past fashionably late—when it was over. I didn't want to cry, and I didn't want to make small talk with a big crowd.

I felt guilty I was there and Stacey was not, and I couldn't seem to muster any joy to make that particular Stacey Day special.

Back home, the house was wrapped in the soft darkness of evening. I sat on the floor in the family room. Suddenly, a shaft of light appeared, then the glow of the upstairs hall light. My then ten-year-old padded down the stairs with a bulging blanket. She sat next to me and unpacked a teddy bear, a doll, and her favorite play tea set. Blanket serving as tablecloth, she set everything up. "Blueberry tea, Mommy. I know it's your favorite."

We talked about little things: How her older brother annoyed her, but how much she secretly adored him. Funny things our Huskies did. How they loved to watch the magpies that were building a nest in the willow next to their kennel. My daughter snuggled in close; I cherished her warmth. I ran my fingers through her hair, caressed her hands, and kissed the freckles on her nose and cheeks. I sipped pretend tea brewed with love and realized it was the best Stacey Day yet.

Find and cherish gratitude for life's sweet, simple pleasures.

NOVEMBER 18
Seeing Is Believing
We all have our own life to pursue, our own kind of dream to be weaving. And we all have the power to make wishes come true, as long as we keep believing. —Lousia May Alcott[258]

"What are you grateful for?" asks author Donna Kozik. In *The Gratitude Book Project: Celebrating 365 Days of Gratitude*, she reveals stories of gratitude from those she asked that question. She finds gratitude for families and pets, hardship and laughter, appreciation for carrot cake and refrigerators.

Others have written books about finding ways to be grateful every day of the year and on ways to express thanks all year long. There are blogs and websites devoted to daily gratitude, written sentiment and emotion expressed through photographs.

How would you like to pay tribute to gratitude? Write a book? Compile a set of essays? Blog about it? Take photos of something you are grateful for each day? If a year seems like a long stretch, try a month. If you take photos, display them on the family bulletin board or refrigerator. However you choose, find a way to express your enthusiasm for gratitude!

NOVEMBER 19
Faith: The Future
I do not want to go back to the past; I want to go back to the past way of facing the future. —Ronald Reagan[259]

The gospel of Jesus Christ contains vital eternal principles and truths. In our day of peril and turmoil, natural devastation, and social, economic, and familial upheaval, there is cause for concern, yet faith can and should always triumph. President Thomas S. Monson promises us that our gospel knowledge will be of comfort through life storms and that there is nothing by which we can be defeated.[260]

Search others' lives for examples of faith during hardship. No matter your current circumstances, anticipate with faith that blessings will come.

NOVEMBER 20
Grateful for Gratitude Lessons
It is a pleasure appropriate to man, for him to save a fellow man, and gratitude is acquired in no better way. —Author unknown

A few things I've learned this year:

Within small epiphanies come big opportunities.

As long as we have time, there is time.

Effort and practice let us know how much more effort and practice we have to undertake.

Getting to where we want to go in the most efficient manner involves resisting twists and turns in favor of the straight and narrow.

Perfectionist tendencies cause despair. Pursuit of eternal perfection is made less painful by trusting and accepting guidance from the Lord.

Things happen for a reason.

The voice of a friend is never so sweet as when it is heard comforting us in times of trouble.

If and when the angels who were sent into our lives get tired of "angeling," others are ready to step in and take their place; we just have to open our eyes and hearts to see them.

We can live the best life we know how to live . . . and still be loved by God.

The chance to love and serve others is invaluable.

Peace comes through forgiveness.

We can love others even when they don't love us back.

Weaknesses show us we're stronger than we thought.

What are you grateful for having learned this year?

NOVEMBER 21
A Tradition of Thanks: Prayers of Gratitude
Give this one day to thanks, to joy, to gratitude! —Henry Ward Beecher[261]

The pilgrims experienced severe hardship, yet they dedicated a day solely to giving thanks. What are your Thanksgiving traditions for expressing gratitude? If you chose to keep a blessing basket this month, read from the submissions.

Tell family members why you are proud of them. How they make the world—and your life—better. How you admire their dedication and examples of love. How you rejoice over their efforts and the contributions they make. For their insight and wisdom. Their willing hearts and kindness, goodwill and good cheer. Their hard work and determination. Their acts of loving kindness that have created a kaleidoscope of joy. Give thanks too for sweet new spirits in the family and loved ones departed. And to Heavenly Father for each choice moment in life, happiness as well as heartache that give you increased strength and courage.

NOVEMBER 22
Family History, Family Needs
If you don't know [your family's] history, then . . . you are a leaf that doesn't know it is part of a tree. —Michael Crichton[262]

My great-uncle Richard never knew he had a family who loved him. Having been separated from his brother at a very early age, my grandfather possessed no memory of him—only a small black-and-white photo of a boy of about six or seven years of age. By all accounts, Richard traveled through many states and lived many places, never truly setting down roots. In 1993, I found he had died all alone almost ten years earlier at the edge of a California desert.

The death of a loved one is painful. The loss of those living can be equally as heartrending. Whether they have strayed from family ideals, whether they are considered different, incompatible, or simply weary from all they have endured, we cannot forget them. Elder Joseph B. Wirthlin noted that with Christ as our example we should be concerned for the one.[263] Matthew 18:11–12 asks a poignant question, "For the Son of man is come to save that which was lost. How think ye? if a man have an hundred sheep, and one of them be gone astray, doth he not leave the ninety and nine, and goeth into the mountains, and seeketh that which is gone astray?"

No matter how those you love have become lost to you, determine how you can help them.

NOVEMBER 23
Planning: Reunions

The lack of emotional security of our American young people is due, I believe, to their isolation from the larger family unit. . . . A child . . . needs to feel himself one in a world of kinfolk, persons of variety in age and temperament, and yet allied to himself by an indissoluble bond which he cannot break if he could, for nature has welded him into it before he was born. —Pearl S. Buck[264]

While everyone is gathered for Thanksgiving, take time to compile ideas for next year's family reunion. Location and budget. Date and duration. Guest list and what to eat. Jot down ideas for games and activities. Discuss what your main objective for the event will be. Togetherness, reconnecting after few years or many, forging unity, getting to know family members who are new to the family. Discuss how many older members there will be versus how many who are teens, toddlers, and babies. Doing so will help you determine a balance for and the types of activities. A planning session to outline the basics will make things easier when firm details are later set in place.

NOVEMBER 24
Where We Need to Be: Little Miracles
What we need somehow always finds us . . .

This weekend I unpacked an old trunk and found treasures long forgotten.

Kitchen utensils, plates, cups, and yellowed but still starch-stiff cotton tablecloths from the days when my grandmother entertained special company or hosted parties for her ladies group. Just holding things she once touched brought tears and cherished memories.

Some things—like a spatula, slotted spoon, and ladle—were still wrapped in plastic and never before used. I smiled. Grandma liked to be prepared. It wouldn't do to be without what she might one day need, so she stocked up on everything. I doubt she imagined the items would be in a tiny kitchen over two hundred miles and a decade away from her home.

But who knows?

Grandma had an innate wisdom that still amazes me.

Maybe she sensed her granddaughter might someday need such items because she had failed to prepare for life in a rustic cabin.

Grandma, as always, thank you.

Today, give thanks for the little miracles in your life. And for the fact that God always leads us to where we need to be.

NOVEMBER 25
Gratitude for Words: Improving Communication
Communication works for those who work at it. —John Powell[265]

As you celebrate this Thanksgiving, keep in mind a few ways to improve communication with others:

✱ Keep a trust. Never share with others what has been shared in confidence with you.

✱ Show respect by looking directly at the other person. Don't read, write, text, or do anything else when you're having a conversation. Show the person you value them.

✱ Decide what you want to say before you say it. Think first and pray for guidance. Be straightforward and honest. Be clear. Speak at a steady rate instead of fast and exasperated. Use a sincere tone of love and concern.

✱ Take notice of nonverbal clues: facial expressions, tone of voice, body language. If someone else seems angry or upset, make sure you remain calm.

✱ Listen for and understand needs and problems. Listen with your heart. Be an active listener. Listen intently to what is being said.

✱ Rather than waiting for your chance to jump in and speak your piece, be patient. Resist the urge to interrupt. If you're not sure you understand something, paraphrase, repeat back what you believe you heard, and ask for clarification.

✱ In a misunderstanding, don't try to cover more than the situation at hand. Find an unhurried time and a neutral, peaceful ground to discuss why you're upset.

✱ Apologize. Be willing to work toward problem resolution. Don't play the blame game.

✱ Resist becoming negative. Strive to understand and be supportive of the other person's point of view.

✱ Extend genuine compliments and praise.

NOVEMBER 26
Twenty Gifts from the Heart
I hate the giving of the hand unless the whole man accompanies it.
—Ralph Waldo Emerson[266]

✱ Give the gift of music. If you play an instrument, volunteer your talent to make someone's holiday brighter. Or share your skill by teaching someone how to play.

✴ Forgive someone and tell them so.

✴ Read to someone in a care center. Make a gift of one of your favorite books.

✴ Write down a memory of favorite Christmases past for a friend or loved one.

✴ Make your own Christmas cards. Don't worry if they're not fancy.

✴ Make a photo collage of treasured memories from varied occasions or vacations.

✴ Offer to care for a busy neighbor's children while she shops.

✴ Make dinner for someone. Deliver it in one of your best dishes; give the dish too.

✴ Turn up the radio, and dance with your sweetheart or child.

✴ Volunteer at a homeless shelter, care center, school, or animal shelter.

✴ Listen to someone who needs to talk. Lend your ear for as long as they need you.

✴ Compile a few of your treasures, and give them away. Write a note explaining why you want the person to have them and what they mean to you. For example: Your grandmother's holiday soup tureen to a newly married niece. The rare Christmas tree ornament you've always loved to a friend. A special piece of jewelry to a child growing into adulthood. A favorite coat, blanket, or other warm article for someone who needs it.

✴ Speak for what you believe in. Remind others of the true meaning of the season.

✴ Be an example. Be kind, patient, and compassionate.

✴ Smile. At everyone.

✴ Visit someone in a hospital. Pray for them.

✴ Donate what you might have spent on a friend or loved one to someone in need. Tell them you did so and why. If they don't understand, just smile and say you hope they'll do the same for you.

✴ Shovel the walk of someone who you don't normally speak to.

✴ Teach your family that true joy doesn't come from how much you accomplish or buy. It comes from little everyday thoughts and actions that define your true character. Decide now what kind of person you want to be, then live up to your own expectations.

✳ Love and accept yourself so that you can grow to more fully love and accept others.

NOVEMBER 27
Hearth and Home for the Holidays
A house is made of walls and beams; a home is built with love and dreams. —Author unknown

On the mantel, faux pine garlands provide a wonderful backdrop for lights and ribbon. Mingle jute or colored raffia along a length of garland. Strings of popcorn, cranberries, or pieces of tinsel lend magic to the scheme, as do pinecones, bows, candy canes, and wooden ornaments. Garlands made of tinsel lend sparkle. Garlands made of real pine boughs (don't forget to wrap the ends with florist tape to guard against leaking sap) lend a nostalgic touch. Intermingle a few pieces of curly willow, or use only curly willow for your garland.

Sprinkle in ornaments that match those on the tree. Christmas stockings, nativities, miniature houses, and candles are additional mainstays of mantel decor. Plan lighting to accent favorite collectibles. A nutcracker collection, assortment of dolls, or grouping of teddy bears add charm. Group by threes, use different textures and colors, and experiment with arranging items from tallest to shortest or largest to smallest. Other items to use are clocks, antique toys, old books, angels, tea sets, stars, nostalgic tins or jars, old gloves, lace hankies, shoes, hats, purses, gingerbread men, or other cookies. Any items and materials that appeal to your emotions. Just as real boughs and cinnamon sticks add a welcoming yuletide scent, photos of family members—both living and deceased—touch the heart. Favorite Christmas cards or postcards from years past give emotional appeal as well. If you don't have a mantel, use the same ideas to decorate shelves or windowsills.

NOVEMBER 28
No-Budget Decorating
I would be the most content if my children grew up to be the kind of people who think decorating consists mostly of building enough bookshelves. —Anna Quindlen[267]

Holiday pictures: Frame old cards to use as inexpensive and easy decor. Dover Publications (http://store.doverpublications.com) offers reprints of holiday images from the eighteenth and nineteenth centuries. You can order CDs of Christmas images (they also come in books), and print them to put in frames. Use dime-store frames painted in holiday colors.

Lighted nativity: To give new life to an old nativity, use a small string of lights to illuminate the stable with a warm glow.

Christmas books: This year I did a bit of rearranging and put a chair by our stairs. Since we have loads of favorite Christmas books, I decided to turn the chair into a special story nook for my youngest daughter and granddaughters. Here, I keep our favorite books ready to read when we need a quiet moment. I've also used Christmas books for decorating other areas of the house.

Use what you have: I decorated the hooks by our back door by adding a few seasonal items: an antique bed warmer, a small tin basket, mittens, and a scarf. In the kitchen, I pulled out old cookie cutters and used them amid lights and garland on the windowsill.

Recycle and enjoy: My favorite project has been finding a new use for an old window. I decided to use it on a keepsake cupboard. I asked my husband to make a 5-inch-deep shadowbox with a shelf in the middle. We used MDF—medium density fiberboard—to build the box. After I painted it, we fastened the window to the box with hinges. Inside, I placed some of my favorite collectables along with old hot chocolate tins, cards, photos, ornaments, and two tiny gingerbread houses my kids made when they were younger.

NOVEMBER 29
Uses for Old Christmas Cards

Christmas is a time when you get homesick, even when you're home.
—Carol Nelson[268]

Gift card holder: Cut a large greeting card lengthwise into two or three equal strips. For each strip cut, fold the bottom half up to meet the middle of the strip. To create a flap, fold the top of the strip down so it overlaps the top edge of the section just folded up. Run a thin line of glue along the sides of the bottom half of the strip to secure it to the back. Embellish with brads, ribbons, jute, buttons, etc. Put a gift tag or gift card inside.

Photo frame: Cut the front off an old card. Mount a smaller photo in the middle. Glue or tape it to the card. Embellish with ribbon or scrapbooking embellishments and hang on the tree.

Stand-up holiday decor: Cut the front off an old card. If desired, cut around any elements to add dimension, and chalk the edges with scrapbooking chalk. Cut a two-inch-wide strip from the back. Fold one-third over flat, and press the fold with your fingernail. Glue this flap to the back of the card.

Card chain: Rummaging through the house for construction paper so the kids can make paper chains? Search no further. If you have a stash of old cards get them out and cut them (a paper cutter works wonderfully) into ½- to 1-inch wide strips. Glue or staple each link as you add it to the chain just as you would with a construction-paper chain. Don't throw away your old gift bags either. You can cut them into strips as well. Let the kids keep adding links as long as the cards and gift bags hold out.

Napkin ring: Cut lengthwise strips out of cards. Glue or staple the ends to form a two-inch-diameter circle. Decorate with pieces from other cards or small ornaments. For my napkin holders, I use glittered snowflakes. Insert your napkins.

Bookmarks: Cut out strips of your favorite parts of the cards into a bookmark. Leave plain or decorate. Use yourself or give as gifts.

Decorative envelopes: Paste selected pieces of cards on the front of new envelopes. Chalk with scrapbooking chalk. Use to store holiday photos, loose gift tags, or scrapbooking elements. Give as gifts with a special message inside or with scented potpourri.

Christmas tree ornaments: Cut cards into shapes: hearts, stars, etc. Add glitter and ribbons and hang on tree.

NOVEMBER 30

So Grateful: The Best Year

For verily I say unto you, If ye have faith as a grain of mustard seed, ye shall say unto this mountain, Remove hence to yonder place; and it shall remove; and nothing shall be impossible unto you. —Matthew 17:20

When I set out to write this book, I wanted to share thoughts and insights. Experiences that have helped me to grow and mature spiritually. I hoped to touch hearts. I prayed to be able to help light the way for others struggling through mists of darkness. What I didn't realize was that my own struggles would grow exponentially.

I never anticipated computer crashes. Serious system and formatting errors left me scrambling to fix problems. The heartache of family trials weighed me down. Challenges of time and circumstance haunted me with a sense of hopelessness. I began to wonder what I could offer when I couldn't even make sense of elements in my own life. Self-doubt kept coming to call. So did fear of failure. Some days I cried. Some days I didn't write at all.

I've never spent as much time on my knees as I have these past months. I honed my listening-to-the-Spirit skills. I was blessed with patience and inner calm. Miracles unfolded. I learned to move forward with faith and confidence. I have come to know that my testimony is sweet and priceless. I can't believe how much I once took it for granted.

This has been the best year of my life. I am thankful for each joy and tender mercy.

The joys and tender mercies you have collected this month are a treasure. Carefully roll the list and tie it with a bow. Tuck it into your Christmas stocking, or put it in a safe place under the tree. On Christmas morning, read and cherish your list and share it with loved ones.

November Recipes

Creamy Shrimp Dip

1 (8 oz.) package cream cheese, cut into small cubes, room temperature
1 (10.75 oz.) can cream of mushroom soup
1 (1 oz.) envelope Knox clear gelatin

1 cup very warm water
¾ cup celery, thinly chopped
1 small onion, sliced very thin
¾ cup mayonnaise
1 cup canned small shrimp, rinsed and drained

In medium saucepan, warm the cream cheese, stirring until melted and creamy. Whisk in soup, and blend well. Dissolve gelatin in the cup of water. In a medium bowl, combine the cream cheese/soup mixture and gelatin water. Blend. Add celery, onion, mayo, and shrimp. Mix well. Turn into a small Jell-O mold or serving bowl. Chill overnight. Serve with corn chips.

Holiday Cheese Log

24 ounces American cheese slices
1 (8 oz.) package cream cheese, softened
1 clove garlic, minced
2 large pimentos

¼ cup paprika
¼ cup sesame seeds
Optional: slivered almonds, crushed to medium consistency

Puree the cheese, cream cheese, garlic, and pimentos in a food processor. Turn into bowl; chill. Form into two logs. Mix together paprika, sesame seeds, and optional almonds. On sections of waxed paper, roll each cheese log in the paprika/sesame seed mixture. Chill until firm.

Hot Artichoke Crab Dip

1 (8 oz.) package cream cheese, softened
1 cup mayonnaise
1 garlic clove, pressed
1 (14 oz.) can artichoke hearts, drained and pressed, diced

1 (8 oz.) package crab meat or imitation crab meat, diced
¾ cup Parmesan cheese
1 teaspoon cracked black pepper
1 teaspoon lemon zest
⅓ cup thinly sliced green onions
⅓ cup red bell pepper, chopped

In small saucepan over low heat, mix cream cheese and mayo until well blended. Add garlic. Chop artichokes; add artichokes and crab to cream cheese mixture. Combine. Add Parmesan cheese, pepper, and lemon zest. Mix well. Turn into buttered baking dish. Top with onion and red pepper. Bake at 350 degrees for 25–30 minutes.

Salmon Puffs

2 (4.5 oz.) packages smoked salmon, chopped
¼ cup grated carrot
2 Tablespoons lemon juice
1 small cucumber, peeled and chopped to make ½ cup
¼ cup mayonnaise

¼ cup sour cream
2 Tablespoons finely chopped white onion
1 Tablespoon dill weed
Puff pastry dough
1 egg, beaten well
1 Tablespoon water

Combine salmon, carrot, lemon juice, cucumber, mayo, sour cream, onion, and dill weed. Refrigerate. Spread pastry dough on cookie sheet. Mix egg and water. Brush dough with egg mixture. Bake according to package directions. Cool. Cut into bite-size pieces with pizza cutter. Spoon salmon mixture onto each piece.

DECEMBER

Destination: Your Divine Promise
Celebrating Life

THE TRANSFORMATIVE POWER OF THE holidays captivates our hearts. A kaleidoscope of wonder awaits. Festive sights and sounds and smells. Presents glitter beneath gilded trees. Snow-covered yards become magical playgrounds. Picture-book scenes of hearth and home rekindle childhood memories of wonder and delight.

As pleased as the senses may be, the real treasures of the season lie not in baubles and beads and glitter-encrusted stars. Plain, simple, subtle. Truth bears riches worth far more than gold. The birth of a babe. Savior. Lord. Crowned with glory, through Him hearts are dusted with new hope. Miracles are wrought. An inner symphony of beauty casts an effervescent glow that lends a sparkle to all eyes. Gratitude extended. Joy burns bright. A Christmas made with love.

Happy celebrating!

Making the Most of December

✱ Make advent envelopes, one to open each day of the month. Inside include quotes or scriptural references to read as a family.

✱ String popcorn and cranberries, cinnamon sticks and marshmallows. Add a new twist: dried lemons, oranges, grapefruits, or apples. Select fully ripened fruits. Wash well. Slice as thin as possible. Dry according to the directions for each fruit in your food dehydrator. To oven-dry, arrange fruit slices in a single layer on a parchment-lined baking sheet. Don't overlap slices. Place in oven set at 150 degrees for approximately 6 hours. Leave the oven door ajar; during the last hours check frequently to prevent browning. For apples, prior to drying, soak slices in a solution of two cups lemon juice and three tablespoons salt. Soak for 30 minutes to an hour, and blot dry with paper towels.

✱ Visit a live nativity or displays of crèches. Make a stable for your yard, and have your own live nativity.

✱ Deck the halls with dime-store decorations. Old flour sifters, cheese graters, and other vintage kitchen gadgets look wonderful tied with colorful Christmas ribbons. Hang delicate teacups on the tree.

✱ Bring color into your house with the flowers of the season. Poinsettias require little care and have blooms all month long; Christmas cactuses and amaryllis are good choices for December blossoms as well. Arrange cut red roses or carnations with variegated holly, pine sprigs, and winter berries. Add a few white chrysanthemums.

✱ Assemble a basket of Christmas books. *Christmas Day in the Morning* by Pearl S. Buck, *Papa Panov's Special Christmas* by Leo Tolstoy, *The Night Before Christmas: The Classic Edition* by Clement C. Moore, or *I Believe in Santa* by Diane G. Adamson. Author Emily Freeman's book *A Christ-Centered Christmas* explains the meaning behind seven gifts of Christmas. Each is based on a figure from the nativity and includes scriptures and simple traditions to help deepen the meaning of the season.

✳ After Christmas, make a photo book. Upload photos to your favorite photo developer or print them yourself. Create a memory book out of a three-ringed binder. As a family home evening activity, talk about experiences and traditions you shared during the holidays. Write down favorite memories, put them in sheet protectors, and insert them in the binder. Add more memories each Christmas. For years to come, you will enjoy reading and reminiscing.

✳ Encourage your family to employ creative writing skills to write songs and poems that express their love for the Christ child.

✳ Instead of exchanging neighbor gifts, involve the neighbors in donating to a cause such as adopting a child or family to help for Christmas. Plan a night for a potluck cookie exchange and have everyone get together to make plans for needed donations and for the delivery.

DECEMBER 1

Heading into the Holidays Knees First

Though I am weak, yet God, when prayed, cannot withhold his conquering aid. —Ralph Waldo Emerson[269]

Before the turkey was even cold and dusk fell the eve of Thanksgiving day, your to-do list grew. And grew. And grew! Time to run, run, run. Black Friday. Cyber Monday. Sales circulars. Presents to buy. Presents to wrap. Put up the tree. Decorate. Rush here. Rush there. Food to cook. Food to eat. Don't forget the lights. The cards. The candles. Clean the house. Enough choices for a year packed into one month! If you don't have a plan, you can hit the ground running every morning and still never catch up. When your stress level skyrockets, your head begins to throb, and you feel like crying; when expectations and emotional pressure threaten to spiral out of control, say to yourself these two simple words: knees first.

Say them silently. Say them out loud. Just say them. Knees first. I am only one woman; how am I going to do everything? Knees first. How am I going to make everyone happy? You know you can't make everyone happy, but when you convince yourself you still have to try . . . knees first. Seclude yourself and pray. Pray too with loved ones. Those who are happy and those who are sad and struggling. Little loved ones who are excited to the point of frenzy. Pray for those who are hard to love. Express gratitude. Ask that peace comfort your mind. Petition mercy for your exhausted body.

Of course, crowds and traffic jams don't afford the ideal time or place to kneel. But you can always offer a prayer in your mind and heart. You can do what you truly need to do this season if you do it knees first.

DECEMBER 2

Simplify Planning: Getting Organized

Behold, mine house is a house of order, saith the Lord God, and not a house of confusion. —D&C 132:8

Organization guru Marilyn Paul, whose clients have included the Kennedy School of Government and the *New York Times*, writes that to manage our time efficiently we must set priorities. "As we do the hard work of time management, we come to understand that we cannot do everything that we want to do. That realization, while disappointing at first, can also yield to an insight that we must learn to make wise choices."[270]

Determining what we really want and don't want to do and developing a realistic view of what we can and can't do is sage advice— especially at this time of year. But where to start when to-dos and obligations begin falling like snow and accumulating faster than we can shovel a clear path? A Christmas planner. Simply print a calendar from the Internet and tape it to the inside front cover of a spiral notebook.

Opposite the calendar on the first pages of the notebook, list and prioritize want-tos, need-tos, and feel-pressure-if-you-don'ts. Color code your activities to provide a quick visual assessment. Use red for activities that make you feel stress or pressure. If many reds begin to appear, reassess your schedule and objectives and shoot for balance in how you'd truly like to celebrate the season. Create basic sections for your planner based on your needs: budget, gift and food shopping lists, card recipient list, etc. Cut a sticky note into strips, and use them as tab dividers at the front of each section.

Once your calendar and lists are established, don't let yourself be pressured into deviating from your schedule. Plan ahead and leave days open with unscheduled time slots when you can complete forgotten shopping or attend to other details. If something doesn't come up to fill those days, enjoy the time off!

DECEMBER 3
Quick Check: Enjoy the Season
Gifts of time and love are surely the basic ingredients of a truly merry Christmas. —Peg Bracken[271]

The ordinary acts we practice every day at home are of more importance to the soul than their simplicity might suggest. —Thomas Moore[272]

To help the season's real treasures become clear:

* Become an expert at finding good cheer—stop, look, and listen.
* Stick to a routine—a schedule will forge order out of chaos.
* Congratulate yourself for your successes—getting through each task is a triumph!
* Don't feel bad for yourself—open your heart and mind to miracles of all shapes and sizes.
* Donate your time to help someone in need—service is where you'll find Christ.
* Do something fun—emulate the joy of a child.
* Smile at everyone you meet—smiles are simple to give and, especially at this time of year, quick to be returned.
* Hang around people who are positive—your determination to be upbeat will set the tone.
* Eat right—remember, all things in moderation . . . even fudge!

DECEMBER 4
Life through the Eyes of a Child (or Puppy!)
Our hearts grow tender with childhood memories and love of kindred, and we are better throughout the year for having, in spirit, become a child again at Christmastime. —Laura Ingalls Wilder[273]

Five-thirty in the morning. Oakleigh needed to go outside. The temperature dipped into the low 20s. While I stood, body and mind numbed to shivering, the puppy forgot her errand and frolicked. When I tugged on the leash with impatience, she sprawled and settled herself into the glory of her first snow. Her tail swished the ground like a windshield wiper. She looked up at me with calm, soulful eyes as if to ask, "Why? Why do we need to stop having fun?"

Chilled to the bone, I could think of lots of reasons why we should immediately retreat to the house. Another wag scattered flakes. She cocked her head. Something in her eyes tugged at my heart, transporting me back to childhood. To a time I ignored cold fingers and frozen toes. A time when I paid no heed to the date on the calendar or the time of day.

A quick trip back inside. Warmer clothing suited for the weather. In minutes, we were out again. This time for an unhurried walk. What began as a hurried errand turned into a relaxing marvel as we ambled through a scene of wintery wonder.

This month, when you feel rushed and harried, stressed and ready to stumble, stop and think like a child. Or a puppy. Live in the moment, not in the stress of the future. Close your eyes. Breathe deeply. Feel the beat of your heart. Remember the sweetness of Christmases past. Carols and cookies. Magic and miracles. Snowmen and snow angels. Sledding and skiing and skating. Days you never wanted to end—even if your nose was as red as Rudolph's! Enjoy the memories, and look forward to the wonders of each new day.

DECEMBER 5
Creating a Christ-Centered Season
God rest ye, little children; let nothing you afright,
For Jesus Christ, your Saviour, was born this happy night;
Along the hills of Galilee the white blocks sleeping lay,
When Christ, the child of Nazareth, was born on Christmas day.
—Dinah Craik[274]

Most of us generally expect more of ourselves during the period between Thanksgiving and New Year's than we do at any other time. December disillusionment occurs as we find ourselves competing in seasonal Olympics. Shopping, decorating, cooking, baking, socializing, wrapping gifts, and sending cards overwhelm us. Deficiencies we might see and forgive in ourselves during other months are suddenly inexcusable. We end up getting run down and compromising our heath. When we find we don't possess superhuman qualities, we feel we've failed. It's easy to lose sight of why we choose to celebrate the season.

Consciously focus on the reason for the season. Set up the nativity set before anything else. Make it the center of your decorating efforts.

If your family tradition dictates that you don't place the nativity figures until the days just prior to Christmas, start with at least the stable, or a star, an angel figurine, or a picture of the baby Jesus. With heartfelt determination and a little effort, the holidays can become holy days.

DECEMBER 6

Seasonal Stress: Avoiding Discouragement over Finances

I've learned that you can tell a lot about a person by the way he/ she handles these three things: a rainy day, lost luggage, and tangled Christmas tree lights. —Maya Angelou[275]

Seasonal stress—yes, there's a name for it—occurs when we worry that we won't meet the expectations of others or when we believe someone else won't meet our expectations. When we fear holiday peace and joy are unattainable, the resulting anxiety can lead us to believe the holidays are something to dread. If you're tired of seasonal stress, the good news is that past holiday history does not have to become unchangeable destiny. The first step is to be aware of the pitfalls of discouragement, discontent, and disillusionment.

Discouragement creeps into the holidays when we compare ourselves to others, particularly when it comes to finances. Just as physically unhealthy habits can at first appear to be attractive, spending too much can seem appealing as well. But the season is not an excuse to indulge financially. Often the media makes it look trendy to go into debt. And the bigger, the more expensive the gift or the more gifts, the more it proves our love for someone or their love for us—right? Um, no. We should consider our real motives for holiday spending.

Separate I-can-afford-it from I-can-buy-it-because-I-have-a-credit-card. By making firm decisions to cut down on expenditures, you're investing in sound financial habits—a priceless gift and healthy example for future generations.

DECEMBER 7

Relationships: A Season of Content

Not to know that any Christian spirit working kindly in its little sphere,
whatever it may be, will find its mortal life too short for its vast means
of usefulness. Not to know that no space of regret can make amends for
one life's opportunities misused! Yet such was I!
—Jacob Marley, from *A Christmas Carol*[276]

Ding, dong.

"Hello? You look familiar. Where have I met you before?"

"Why, ma'am. My name is Discontent. Don't you remember me?"

"Come to think of it, I do. You're the one who caused the conflict with my sister last year and absolutely ruined Christmas Eve because no one could get along."

Heavenly Father expects you to be kind and patient with your relatives. He doesn't expect you to be emotionally berated or guilt yourself into depression. While it's true the holidays can help soften hearts and heal fractured relationships, the anticipation that all wrongs will be set right is unrealistic. And if emotions run high, problems and differences of opinion are unlikely to be resolved. Cultivate realistic expectations of family and friend time. Determine to change your reaction to criticism or careless remarks from others who may be stressed. Avoid comparisons and bringing up old wounds, mistakes, or failures—yours or those of others. Be kind to yourself and realize that even with planning, some things go smoothly and some don't.

Patience and faith are key elements that will shut and lock the door on discontent. Whether it's a feeling of peace that remains in the house long after everyone's gone, seeing wonder in—or through—the eyes of a child, or kindling hope and good cheer, celebrate and congratulate yourself on each and every success!

DECEMBER 8

Example and Attitude

Christmas is not a time nor a season, but a state of mind. To cherish
peace and goodwill, to be plenteous in mercy, is to have the real spirit of
Christmas. —Calvin Coolidge[277]

The timeless, classic Christmas movie *It's a Wonderful Life* tells the story of unsung hero George Bailey. An icon of selflessness, George's unshakable belief is that people come before money. As personal and financial troubles mount, however, George's optimism splinters. He contemplates taking his own life. It requires a visit from his bumbling guardian angel, Clarence, to convince George of his worth and help him see that the abundance of love in his life is a priceless asset.

Unlike material goods, happy memories are irreplaceable and don't need to cost a cent. True love is shown with gifts that last a lifetime:

Unrushed time together. Pray together. Read together. Plan special one-on-one activities that show family and friends they are important and worth your time and attention. Tell them why they are important to you. Make sure they know how much you value them and how they enhance your life and the lives of others.

Your attitude toward the holidays. Tell others what Christ's birth means to you and of your love for Him. Do you believe that people come before money? Explain why. Start now to shift the focus of the holidays to giving instead of getting. Don't be guilted into buying.

Your positive example of strength and conviction. It's normal for seasonal stress to cause us to stumble into frustration, to feel overwhelmed, or to become sad. It's natural to cry and vent a little. Let yourself experience the feelings you encounter, but don't flounder in them. Move on. Teach your children to do the same.

Like George Bailey learned, what matters isn't money or fame. We have the power to make a difference for the better; our examples and attitudes become our legacy.

DECEMBER 9
Nope, Can't, Sorry Not This Time: Gracefully Saying No
Learn to say "No," and it will be of more use to you than to be able to read Latin. —Charles Haddon Spurgeon[278]

Everybody loves the good guy (or girl), right? We want to be that person. Everybody loves us when we give of ourselves. We want to be helpful. Well regarded. Valued. We want to please but at what cost to ourselves? Constantly saying yes buries us neck deep in commitments and obligations we have no idea how we'll meet or complete. (We all know it's true because we've done it.) There are times when we simply need to decline an offer or offers in order to set and maintain healthy boundaries—and to preserve our own health and sanity.

Decide what you really want—Be honest with yourself. Are you doing something simply because you enjoy the compliments? Is it worth it? Does someone want you to buy them a certain gift? Does it feel right? If you don't know how you feel or aren't certain of other commitments, say you need time to think things over.

Be polite—Be honest with others. Misunderstandings can be prevented by stating our true feelings. While beating around the bush may save a negative emotional response in the present, it often brews problems for the future. If we hem and haw and toss excuses like a juggler, it leaves the door wide open for misinterpretation.

When asked to do something you know you can't do, express thanks for the offer, then state your response and intentions in a clear and concise manner. I'm sorry, I can't. I don't feel comfortable being in front of that many people. I need time for myself. I need to focus on my family. I'm not able to bake that many cookies, but I can bring punch. Restate your intentions if necessary, but if you've decided your answer is no, stick to it and don't back down.

Don't apologize—there's nothing wrong with saying no to something you can't do. Your time and health are important. If others truly have your best interests in mind, they'll understand.

Consider the fact that if you decline to pitch in every time something is needed, others will be given the chance to discover their own talents and strengths.

DECEMBER 10
Prioritize, Plan, Prepare: Celebrating What's Most Important
Prepare ye the way of the Lord. —Isaiah 40:3

Prioritize: Think back to years past. What brought true happiness and a lasting sense of peace? What is your definition of the perfect Christmas? What things do you think should stay the same? What would you like to change? Are there new traditions you'd like to incorporate?

Plan: Set goals for where you want to be and how you want to feel after the holidays, financially, physically, emotionally, and spiritually. Don't overburden yourself with shoulds—the I should make, take, bake, etc. Try not to be a perfectionist. Strive for quality instead of quantity.

Prepare: Even with priorities and plan in place, you need proper rest, nutrition, and exercise to help you stay on your game. Taking care of your body will equip you for unforeseen obstacles. Decide beforehand to give everyone—including yourself—the benefit of the doubt. Try to find common ground with others, even if it's only a tiny island in a vast sea of difference. Choose to maintain healthy boundaries, dismiss criticism, and show respect and kindness. Look for the silver lining in every crowd.

The solutions to avoiding seasonal stress can be as simple as they are complex but well worth the effort when it comes to celebrating the holidays.

DECEMBER 11
The Comfort of a Loving Home
Love not the world, neither the things that are in the world. If any man love the world, the love of the Father is not in him. —1 John 2:15

As a teenager, I spent one winter with my grandparents on their farm in rural Idaho. Each day was cold and tiring. I woke at 3 a.m. and walked a quarter mile to a small cinderblock store, where I waited to board a chattering and hopefully dependable school bus. In winter, the roads where my grandparents lived were hazardous. Black ice beneath thick frosty snow. The pass the bus needed to climb to get out of the valley was steep, narrow, and winding. Often we followed behind a snow plow. Windblown drifts built to numerous feet in height.

At the end of the day, we returned down the ice-covered pavement of Granite Pass. Back at the old store, I got off the bus and made the quarter-mile trek home. My boots crunched on the icy gravel drive that led to my grandparents' farm. My fingers near frozen,

I shoved open the back door to enter a warm house where a hot meal was being prepared and where love was expressed abundantly. It was in those precious days that I first began to understand and appreciate the intricacies of life and what gives it depth and meaning.

I count myself blessed to have spent that winter with my grandparents. Experiences that hew existence down to its simplest form bring the greatest focus. When I feel tempted to allow my holiday planning to become complex, I remind myself of those days, where expressions of faith and sacrifice—and the basic comforts of a loving home—were the things that meant the most.

DECEMBER 12
Deepening the Meaning: Traditions
Christmas, my child, is love in action. When you love someone, you give to them, as God gives to us. —Dale Evans Rogers[279]

* Prepare an empty manger for the Christ child. If your nativity set doesn't have a manger separate from the baby, make one out of popsicle sticks, tongue depressors, twigs, or a matchbox. Each evening invite members of your family to place pieces of straw (or shreds of paper) representing good deeds they have done during the day into the manger. When Christmas Eve arrives, the babe will have a soft bed to lie on.

* Start each day by having everyone share an idea for what they can give to Jesus. For example, smile at someone, be kind, read an extra verse or two of scripture, volunteer to say family prayer, or show compassion to a sibling.

* Keep a small pad of paper and pencil near the nativity. Encourage family members to write anonymous notes of gratitude to Jesus and place them in a box or basket. Decide whether to read them this year or look forward to reading them next year.

* On Christmas Eve, have everyone write down their testimony. Make sure to sign and date it. Put the testimonies in a binder to read in coming years.

✷ Prepare and send packages for missionaries in your family or ward. Some helpful items might include sticky notes, packets of hot cocoa and oatmeal, water filtration bottles, highlighters, pictures of the Savior or the prophet, breath mints, gum, hand warmers, a recorded message from home, socks, beef jerky, Article of Faith cards, stationery and envelopes, CTR rings, hand sanitizer, small flashlights, hard Christmas candies, a pillowcase with messages of encouragement written in indelible ink, or Band-Aids. Or have a brunch for the missionaries serving in your area.

DECEMBER 13
Kidnapping Mary
And she shall bring forth a son, and thou shalt call his name Jesus: for he shall save his people from their sins. —Matthew 1:21

We had a simple plan: leave a piece of a nativity set at the doorstep of an unsuspecting recipient on each of the twelve nights preceding Christmas. On Saturday evening, a delicately painted figurine depicting Mary was the first to be sent. Sunday morning we celebrated supposed success. With excited tones and smiles, we spoke of how Joseph would be next. We elected a person to deliver him. While we compared notes on directions to the intended family's house, we discovered the awful truth: Mary had been delivered to the wrong address! We had no choice. We had to kidnap Mary—somehow get her back.

Then someone felt inspired to present a differing opinion: What if we were supposed to take Mary to that address? A few phone calls and questions to others in the neighborhood, and we were humbled to discover that by any standard—mortal or heavenly—the people who had received Mary very much needed her. Those who knew them, we found, had been praying that family's life would be blessed and their hearts somehow touched by the Christmas spirit. A second nativity was purchased for the original family we had selected.

The Joseph from the first nativity went to join his Mary that night.

Is there a twelve days of Christmas family you'd like to adopt in your town?

DECEMBER 14
Comfort Days
It is not enough merely to live. One must have sunshine, freedom, and a little flower. —Hans Christian Andersen[280]

Buy. Shop. Deal. Save. Beep. Buzz. Flash. Pop. Too much sensory sugar. A glitz of sight and sound. Plain and simple comforts of the season get lost. Before you know it, Christmas will be packing up and heading out of town. Create and savor comfort days that herald in wonder and joy. Learn about the Christmas customs, traditions, and foods in the countries your ancestors are from. Or pick a country that interests you and discover their Christmas customs and foods.

Mix and match newfound traditions with your own. Arrange an old-fashioned sleigh ride for family and friends. Sleep in. Have breakfast in bed. Take the phone off the hook for a cookie night. Gather everyone together and make special breads or jams. Make gingerbread men or gingerbread houses. Sleep in the living room together. Light candles. Line the walks with luminarias. Make stars out of paper or twigs. Adopt a Christmas family or child.

Celebrate the little things: the smiles and laughter of children, an unexpected call from a friend, the smell of a real Christmas tree, the aroma and warmth of hot cocoa. Remember snow angels? They're just as fun when you're an adult. Make a snowman or provide something for someone who's making one: an old hat, a carrot for a nose, sticks for arms. Journal your thoughts.

Family. Home. Peace. Calm. Joy. Wonder. Beauty. Love. The comfort words of Christmas!

DECEMBER 15
Abundance: Always Counting Blessings
A faithful man shall abound with blessings. —Proverbs 28:20

"It's just another Saturday," I sighed as I swung my feet over the edge of the bed. Outside, thick gray clouds loomed, signaling another winter storm. Viewing the impending snowstorm from my bedroom window, my mood sank to meet the dimness of the cold morning. Yet, walking around the edge of the bed it struck me: I was alive and walking. What a blessing! My mind flashed back to December 15, 2007—not just another Saturday. It was the last Saturday my friend Stacey had on earth. After a four-year battle with leukemia, she'd died two days later. I'd lost count of all the Saturdays that followed. Like a careless child, I'd let them slip through my fingers.

Walking through the house, I looked past piles of laundry, crumbs hiding in corners on the floor, and dishes everyone somehow forgot to do. Such things—plus my ever-burgeoning list of Saturday chores— were only mundane and tedious if I let them be. They were, in reality, signs that all in our household was bustling with life and living.

What a blessing.

During the hectic days this month, don't forget to count and celebrate your blessings. You'll rediscover them in abundance!

DECMEBER 16
Entertaining with Ease
From home to home, and heart to heart, from one place to another the warmth and joy of Christmas, brings us closer to each other.
—Emily Matthews[281]

Often we feel stressed during the holidays as we attempt to forge memories that yield happiness. Prioritize. Pick what means the most, what you look forward to, what you enjoy. Skip the rest.

Limit the size of your gatherings and concentrate on making them memorable. Small get-togethers that leave you feeling satisfied are much better than huge extravaganzas that deplete you physically and emotionally. Accept help and delegate responsibilities. Go potluck, and ask your guests to bring either a main dish, side, or dessert.

Holiday brunches with simple breakfast casseroles, frozen waffles, premade muffins, fruits, and juices are fast and easy to host. In lieu of parties heavy on feasting and presents, have a special memory night where family and friends come prepared to share stories of the season, recount personal anecdotes, read Christmas books together, or view old photos and home movies. Have eggnog or cocoa ready, or serve a selection of homemade candies you've invited your guests to bring.

Take everyone to see the lights downtown. Carol at a nursing home. Volunteer to serve a meal at a homeless shelter. All are ways of commemorating the spirit of the season. So is skipping a social event to stay home and listen to Christmas music or engaging family members in creating a holiday memory book with reminiscences from years past.

DECEMBER 17
Simple Decor
I love Christmas, not just because of the presents but because of all the decorations and lights and the warmth of the season.
—Ashley Tisdale[282]

Contrary to popular belief, you don't have to decorate every room in the house. Remember that every room and surface you decorate will end up needing to be undecorated! Decorating can be as simple as adding distinctive touches your guests will remember. Even during the holidays, less is more. Old family photos, cherished holiday cards, a few pinecones or old ornaments on the mantel, piano, or windowsill—all add understated yet calming cheer.

Bright napkins help create an inviting atmosphere, as does Christmas music. A few candles or a string of indoor lights are simple touches that yield comfort; so are fresh pine boughs and ribbons. Delegate one of your guests to bring a centerpiece. Kids love to help. Let them. And don't worry about what anyone might think of their efforts. Stringing together popcorn, cranberries, and marshmallows can keep kids as happy now as it did years ago—especially when their work is proudly displayed.

The easiest way to simplify decorating is to cut down. If you have boxes and boxes of things and increasingly find you have no time to display them, consider donating them to a charity, a nursing home, or a homeless shelter.

DECEMBER 18
That's a Wrap: Easy Gift Wrapping
The Christmas tree is a symbol of love, not money. There's a kind of glory to them when they're all lit up that exceeds anything all the money in the world could buy. —Andy Rooney[283]

The Chinese invented paper. The Hall brothers (Hallmark) are said to have invented modern gift wrap. In 1917 during the Christmas rush, the brothers ran out of solid-colored gift wrapping and instead had to use elaborately decorated French envelope linings—which became so popular the brothers elected to start printing their own. The rest, as they say, is history.

Designate an area away from heavy traffic zones in your home as a gift wrap center. Empty oatmeal containers are great for storing bows, ribbons, and gift tags. Use a small box or container to stash pens or felt-tip markers, tape, and scissors, and keep it alongside everything else. Or keep everything, rolls of wrapping paper included, in a plastic storage container that can easily slide under a bed. The lid of such containers makes a handy surface for wrapping.

Old panty hose can be cut into sections (like large rubber bands) and stretched over rolls of wrapping paper to keep them from coming unrolled. Two or three rolls of gift wrap can be joined for organized storage by securing them together in a similar fashion. To save expense, wrap gifts with old newspaper, calendar or magazine pages, or colorful fabric. Twine or string adds a vintage touch.

DECEMBER 19
Simplify Cooking and Baking
Remove far from me vanity and lies: give me neither poverty nor riches; feed me with food convenient for me. —Proverbs 30:8

Are there main dishes or sides you can make beforehand and freeze? Use freezer-to-oven containers so you can quickly heat and serve on days when you have big meals and lots of guests. Use disposable serving dishes, Crock-pot liners, and pans. Disposable baking pans are not only great for easy clean up but for sending leftovers home with guests.

If you don't enjoy baking or don't have time, use store-made cookie dough and frosting. The fun of cookie decorating isn't diminished when you don't make the dough yourself. Use a straw to cut out a hole in your creations so they can later be used as ornaments. Even already-baked cookies from the store can quickly be made to look festive by using colorful premade icings and gels, or by dipping them in melted chocolate and sprinkling with nuts, dried fruits, or crushed candies. Muffins in decorative cups and dipped pretzel rods are also fast and easy alternatives to making, baking, and decorating dozens of cookies.

Bake cakes in disposable pans or in thrift-store bakeware finds (well washed, of course) that you can give away. Cakes baked into mugs and cups (check the Internet for how-to instructions and advice on choosing the right containers) covered with plastic wrap secured by a festive ribbon yield fast and attractive gifts.

DECEMBER 20
Remember: Honoring Loved Ones Who Have Passed On
And he shall turn the heart of the fathers to the children, and the heart of the children to their fathers. —Malachi 4:6

I've never visited the polar ice cap, but I think it must look much like our local cemetery did one Christmas Eve. It was nearly eleven p.m. when we donned coats, gloves, hats, and scarves and set out. Blowing and drifting snow obscured most of the headstones and made navigation difficult. Several times we thought we'd located the right grave only to find, after digging and scraping away snow, that we were in the wrong place. Persistence paid off. At each of the six graves of our loved ones, we dug down to frozen grass, created a partial snow cave, and nestled a lighted lantern next to the shelter of the headstone. We scooped and packed snow into little walls, working until each wick burned brightly.

Hands, fingers, faces, and toes numb from the cold, we left the last grave and clambered back into the truck just before midnight. Those we loved had passed on, but the lanterns represented our remembrance of how they had brightened our lives.

Lighting lanterns or luminarias are only two of several ways you can celebrate the lives of those you love who have passed on. Some families hang stockings for deceased loved ones and write messages of devotion and hope to place inside. Special ornaments on the tree, stories told at family gatherings, and old photos on the mantel are additional ideas to demonstrate honor and family unity.

DECEMBER 21
Celebrating What We Have: Happiness Is in the Heart of the Beholder
Happy is the man that findeth wisdom, and the man that getteth understanding. —Proverbs 3:13

The first Christmas after my grandma Esther's death, I found myself in possession of her box of gold-colored ornaments. To those that still bore their silver caps but had no hanger, she'd fastened green thread or plastic bread ties. For one without a cap, she'd bent the prongs of a bobby pin out and gently pushed it inside. I wondered what people would think if I used the decorations on my tree. I contemplated removing Grandma's innovations and hanging the ornaments with my own hooks. Somehow that seemed disloyal; so did not displaying the ornaments at all. I decided to use them as they were. Days later, their message hit home.

I'd noticed throughout the holidays, two distinct types of people: those intent on finding just the right—often extravagant—gifts to evoke happiness in themselves and the recipients, and those who concentrated their efforts on being grateful for what they had, even if it was very little. Among the second set of people, I'd observed the efforts of a man and his wife who used their limited means to clothe the homeless. I'd seen the tears of an old man over a simple but heartfelt gift. Those people, my heart confirmed, were genuinely happy.

In the stillness of evening, I sat next to our Christmas tree. Its white lights illuminated Grandma's ornaments; the one with the bobby pin was nearest me. How could I have thought of not displaying them? They were a symbol of Grandma's wisdom: true happiness isn't dependent on the nature of anything external. Happiness at Christmas—or at any time of year—is in the heart of the beholder, the manner in which we choose to perceive our circumstances.

DECEMBER 22
A Wish Tree

This is my wish for you: comfort on difficult days, smiles when sadness intrudes, rainbows to follow the clouds, laughter to kiss your lips, sunset to warm your heart, hugs when spirits sag, beauty for your eyes to see, friendships to brighten your being, faith so that you can believe, confidence for when you doubt, courage to know yourself, patience to accept the truth, love to complete your life. —Author unknown

Create a wish tree for the holidays. A pine bough or tree branch works well. Suspend the bough or branch by a length of ribbon hung on a wall. Cut lengths of ribbon or cording. Card stock can be used to create rectangles or various shapes such as doves, holly leaves, or snowflakes. Punch holes in the shapes. Display "The Wish Tree Poem." Place the ribbon and shapes near the tree along with a pen. Invite family, friends, and holiday guests to write messages of hope, good cheer, love, forgiveness, happy thoughts, and wished-for blessings. Signing names is optional. Thread the lengths of ribbon through the holes, and tie the shapes to the tree. Make it a challenge to fill the tree with wishes by Christmas Day!

When the holidays end, remove the shapes and burn them in the fireplace to symbolize the wishes going to heaven. Or store them in a memento box.

The Wish Tree Poem

Take a moment. Stop and share.
Happy thoughts, a poem, a quote.

Well wishes and good cheer.
From your heart, your words—a note!
Love, blessings, forgiveness, hope.
Sentiment adorns the tree.
Christmas wishes so dear.
Miracles. Just wait and see!

DECEMBER 23
A Recipe for Christmas Joy

*Are you willing to forget what you have done for other people, and to
remember what other people have done for you. . . . Are you willing to
stoop down and consider the needs and the desires of little children; to
remember the weakness and loneliness of people who are growing old. . . .
Are you willing to believe that love is the strongest thing in the world . . .
stronger than hate, stronger than evil, stronger than death. . . . Then
you can keep Christmas. And if you keep it for a day, why not always?*
—Henry Van Dyke[284]

Recipe for Christmas Joy:

2 cups Love
2 cups Gratitude
1 cup Selfless Giving
1 cup Forgiveness
¾ cup Prayer
½ cup each Compassion and Hope
¼ cup Hugs
3 Tablespoons Joy, Peace on Earth, and Goodwill toward Men
A dash of Wonder
Dozens of Smiles

Mix Love, Gratitude, Selfless Giving, Forgiveness, and Prayer.
Blend in Compassion and Hope. Sprinkle in Hugs. Stir in Joy, Peace
on Earth, and Goodwill toward Men. Add the dash of Wonder. Top
with smiles. Store in a warm heart. Will last all year long. Yield:
Countless miracles. Serve to one and all.

DECEMBER 24
The True Meaning of Christmas
O little town of Bethlehem,
How still we see thee lie!
Above thy deep and dreamless sleep
The silent stars go by;
Yet in thy dark streets shineth
The everlasting Light;
The hopes and fears of all the years
Are met in thee to-night.
—Phillips Brooks[285]

Throughout my life, I enjoyed the blessing of experiencing with my grandparents what I can best term as Hallmark Hall of Fame Christmases. Each Christmas, a fragrant evergreen was cut from a nearby hillside and adorned with inexpensive decorations. Stockings were hung by the woodstove, and a brilliant lighted wooden star illuminated the yard and shone as a beacon to travelers on dark, snowy nights. Material gifts were few, but love was abundant.

On Christmas morning 2006, my uncle phoned. "Lori," he sobbed, "your grandmother has died." Five days later, my grandfather passed away as well. My life, and Christmas, seemed to shatter into a thousand tiny pieces. I looked forward to bleak days filled with sadness. How could I ever look at Christmas the same way again?

Over the ensuing weeks, truth flickered then burned brightly deep within my heart: Grandpa and Grandma were gone from this world, but Christmas was still Christmas. It remained a precious time to celebrate the birth of the Savior and His gift of love that extends to all. It was still a time to count and fully comprehend my many blessings, a time to share what was in my heart with family and friends. It remained the very Christmas my grandparents had commemorated each year with joy and anticipation, though they too had suffered losses.

My grandparents had given me a blueprint I wanted to follow. Humbled, I realized I wanted to construct a legacy that would bless the lives of future generations, just as my life had been blessed.

Bless the lives of your family with hope and happiness.

DECEMBER 25

Faith, Hope, and Charity

With malice toward none, with charity for all, with firmness in the right as God gives us to see the right, let us finish the work we are in.
—Abraham Lincoln[286]

During this wonderful Christmas season, discuss with your family what the words faith, hope, and charity mean to you. Perhaps you will want to write down your impressions so future generations can know what is in your heart. Christmas is a magical time and will always be so. Choosing to fully embrace the season despite trials will yield the true joy the holiday was intended to bring. The greatest gifts are indeed as simple and heartfelt as was the gift of a baby born in a stable.

Remember your gift to yourself from November: your list of joys and tender mercies. Read and savor it!

DECEMBER 26

Simple Faith: Miracles All Year Long

A prophet has been described as a great torchlight striding through the earth lighting the lamps of truth. Your candle has been lit; mine has been lit; it is up to us to keep the flame burning and thereby light many more. —Marjorie Pay Hinckley[287]

Another Christmas has come and gone. For most of us, it has done so much too quickly. The spirit the season brings, however, does not need to end when ribbons and bows and decorations are put away. Magic and wonder can fill our lives year-round. Hope, joy, and love continue to await discovery. You can step confidently into the new year and light the way for others.

Use the following instructions to make ice candles this week. These are great for the table, front porch, or yard. Let their light remind you that simple faith yields great miracles regardless of the date on the calendar.

Ice Candles

Large (24-oz. or 22-oz.) cottage cheese containers
An equal number of medium-sized (6 oz.) yogurt containers
Pea gravel or other small rocks
Fresh cranberries
Sprigs of holly, mistletoe, or pine
Curly willow
Tea candles

Wash containers and dry. Pour two inches of water into each cottage cheese container and freeze.

Fill each yogurt container half full with gravel or other small rocks. Center the yogurt containers on the ice inside the cottage cheese containers. Arrange cranberries and foliage in the space between the two containers. Fill the cottage cheese containers with water to the top rims of the yogurt containers—don't fill the yogurt containers with water—and carefully place in the freezer. Double check to ensure the yogurt containers are still centered in the cottage cheese containers. Freeze overnight. Pour the gravel or rocks out of yogurt containers. Add warm water to the yogurt containers—just enough to loosen them from the ice. Briefly run the cottage cheese containers under warm water until the ice vase slides out. Place the vases on a decorative tin tray or aluminum pie plate. Put tea candles into the vases and light.

DECEMBER 27
A Family Quilt
Blankets wrap you in warmth, quilts wrap you in love.
—Author unknown

While everyone is still gathered for the holidays, make a family quilt. Cut six-inch squares of fabric. Depending on the quilt size and the number of those contributing, figure out how many blocks to give each family member. Have them draw in pencil on their square or squares. They can write their name, use a block letter for their given name or surname, write down a short quote, or sketch an object.

After they have finished this step, have them use fabric paints or a needle and embroidery threads to trace over what they have drawn.

When all the squares are completed, assign a family member to piece them together. Use your quilt at home or give it to someone in need.

DECEMBER 28
Listen, Listening, Listened

For behold, thus saith the Lord God: I will give unto the children of men line upon line, precept upon precept, here a little and there a little; and blessed are those who hearken unto my precepts, and lend an ear unto my counsel, for they shall learn wisdom; for unto him that receiveth I will give more. —2 Nephi 28:30

Today the request was simple. A family member asked me to accompany them on a drive. The Spirit strongly indicated I should not go. Logically, there was no reason why. Though my heart was troubled, I knew I'd received counsel that was for my benefit. I didn't go. Hours later, a call came to my husband. The vehicle I would have been traveling in had broken down in a dangerous area. Eventually, all turned out well. Would things have turned out the same had I gone along? Or for some reason—timing or course of travel—worse? I will never know. I do know, however, that the Spirit is never wrong.

Elder Russell M. Nelson has taught that blessings come as we learn to listen then strive to learn from the Spirit what the Lord instructs. In doing so, we find truth and peace.

DECEMBER 29
Faith: Confidence in the Future

New Year's Eve is like every other night; there is no pause in the march of the universe, no breathless moment of silence among created things that the passage of another twelve months may be noted; and yet no man has quite the same thoughts this evening that come with the coming of darkness on other nights. —Hamilton Wright Mabie[288]

At the beginning of each new year, we traditionally sum up our lives and determine new goals and aspirations—contrasted with where we have been, and what we have done or accomplished in the past. In considering the past, Elder Jeffrey R. Holland asks us what the wife of Lot did wrong when she looked back. He asserts it wasn't merely the act of looking back, but that she yearned for her past. Just steps into her departure from Sodom and Gomorrah, she already missed her old life. Her affection for where she had been overshadowed her belief in the possibilities of a better future.[289]

The past is to be learned from, not lived in. As we move forward with faith, Elder Holland points out that we should carry the best forward with us but forsake what might drag us down or impede our progress. We should expect and trust that God's love will have a transformative power over our lives.[290]

As Elder Holland counsels, focus on the future with faith. Anticipate "trust and divine love that will transform your life today, tomorrow, and forever."[291]

DECEMBER 30
New Year's Resolutions: Seek Things of Eternal Value
Seek ye the kingdom of God; and all these things shall be added unto you. —Luke 12:31

In the coming year, instead of resolutions that focus on your exterior self, turn to your inner self, your spiritual self. Remember all you have learned about your potential. You can accomplish all you set your mind to when you focus on what's most important: you are a daughter of God. Do you want to lose weight to improve your health because you value yourself or only so others will admire you? Do you want to make more money to get out of debt or because you want things that will bring mortal regard and status? Do you dream to search for isles of transitory mortal pleasures or to discover the fullness of the promise God designed you to have as an eternal being?

We are of the highest quality workmanship. Heavenly Father designed us to be around forever. He didn't make us just to simply accumulate material things that "moth and rust doth corrupt." Our underpinnings of royal, heavenly heritage predispose us on the deepest level of our being to yearn for things of eternal value. If we dismiss that, we do ourselves a great disservice. We can't settle for less, for things of little or no significance. We desire, need, and deserve true and lasting happiness.

As the new year approaches, take time to contemplate goals that are in line with your eternal priorities.

DECEMBER 31
The Gifts of the Journey

And, if you keep my commandments and endure to the end you shall have eternal life, which gift is the greatest of all the gifts of God.
—D&C 14:7

Full of wonder, promise, and hope. Gifts. Carefully wrapped and adorned. Given in love they awaited. Did you leave any of your Christmas presents unopened? Hopefully by now they are not only opened but enjoyed. The moment you unwrapped that box of fine candy, you knew you'd have to avoid the scales for a while. But, oh, those chocolates were good! The sweater you wanted, just your size and color, is warm and cozy. You'll wear it often with pride. The bright red socks with dancing reindeer whose noses light up? Warm too, but you'll only wear them at home!

What about the spiritual gifts you found along your journey this year? Have you opened those as well? Are you enjoying them to the fullest? Unlike some material gifts, all spiritual gifts have purpose that will bless your life.

This year we've discussed steps to strengthen our belief that we are God's daughters, divine and full of potential. Through prayer and scripture study, we've gleaned determination to travel. We've talked about dancing through both joys and challenges and learned a little more about walking in the light. No doubt, through your faith, obedience, and diligence, your light shines brighter. I pray that you've gathered armfuls of love, harvested blessings, defined what you stand for, and experienced a greater depth and breadth of gratitude—all in pursuit of realizing the fullness of possibilities inherent in your birthright.

You've become aware of other gifts waiting along the way. The gift of knowing that God is your Father and Jesus Christ is His Son and your beloved Brother. The gift of knowing yourself better, of loving yourself, and of forgiving yourself for mistakes, misconceptions, and imperfections. The gifts of friendship and family, of knowledge, and of teaching your children. The gifts of emotional healing that can be yours through the Atonement. Gifts of miracles to record as Mindful of Me entries.

You have likely become conscious that even problems are gifts because working on their solutions illuminates your strengths. Some gifts you have perhaps found without much effort. Others have required attentive work and much prayer and fasting. As you've sought spiritual gifts to help and guide you—working in obedience and trusting your Father in Heaven—you've become mindful of how they can benefit your life and the lives of others.

Your spiritual gifts bring great blessings but only when diligently sought, carefully unwrapped—sometimes layer by delicate layer— then used and enjoyed in gratitude. Once they are yours and opened, what then?

Do you allow your good silver to be used as garden tools? Do you use your grandmother's crystal or china as pet dishes? I hope not! Spiritual gifts should be guarded just as fine silver or china. Much more so, they should be honored, revered, and cherished for their infinite, priceless value.

This coming year, every precious day, each moment will bring marvelous gifts. Filled with hope, wonder, and promise, they await you. Discover them. Hold them to your heart, and celebrate each one!

Recipes for December

Savory Sausage and Egg Pie

1 lb. turkey Italian sausage
1 medium red pepper, chopped
1 small white onion, chopped
1 package (16 oz.) small curd 1% cottage cheese

2 cups shredded Monterey Jack cheese
6 eggs, beaten
1 cup milk
1 cup Bisquick
1 cup shredded pepper jack cheese

Cook sausage, pepper, and onion until sausage is browned. Drain. In a large bowl, mix together cottage cheese, Monterey Jack cheese, eggs, milk, and Bisquick. Blend in sausage mixture. Coat a 9x13 baking dish with cooking spray, and pour mixture into it. Sprinkle top with with pepper jack cheese. Bake at 350 degrees for 40 minutes or until set. Allow to cool slightly before cutting.

Quick Holiday Breakfast Bake

1 medium white onion, diced
1 medium red onion, diced
1 large clove garlic, minced
2 cups fresh mushrooms, sliced
4 cups frozen hash brown potatoes, thawed
1 pound bacon, cooked, drained, and crumbled

4 eggs
1 ½ cups half and half
1 teaspoon cracked black pepper
1 cup shredded Monterey Jack cheese
½ cup shredded cheddar cheese

Sauté onions, garlic, and mushrooms until tender. Spray 9x13 casserole dish with nonstick spray. Layer hash browns on bottom of dish. Top with bacon, sautéed onions, garlic, and mushrooms. Beat eggs, half and half, and pepper. Pour over other ingredients in dish. Sprinkle with cheeses. Cover tightly with foil. Refrigerate overnight. Bake 1 hour at 400 degrees or until set.

Tortilla Breakfast Casserole

2 cups diced cooked ham
1 cup white onion, finely diced
½ cup green onions, chopped
10 eight-inch flour tortillas
4 cups shredded mozzarella cheese
2 (15 oz.) cans Stokes Green Chile Sauce

2 cups half and half
1 Tablespoon Greek yogurt
1 small can green chilies
1 dash Tabasco sauce
6 eggs, beaten

Preheat oven to 350 degrees. Combine ham, onion, and green onions. Put ¼ to ⅓ cup of mixture lengthwise down the center of each tortilla. Divide and sprinkle 2 cups of cheese into each tortilla over the ham mixture. Add 2–3 Tablespoons Stokes Green Chile Sauce. Roll tortillas and put seam side down in a well-greased 9x13 baking dish. Combine half and half, yogurt, green chilies, Tabasco, and eggs. Mix until smooth. Pour over tortillas in dish. Cover tightly with foil, and refrigerate overnight. Bake at 350 degrees for 25 minutes, covered.

Uncover and bake for 10 minutes more. Sprinkle on the remaining 2 cups cheese; bake until cheese melts.

Christmas Morning Lemon French Toast with Berries

1 (8 oz.) package reduced-fat cream cheese (Neufchatel), softened
⅓ cup powdered sugar
1 teaspoon lemon extract
1 teaspoon vanilla
1 (22 oz.) can lemon pie filling
8 eggs
2 cups milk or half and half

1 loaf French bread, cut into slices (approx. 16)
¾ cup quick-cooking rolled oats
¼ cup packed brown sugar
1 teaspoon ground cinnamon
½ teaspoon nutmeg
3 Tablespoons butter, soft
Powdered sugar
Fresh blueberries or raspberries

Preheat oven to 350 degrees. Spray a 9x13 baking dish with nonstick spray. In a large bowl combine cream cheese, sugar, lemon extract, and vanilla until smooth. Add the pie filling. Mix until well blended. In a separate bowl, whisk eggs and milk until blended. Arrange eight of the bread slices in the dish. Pour half the egg mixture over the top, ensuring it is spread evenly. Spoon lemon filling onto each bread slice, and cover evenly. Top with remaining slices. Pour in remaining half of the egg mixture. Combine oats, sugar, cinnamon, and nutmeg. Cut in butter until crumbly. Sprinkle over ingredients in the baking dish. Bake 40–50 minutes until set. Cool before serving. Sprinkle with powdered sugar. Top with berries.

Notes

1. C. S. Lewis, *Mere Christianity*, Harper San Francisco; Revised & Enlarged edition, 2009, pp. 136-137.
2. Elder M. Russell Ballard, "Pioneer Faith and Fortitude—Then and Now," From an address delivered in Ogden, Utah, on July 15, 2012.
3. Joseph Langford, *Mother Teresa's Secret Fire: The Encounter That Changed Her Life, and How It Can Transform Your Own*, Our Sunday Visitor; First Printing edition 2008, p. 145.
4. Spencer W. Kimball, "The Role of Righteous Women," October 1979 General Conference.
5. Elie Wiesel, "Oprah Talks to Elie Wiesel," *O: The Oprah Magazine* (November 2000), http://www.oprah.com/omagazine/Oprah-Interviews-Elie-Wiesel/2.
6. Gordon B. Hinckley, *Way to Be! 9 Ways to Be Happy and Make Something of Your Life*, Simon & Schuster, 2002.
7. James E. Faust, "An Attitude of Gratitude," April 2009 general conference.
8. Henry B. Eyring, "Trust in God, Then Go and Do," October 2010 general conference.
9. Jane Austen, *Mansfield Park*, W. W. Norton & Company, 1998, p 81.
10. Epictetus, *The Discourses of Epictetus: With the Enchirdion and Fragments*, London, William Clowes and Sons, Limited, Stamford Street and Charing Cross, 1890, p. 429.
11. www.megjohnsonspeaks.com/meet-meg.html
12. Virginia U. Jensen, "Lead, Kindly Light," *Ensign*, November 2000.
13. Ann Morrow Lindbergh, *Gift from the Sea*, Pantheon, 1991, p. 50.
14. Bob Votruba, http://www.onemillionactsofkindness.com/about.
15. Ralph Waldo Emerson, Journals (1822–1863), 12 April 1834.
16. Oswald Chambers, *The Golden Book of Oswald Chambers: My Utmost for His Highest*; Selections for the Year, Dodd, Mead, 1935, University of Virginia, p. 241.
17. Erma Bombeck, *The Erma Bombeck Collection: If Life Is a Bowl of Cherries, What Am I Doing in the Pits?*
18. Helen Keller, *We Bereaved*, 1929, Reprinted in *The International Thesaurus of Quotations: Revised Edition*, HarperCollins Publishers, Inc.
19. Spencer W. Kimball, "The Lord Expects Righteousness," October 1982 general conference.
20. http://www.nytimes.com/2010/02/16/health/16real.html?_r=3&.

352   SIMPLE THINGS

21. Grandma Moses, *Grandma Moses: My Life's History*, 1951.
22. James Frances Dwyer, "The Citizen," From *Collier's Weekly*, Reprinted in *The Best American Short Stories and the Yearbook of the American Short Story*, Edited by Edward Joseph Harrington O'Brien, Martha Foley, Houghton Mifflin Company, 1916, p. 75.
23. Brigham Young, *Journal of Discourses*, p. 250.
24. Jewel Adams, personal interview with Lori Nawyn, August 5, 2001.
25. Dallin H. Oaks, "Good, Better, Best," October 2007 general conference.
26. Robert Frost, "Stopping by Woods on a Snowy Evening," *The Poetry of Robert Frost*, edited by Edward Connery Lathem, by Henry Holt and Company, Inc., 1969.
27. As quoted in *Long May You Run: all. things. running.* by Chris Cooper, Simon and Schuster, 2010, p. 6.
28. As quoted in *The 7 Habits of Highly Effective Teens* by Sean Covey, Simon and Schuster, 2011, p. 38.
29. As quoted by John Alexander Dowie in *Leaves of Healing*, Volume 37, Zion House Publishing, 1915, p. 12.
30. Dallin H. Oaks, "Faith in the Lord Jesus Christ," April 1994 general conference.
31. As quoted in *Take 2: Your Guide to Creating Happy Endings and New Beginnings*, by Leeza Gibbons, Hay House, Inc., 2013.
32. Ibid.
33. Epictetus, as quoted in *The Air Up There: More Great Quotations on Flight*, McGraw Hill Professional, 2003, p. 155.
34. Helen Keller and Annie Sullivan, *The Story of My Life*, Grosset and Dunlap, 1905, p. 113.
35. Ralph Waldo Emerson, *Essays and Poems by Ralph Waldo Emerson*, Spark Educational Publishing, 2004, p. 280.
36. As quoted in Theodore Roosevelt, *An Autobiography, by Theodore Roosevelt*, Charles Scribner and Sons, 1913, p. 337.
37. Henry Ford, *My Life and Work*, Doubleday, Page & Company, 1922, p. 220.
38. Dr. Norman Vincent Peale, *You Can If You Think You Can*, Simon and Schuster, 2013, p. 36.
39. Viktor E. Frankl, *Man's Search for Meaning*, Beacon Press, 2006.
40. Elder Robert D. Hales, "Waiting Upon the Lord: Thy Will Be Done," October 2011 general conference.
41. http://www.cnn.com/2007/HEALTH/07/09/antidepressants/.
42. *Tuck Everlasting*, 2002.
43. http://www.goodreads.com/author/show/18732.Masaru_Emoto
44. Louisa May Alcott, *Little Women*, Simon and Schuster, 2013, p. 846.
45. G. K. Chesterton, *The Wit and Wisdom of G. K. Chesterton*, p. 243.
46. Elder Gary E. Stevenson, "Sacred Homes: Sacred Temples," April 2009 general conference.
47. As quoted by Stephen R. Covey in *Daily Reflections for Highly Effective People: Living the Seven Habits of Highly Successful People*, Simon and Schuster, 1994, p. 319.
48. Marianne Williamson, *A Return to Love: Reflections on the Principles of "A Course in Miracles,"* HarperCollins, 1992, p. 190.
49. Henry David Thoreau, *Walden: A Fully Annotated Edition*, Yale University Press, 2004, p. 315.

50. Helen Keller, *The Open Door*, Doubleday, 1957.
51. Henry David Thoreau, *Walden and Other Writings*, Random House, 2004, p. 79.
52. H.L. Wiese, personal interview with Lori Nawyn, 2005.
53. Miriama Kallon, "Learning to Hope," *New Era*, November 2006.
54. Pat Williams, *How to Be Like Walt: Capturing the Magic Every Day of Your Life*, HCI, 2004, p. 63.
55. From an interview with Anne Stevenson by Lidia Vianu, *Desperado Essay-Interviews*, Editura Universitatii din Bucuresti, 2006.
56. Presented as a statement of 1877, as quoted in *From Telegraph to Light Bulb with Thomas Edison*, 2007, by Deborah Hedstrom-Page, B&H Books, p. 22.
57. Mark Victor Hansen, http://markvictorhansen.com/about-us/.
58. Henriette Anne Klauser, *Write It Down, Make It Happen: Knowing What You Want—And Getting It!*, Simon and Schuster, 2012.
59. As quoted in *Rediscovering Your Happily Ever After: Moving from Hopeless to Hopeful as a Newly Divorced Mother* by Peggy Sue Wells, Kregel Publications, 2010, p. 199.
60. President Gordon B. Hinckley, "Stand Up for Truth," BYU Devotional, September 1996.
61. William Stixrud, PhD, http://www.scholastic.com/parents/resources/article/homework-project-tips/perils-multitasking.
62. As quoted in *Stories That Move Mountains: Storytelling and Visual Design for Persuasive Presentations* (Google eBook), Martin Sykes, Nick Malik, Mark D. West, Published by John Wiley & Sons, 2012, p. 89.
63. As quoted in *The Athlete's Way: Sweat and the Biology of Bliss*, by Christopher Bergland, Macmillan, 2007, p. 293.
64. Speech given at Harrow School, Harrow, England, October 29, 1941. Quoted in *Churchill by Himself: The Definitive Collection of Quotations*, 2008, editor Richard Langworth, Published by PublicAffairs, 2008, p. 23.
65. Philip James Bailey, *Festus*, 1839, scene "A Country Town."
66. As quoted in *The Mountain Within: Leadership Lessons and Inspiration for Your Climb to the Top*, McGraw Hill Professional, 2011, p. 166.
67. Thomas Moore, *SoulMates*, HarperCollins, 1994, p. 95.
68. As quoted in *My Favorite Quotations*, by Norman Vincent Peale, HarperCollins, 1990.
69. *The Dramatic Works of William Shakespeare*, "All's Well That Ends Well," Phillips, Sampson, and Co., 1850, p. 240.
70. Katie Shepherd, personal interview with Lori Nawyn, 2012.
71. As quoted in *Elizabeth Taylor, A Passion for Life: The Wit and Wisdom of a Legend* (Google eBook), by Joseph Papa, HarperCollins, 2011, p. 179.
72. President James E. Faust, "Welcoming Every Single One," *Ensign*, August 2007.
73. As quoted in *The Parent You Want to Be* by Les and Leslie Parrot, Zondervan, 2009.
74. As quoted in *How to Be Lovely: The Audrey Hepburn Way of Life*, by Melissa Hellstern, Penguin, 2004.
75. *Teachings of Presidents of the Church: Brigham Young*, 1997, pp. 183–91.
76. As quoted in *Chicken Soup for the Sister's Soul 2: Celebrating Love and Laughter Throughout Our Lives*, by Jack Canfield, Mark Victor Hansen, Patty Aubery, and Kelly Zimmerman, Open Road Media, 2012.
77. As quoted in *Phillips' Book of Great Thoughts and Funny Sayings* by Bob Phillips, Tyndale House Publishers, Inc., 1993, p. 136.

78. Suzy Toronto, From her artwork.
79. Speech of Senator John F. Kennedy, Raleigh, NC, Coliseum, September 17, 1960.
80. Elizabeth Barrett Browning, *Aurora Leigh*, 1856, Book II.
81. As quoted in *Winning with People: Discover the People Principles That Work for You Every Time* by John C. Maxwell, Thomas Nelson, Inc., 2005, p. 245.
82. As quoted in *Chicken Soup for the Teenage Soul III*, Jack Canfield, Mark Victor Hansen, Kimberly Kirberger, Open Road Media, 2012.
83. Helen Keller, *To Love This Life: Quotations by Helen Keller*, American Foundation for the Blind, 2000, p. 33.
84. As quoted in *Ancestry Magazine*, Ancestors Special Edition, 1996.
85. Letter to William Hamilton, April 22, 1800.
86. As quoted in *The Power of a Woman's Words* by Sharon Jaynes, Harvest House Publishers, 2007, p. 96.
87. As quoted in *One Year of Sunday School Lessons for Young Children* by Florence Ursula Palmer, The Macmillan Company, 1899, p. 204.
88. President Spencer W. Kimball, "President Spencer W. Kimball Speaks Out on Service to Others," *New Era*, March 1981.
89. Marvin J. Ashton, "What Is a Friend?" *Ensign*, January 1973, p. 41.
90. Henry David Thoreau, *The Writings of Henry David Thoreau*, Volume 8, Houghton Mifflin, 1887, p. 346.
91. John Greenleaf Whittier, *The Complete Poetical Works of John Greenleaf Whittier*, Volume 1, Houghton, Mifflin, 1895, p. 290.
92. Anne Frank, The Diary, 12 June 1942–1 August 1944.
93. *Ratatouille*, 2007.
94. As quoted in *The Harper Books of Quotations*, HarperCollins, 1993, p. 162.
95. Betsie Ten Boom as quoted in *The Hiding Place* by Corrie Ten Boom, Hendrickson Publishers, 2009, p. 240.
96. As quoted in *Dictionary of Burning Words of Brilliant Writers* by Josiah Hotchkiss Gilbert, 1895, p. 251.
97. As quoted in *A Dictionary of Thoughts*, Tyron Edwards, F. B. Dickerson Company, 1908, p. 458.
98. As quoted in *The Harper Book of Quotations*, Revised Edition, Harper Collins, 1993, p. 215.
99. President James E. Faust, "The Healing Power of Forgiveness," April 2007 general conference.
100. As quoted in *Taking Flight: Inspiration and Techniques to Give Your Creative Spirit Wings* by Kelly Rae Roberts, North Light Books, 2008, p. 83.
101. President James E. Faust, "Five Loaves and Two Fishes," April 1994 general conference.
102. Mahatma Gandhi, "Interview to the Press," 23 March 1931; published in *Young India*, 2 April 1931.
103. Gordon B. Hinckley, "Forgiveness." October 2005 general conference.
104. As quoted in *A Dictionary of Thoughts* by Tyron Edwards, F. B. Dickerson Company, 1908, p. 582.
105. As quoted in *The One Year Love Talk Devotional for Couples* by Les and Leslie Parrot, Tyndale House Publishers, Inc., 2011.
106. Elder Russell M. Nelson, "Blessed Are the Peacemakers," October 2002 general conference.

107. As quoted in *The Oxford Dictionary of American Quotations*, Oxford University Press, 2006, p. 213.

108. President Thomas S. Monson, "A Doorway Called Love," October 1987 general conference.

109. Stephen E. Robinson, *Believing Christ*, Deseret Book, 2002, pp. 5, 7, 9–10.

110. Martin Luther King, Jr., *The Essential Martin Luther King, Jr.: "I Have a Dream" and Other Great Writings*, Beacon Press, 2013.

111. Advice from *Poor Richard's Almanac*, Benjamin Franklin, 1757, Penguin, 2011.

112. As quoted in *If Ignorance Is Bliss, Why Aren't There More Happy People?*, Random House, 2009, p. 294.

113. President Dieter F. Uchtdorf, "The Way of the Disciple," April 2009 general conference.

114. Thomas à Kempis, Imitation of Christ.

115. Elder Jeffery R. Holland, "Amazed at the Love Jesus Offers Me," address given to Salt Lake Temple workers on November 24, 1985.

116. H. Jackson Brown, Jr., *Life's Little Instruction Book*, Thomas Nelson; Revised edition, September 29, 2000.

117. As quoted in *The Words of Extraordinary Women*, HarperCollins, 2010.

118. As quoted in *Spirit of Service*, HarperCollins Publishers, 2009, p. 138.

119. *The Journal of Henry David Thoreau*; March 31, Thursday, 1841, New York Review of Books, 2011, p. 26.

120. Henry David Thoreau, *Thoreau and the Art of Life*, Heron Dance Press, 2006, p. 83.

121. President Spencer W. Kimball, "Small Acts of Service," *Ensign*, First Presidency Message, December 1974.

122. As quoted in *The Words of Extraordinary Women* by Carolyn Warner, HarperCollins, 2010.

123. As quoted in *1001 Smartest Things Teachers Ever Said* by Randy Howe, Globe Pequot, 2010, p. 251.

124. Elder David A. Bednar, "More Diligent and Concerned at Home," October 2009 general conference.

125. President Henry B. Eyring, "Prayer," October 2001 general conference.

126. Joel Osteen, *Your Best Life Now: Seven Steps to Living Your Full Potential*, Hachette Digital, Inc., 2007.

127. Walt Whitman, *Walt Whitman: Selected Poems 1855–1892*, Macmillan, 2000, p. 8.

128. Elizabeth Barrett Browning, *The Poetical Works of Elizabeth Barrett Browning*, Oxford University Press, 1920, p. 543.

129. Dallin H. Oaks, "Following the Pioneers," October 1997 general conference.

130. Martin Luther King Jr., *Strength to Love*, Fortress Press, 1977, p. 53.

131. As quoted in *What Makes a Woman Feel Loved* by Emilie Barnes, Harvest House Publishers, 2007, p. 54.

132. As quoted in *The Artist's Way at Work: Riding the Dragon* by Mark A. Bryan with Julia Cameron and Catherine A. Allen, William Morrow Paperbacks, 1999, p. 160.

133. Ann Taylor, "My Mother," From *The Taylors of Ongar* by Doris Mary Armitage, Cambridge: W. Heffer & Sons, Ltd., 1938, pp. 181–182.

134. Helen Steiner Rice, *The Poems and Prayers of Helen Steiner Rice*, Revell, 2004, p. 37.

135. Eberhard Arnold, *God's Revolution*, The Plough Publishing House, 1997, p. 137.

136. President Dieter F. Uchtdorf, "Continue in Patience," April 2010 general conference.

137. As quoted in *How to Remember Everything in the Old Testament*, by David R. Larsen, Cedar Fort, 2006, p. 93.

138. As quoted in *Kiplinger's Personal Finance*, The Kiplinger's Service for Families, September 1961, p. 48.

139. Quoted at http://www.biography.com/people/wilma-rudolph-9466552?page=1.

140. As quoted in *Flying Lessons: 122 Strategies to Equip Your Child to Soar into Life with Confidence and Competence*, Thomas Nelson, Inc., 2007, p. 143.

141. Beppie Harrison, "Giving Children Quantity and Quality Time," *Ensign*, July 1982.

142. Elder M. Russell Ballard, "Daughters of God," April 2008 general conference.

143. Ralph Waldo Emerson, *Society and Solitude*, Works and Days, James R. Osgood and Company, 1870, p. 143.

144. As quoted in *The Magazine of Poetry*, Volume 4, by Charles Wells Moulton, 1892, Charles Wells Moulton, p. 297.

145. Lori Nawyn, "Blessings in Disguise," *Segullah*, Fall 2009.

146. Jeffery R. Holland, "Because She Is a Mother," April 1997 general conference.

147. Erin Herrin, *When Hearts Conjoin*, Brigham Distributing, 2009, pp. 178–179.

148. *Comforting Thoughts*, Henry Ward Beecher, Irene H. Ovington, Fords, Howard, and Hulbert, 1901, p. 141.

149. Elder Neil L. Anderson, "Tell Me the Stories of Jesus," April 2010 general conference.

150. As quoted in *Women's Rites of Passage: How to Embrace Change and Celebrate Life* by Abigail Brenner, Rowman & Littlefield, 2007, p. 93.

151. Marjorie Pay Hinckley, *Small and Simple Things*, Deseret Book, 2003, p. 141.

152. As quoted in *Chicken Soup for the Parent's Soul* by Jack Canfield, Mark Victor Hansen, Raymond Aaron, Kimberly Kirberger, Open Road Media, 2012.

153. Wayne W. Dyer, *Your Erroneous Zones*, HarperCollins, 2009, p. 28.

154. As quoted by Lily and Thistle, http://lilyandthistle.blogspot.com/2010/10/favorite-on-friday-stephanie-nielson.html.

155. Karen Eddington, personal interview with Lori Nawyn, 2011.

156. As quoted in *The Evidence-Based Parenting Practitioner's Handbook* by Kirsten Asmussen, Routledge, 2012.

157. As quoted in *Art Teaching: Elementary through Middle School* by George Szekely and Julie Alsip Bucknam, Routledge, 2013, p. 229.

158. As quoted in *The Complete Idiot's Guide to the Psychology of Happiness*, Penguin, 2008, p. 189.

159. David A. Bednar, "Things as They Really Are," CES Fireside, May 2009, BYU.

160. As quoted in *Psychology around Us* by Ronald Comer and Elizabeth Gould, John Wiley & Sons, 2012, p. 82.

161. Pearl S. Buck, "To You on Your First Birthday," *To My Daughters with Love*, 1967, p. 138.

162. Joyce Maynard, her first column, June 15, 1991, as quoted in *She Said What?*, University Press of Kentucky, 1993, p. 161.

163. As quoted in *The International Thesaurus of Quotations*, 1996, Eugene Ehrlich and Marshall De Bruhl, HarperCollins, 1996, p. 86.

164. Oliver Wendell Holmes, *The Complete Works of Oliver Wendell Holmes*, Volume 2, Sully and Kleinteich, 1891, p. 124.

165. As quoted in *From a Daughter's Heart to Her Mom: 50 Reflections on Living Well* by Thomas Nelson, Thomas Nelson, Inc., 2006, p. 31.

166. As quoted in *Mother Teresa: An Authorized Biography* by Kathryn Spink, HarperCollins, 2011, p. 172.

167. As quoted in *The Columbia Dictionary of Quotations* by Robert Andrews, Columbia University Press, 1993, p. 315.

168. Erma Bombeck, *Family—The Ties That Bind . . . And Gag!*, New York: Random House, 1988, p. 11.

169. As quoted by President Thomas S. Monson, "Hallmarks of a Happy Home," *Ensign*, First Presidency Message, October 2001.

170. President Thomas S. Monson, "Hallmarks of a Happy Home," *Ensign*, First Presidency Message, October 2001.

171. Mitt Romney, From the press conference announcing his candidacy for presidency, 2007.

172. President Gordon B. Hinckley, "The Blessings of Family Prayer," *Ensign*, First Presidency Message, February 1991.

173. As quoted in *A Little Book of Thank Yous* by Addie Johnson, Conari Press, 2010, p. 100.

174. Vaughn E. Worthen, PhD, "The Value of Experiencing and Expressing Gratitude," *Ensign*, March 2010.

175. As quoted in *Love Works: Seven Timeless Principles for Effective Leaders*, Zondervan, 2012.

176. Elder Donald L. Staheli, "Striving for Family Unity," *Ensign*, September 2007.

177. Peter Buffett, *Life Is What You Make It*, Random House, 2011, pp. 10–12.

178. From his 2012 speech http://www.cambridge-news.co.uk/News/Hawkings-speech-Remember-to-look-up-at-the-stars-and-not-down-at-your-feet-08012012.htm.

179. Stephen E. Robinson, *Believing Christ*, Deseret Book, 2002, pp. 13–14.

180. From the *Nicomachean Ethics*, Book II, 4; Book I, 7, as quoted by Will Durant in *The Story of Philosophy: The Lives and Opinions of the World's Greatest Philosophers*, Simon & Schuster/Pocket Books, 1991.

181. Morrie Schwartz, as quoted by Mitch Albom, *Tuesdays With Morrie*, Random House, 2007.

182. *Public Papers of the Presidents of the United States*, Administration of George Bush, 2001, Government Printing Office, 2004.

183. As quoted in the *Dictionary of Quotations from Ancient and Modern English and Foreign Sources*, F. Warne and Company, 1899, p. 549.

184. *History of the Church*, 5:134–35.

185. John C. Nelson, "A Conversation on Spouse Abuse," *Ensign*, October 1999, p. 22.

186. As quoted by The Foundation for Family Life, http://foundationforfamilylife.com/about.html.

187. As quoted in *Christmas Prayers: A Heartwarming Collection of Holiday Blessings* by Paul M. Miller, Barbour Publishing, 2013.

188. Ezra Taft Benson, *Come Listen to a Prophet's Voice*, Deseret Book, 1990, pp. 32–36.

189. David A. Bednar, "Watching with All Perserverance," April 2010 general conference.
190. President James E. Faust, "Enriching Our Homes through Family Home Evening," *Ensign*, First Presidency Message, June 2003.
191. As quoted in *100 Ways to Simplify Your Life* by Joyce Meyer, Hachette Digital, Inc., 2008.
192. http://speeches.byu.edu/?act=viewitem&id=792.
193. Gordon B. Hinckley, "The Marvelous Foundation of Our Faith," October 2002 general conference.
194. Marjorie Pay Hinckley, *Small and Simple Things*, Deseret Book, 2003, p. 32.
195. As quoted in *The Mackay MBA of Selling in the Real World*, by Harvey Mackay, Penguin, 2011, Chapter 30.
196. Baron Edward Herbert of Cherbury, *Autobiography of Edward Lord Herbert of Cherbury*, A. Murray, 1870, p. 32.
197. Lori Nawyn, "Cream of Wheat," *Segullah*, Spring 2008.
198. F. Burton Howard, *Eternal Marriage and the Parable of the Silverware*, 2004, Deseret Book, 2004, pp. 20, 53, 54, 57.
199. William Shakespeare, *William Shakespeare: The Complete Works*, Barnes and Noble Publishing, 1994, p. 518.
200. Henry B. Eyring, "Our Perfect Example," October 2009 general conference.
201. Ibid.
202. As quoted in *The Complete Idiot's Guide to the Psychology of Happiness* by Arlene Uhl, Penguin, 2008, p. 180.
203. Philip James Bailey, *Festus*, 1813, scene "A Party and Entertainment."
204. Dallin H. Oaks, "Divorce," April 2007.
205. Nathaniel Hawthorne, *The Complete Works of Nathaniel Hawthorne*, Houghton Mifflin, 1910, p. 256.
206. As quoted in *The Words of Extraordinary Women* by Carolyn Warner, HarperCollins, 2010.
207. Laura Ingalls Wilder, *Little House in the Big Woods*, HarperCollins, 2007, p. 18.
208. Laura Ingalls Wilder, *The Long Winter*, HarperCollins, 2007, p. 390.
209. Stephen R. Covey, *Daily Reflections for Highly Effective People*, Simon and Schuster, 1994, p. 264.
210. As quoted in *101 Success Secrets for Women* by Sue Augustine, Harvest House Publishers, 2011, p. 112.
211. Amelia Earhart, "Courage Is the Price," *Amelia Lost: The Life and Disappearance of Amelia Earhart*, by Candace Fleming, Random House, 2011, p. 76.
212. As quoted in *Self Care for Life* by Alexander Skye and Lester Meera, Adams Media, 2011.
213. Eleanor Roosevelt, *You Learn by Living*, Fiftieth Anniversary Edition, HarperCollins, 2011.
214. Marianne Williamson, *A Return to Love: Reflections on the Principles of a Course in Miracles*, HarperCollins, 2009.
215. As quoted in *Quotable Quotes* by the Editors of *Reader's Digest*, Penguin, 1997.
216. As quoted in *Evel: The High-Flying Life of Evel Knievel: American Showman, Daredevil, and Legend*, by Leigh Montville, Random House, 2012, p. 61.

217. Gordon B. Hinckley, *Stand A Little Taller*, Eagle Gate, 2001, p. 2.

218. From "Faith Is the Pierless Bridge," as quoted in *Famous Lines: A Columbia Dictionary of Familiar Quotations*, Columbia University Press, 1997, p. 163.

219. As quoted in *Quotable Quotes* by the Editors of *Reader's Digest*, Penguin, 1997.

220. As recalled by Rebecca R. Pomroy in *Echoes from Hospital and White House*, 1884, by Anna L. Boyden, p. 61.

221. As quoted in *In God We Still Trust: A 365 Day Devotional by Richard Lee*, Thomas Nelson, Inc., 2011, p. 17. Dr. Norman Vincent Peale, *The Power of Positive Thinking*, Simon & Schuster, 2003.

222. Dr. Norman Vincent Peale, *The Power of Positive Thinking*, Simon & Schuster, 2003

223. As quoted in *Don't Take My Lemonade Stand* by Janie Johnson, Hillcrest Publishing, 2010.

224. President Henry B. Eyring, "Moral Courage," *Ensign*, First Presidency Message, March 2010.

225. J. C. Watts from the 1996 Republican convention. As quoted in *If Ignorance Is Bliss, Why Aren't There More Happy People?* by John Lloyd and John Mitchinson, Random House, 2009, p. 46.

226. *The Political Writings of Thomas Paine*, G. Davidson, 1824, p. 259.

227. Mark Twain in a letter to George Bainton, 15 October, 1888, *The Art of Authorship: Literary Reminiscences, Methods of Work, and Advice to Young Beginners*, 1890, pp. 87–88.

228. President James E. Faust, "Spiritual Nutrients," October 2006 general conference.

229. Ibid.

230. Louisa May Alcott, *Little Women*, Simon and Schuster, 2013.

231. Elder Robert D. Hales, "Modesty: Reverence for the Lord," August 2008 general conference.

232. "The Hidden Power of the Heart" from http://www.heartquotes.net/Hope.html.

233. Winston Churchill, *My Early Life*, as quoted in the *Yale Book of Quotations*, edited by Fred R. Shapiro, Yale University Press, 2006, p. 152.

234. As quoted in *Ralph Waldo Emerson* by Oliver Wendell Holmes, Houghton Mifflin, 1884, p. 383.

235. Phillips Brooks, "Going Up to Jerusalem," *Twenty Sermons*,1886, p. 330.

236. As quoted in *The Art of Deliberate Success* by David Keane, John Wiley and Sons, 2012, p. 71.

237. Elder Russell M. Nelson, "Now Is the Time to Prepare," April 2005 general conference.

238. As quoted in *The Columbia Dictionary of Quotations* by Robert Andrews, Columbia University Press, 1993, p. 683.

239. Jane Brody, http://well.blogs.nytimes.com/2009/03/20/planning-for-death-when-youre-healthy/?_r=0.

240. As quoted in *Winning Balance: What I've Learned So Far about Love, Faith, and Living Your Dreams* by Shawn Johnson, Tyndale House Publishers, 2012, p. 3.

241. Louisa May Alcott, *Louisa May Alcott: Her Life, Letters, and Journals*, Little, Brown & Company, 1914, p. 95.

242. As quoted in *Elbert Hubbard's Scrapbook*, Pelican Publishing, 1999, p. 172.

243. Elder David A. Bednar, "The Tender Mercies of the Lord," April 2005 general conference.

244. As quoted in *Bless This Food: Ancient and Contemporary Graces from around the World* by Adrian Butash, New World Library, 2010, p. 86.

245. Bonnie D. Parkin, "Gratitude: A Path to Happiness," April 2007 general conference.

246. As quoted in *Gratitude—A Daily Journal: Honor and Appreciate the Abundance in Your Life* by Jack Canfield and D. D. Watkins, HCI, 2007.

247. Henry B. Eyring, "Remembrance and Gratitude," October 1989 general conference.

248. As quoted in *The Oxford Handbook of Positive Psychology* by Shane J. Lopez and C. R. Snyder, Oxford University Press, 2011, p. 444.

249. As quoted in *One Life to Give: A Path to Finding Yourself by Helping Others* by Mary Akers and Andrew Bienkowski, Workman Publishing, 2010.

250. As quoted in *The International Thesaurus of Quotations: Revised Edition* by Eugene Ehrlich and Marshall De Bruhl, HarperCollins, 1996.

251. As quoted in *The Juggling Act: The Healthy Boomer's Guide to Achieving Balance in Midlife* by Peggy Edwards, Miroslava Lhotsky, and Judy Turner, Random House, 2011.

252. Mother Teresa, *Love, A Fruit Always in Season: Daily Meditations from the Words of Mother Teresa of Calcutta*, Ignatius Press, 1987, p. 122.

253. Sister Julie B. Beck, "There Is Hope Smiling Brightly before Us," April 2003 general conference.

254. Cecil Francis Alexander, *Hymns for Little Children*, "All Things Bright and Beautiful," 1848.

255. As quoted in *Do More Great Work: Stop the Busywork. Start the Work That Matters* by Michael Bungay Stanier, Workman Publishing, 2010, p. 10.

256. As quoted in *The Latter-Day Saints' Millennial Star*, Volume 43, Parley P. Pratt, 1881.

257. J. M. Barrie, "Courage," *Chicken Soup for the Soul: Woman to Woman* by Jack Canfield, Mark Victor Hansen, and Amy Newmark, Simon and Schuster, 2011.

258. George Canning, "The Pilot That Weathered the Storm," *Select Speeches of the Right Honorable George Canning* by James Crissy, 1846.

259. As quoted by Carolyn Rubenstein in *Perseverance*, Macmillan, 2010, p. 235.

260. As quoted by L. Tom Perry in "The Past Way of Facing the Future," October 2009 General Conference.

261. President Thomas S. Monson, "Be of Good Cheer," April 2009 general conference.

262. Henry Ward Beecher, *The Original Plymouth Pulpit: Sermons of Henry Ward Beecher in Plymouth Church, Brooklyn*, Volumes 1–2, Henry Ward Beecher, Pilgrim Press, 1897.

263. *Ready Resource for Relief Society*, Part 2, Cedar Fort, 2010, p. 95.

264. Elder Joseph B. Wirthlin, "Concern for the One," April 2007 general conference.

265. As quoted in *World Family Policy Center Newsletter*, Volume 8 Issue 173–January 14, 2008, BYU J. Reuben Clark Law School.

266. John Joseph Powell, *The Secret of Staying in Love*, Argus Communications, 1974, p. 194.

267. As quoted in *The Harper Book of Quotations: Revised Edition* by Robert I. Fitzhenry, HarperCollins, 1993, p. 179.

268. As quoted in *Quotable Quotes: Wit and Wisdom from the Greatest Minds of Our Time* by the Editors of *Reader's Digest*, Penguin, 2012.

269. As quoted in *Chicken Soup for the Soul: Christmas Magic* by Jack Canfield, Mark Victor Hansen, and Amy Newmark, Simon and Schuster, 2010.

270. Ralph Waldo Emerson and Mary Moody Emerson, "The Nun's Aspiration," *Lectures and Biographical Sketches, The Complete Works of Ralph Waldo Emerson*, XV. New York, Houghton Mifflin and Company, The Riverside Press, Cambridge, 1904, p. 397.

271. Marilyn Paul, *It's Hard to Make a Difference When You Can't Find Your Keys: The Seven-Step Path to Becoming Truly Organized*, Penguin Books, 2003.

272. http://www.searchquotes.com/quotation/Gifts_of_time_and_love_are_surely_the_basic_ingredients_of_a_truly_merry_Christmas./217132/

273. As quoted in *The Gift of an Ordinary Day: A Mother's Memoir*, Hachette Digital, Inc., 2009.

274. Laura Ingalls Wilder, *Missouri Ruralist* "As a Farm Woman Thinks," December 15, 1924.

275. Dinah M. Craik in "Christmas Carol," St. 2.

276. As quoted in *If Ignorance is Bliss, Why Aren't There More Happy People?*, by John Lloyd and John Mitchinson, Random House, 2009, p. 79.

277. "A Christmas Carol," in *The Best Short Stories of Charles Dickens*, New York: Charles Scribner's Sons, 1947, p. 435.

278. As quoted in *Chicken Soup for the Soul: Christmas Treasury for Kids* by Jack Canfield, Jack, Mark Victor Hansen, Patty Hansen, and Irene Dunlap, 2002, HCI, p. 1.

279. *The Sword and the Trowel*, ed. by C. H. Spurgeon, 1867, p. 342.

280. Roy Rogers and Dale Evans, *A Happy Trails Christmas*, Revell; Reprint Edition, 2012.

281. Hans Christian Andersen, "The Butterfly," *The Complete Fairy Tales*, Wordsworth Editions Ltd., 1998, p. 840.

282. As quoted in *Christmas Celebration* by Thomas Kinkade, Andrews McMeel Publishing, 2003.

283. As quoted in *Ashley Tisdale: Life Is Sweet!* by Grace Norwich, Penguin, 2006, p. 90.

284. Andy Rooney, *Andy Rooney: 60 Years of Wisdom and Wit*, PublicAffairs, 2010, p. 199.

285. Henry Van Dyke, "The Spirit of Christmas," *The American Blacksmith: A Practical Journal of Blacksmithing and Wagonmaking*, Volume 16, December 1916, p. 66.

286. Phillips Brooks, "O Little Town of Bethlehem, 1868, reported in *Bartletts' Familiar Quotations*, 10th ed. 1919.

287. Abraham Lincoln, Second Inaugural Address, 4 March 1865.

288. Marjorie Pay Hinckley, *Glimpses into the Life and Heart of Marjorie Pay Hinckley*, Deseret Book, 1999, p. 18.

289. Hamilton Wright Mabie, *My Study Fire*, Dodd, Mead, 1890, p. 42.

290. Jeffrey R. Holland, "The Best Is Yet to Be," Brigham Young University Devotional Address, January 13, 2009.

291. Ibid.

292. Ibid.

About the Author

LORI NAWYN'S AWARD-WINNING FICTION AND nonfiction reflect her desire to help others recognize their own unique talents and abilities and overcome adversity. Her essays, articles, and short stories have appeared in regional and national print publications, including the *Desert News*, *Outside Bozeman*, *Segullah*, and the *SCBWI Bulletin*. She is the author of the novel *My Gift to You*. Her book for girls and women, *Fill Your Day with Hope*, was released August 2013. An artist and graphic designer, she is also the illustrator of the book *Love, Hugs, and Hope: When Scary Things Happen*. Lori believes in the wisdom taught by her grandmothers: if your heart is in the right place, your hands can work miracles. She is the mother of four, grandmother of four, and is married to a fireman.